TOURISTS AT THE TAJ

The Taj Mahal is seen by many as a symbol of India, the world's greatest monument to love and the ultimate icon of splendid extravagance. Yet for many others it represents something quite different; a centre of Islamic power, or a national symbol of India.

For the first time, *Tourists at the Taj* presents an analysis of this conflict and demonstrates how the qualities which are recognised by contemporary Western tourists remain largely rooted in British colonial knowledge, contrasting with other narratives which contest these ethnocentric dispositions. Furthermore, by analysing a wide range of tourist practices at the Taj and by regarding tourist sites as stages, using the metaphor of 'performance' to describe the culturally situated practice of travel, the author demonstrates that tourism is a continually changing set of processes rather than an epitome of particular social characteristics.

Clearly written and fascinatingly illustrated, *Tourists at the Taj* will be of interest to students in a wide variety of disciplines, including sociology, cultural studies and tourism. It will also appeal to anyone with an interest in India and to professionals in the travel industry.

Tim Edensor is lecturer and researcher in the department of cultural studies at Staffordshire University. He has researched extensively in tourist practices and popular culture.

INTERNATIONAL LIBRARY OF
SOCIOLOGY
Founded by Karl Mannheim
Editor: John Urry
Lancaster University

TOURISTS AT THE TAJ

Performance and meaning at a symbolic site

Tim Edensor

London and New York

First published 1998
by Routledge
11 New Fetter Lane, London EC4P 4EE

Simultaneously published in the USA and Canada
by Routledge
29 West 35th Street, New York, NY 10001

© 1998 Tim Edensor

Typeset in Bembo by Routledge
Printed and bound in Great Britain by
Biddles Ltd, Guildford and King's Lynn

All rights reserved. No part of this book may be reprinted or reproduced or utilised in any form or by any electronic, mechanical, or other means, now known or hereafter invented, including photocopying and recording, or in any information storage or retrieval system, without permission in writing from the publishers.

British Library Cataloguing in Publication Data
A catalogue record for this book is available from the British Library

Library of Congress Cataloguing in Publication Data
Edensor, Tim. Tourists at the Taj (International library of sociology) Includes bibliographical references and index.
1. Taj Mahal (Agra, India). 2. Tourist industry – India.
3. Popular culture – India. 4. Architecture and state – India. 5. Symbolism in architecture – India. 6. Great Britain – colonies. 7. India – civilization – British influences. 8. India – politics and government – 1765 – 1947. 9. India – public opinion. 10. Public opinion – Great Britain. I. Title. II. Series.
DS 486. A3E34 1998 98–5286
954' .2–dc21 CIP

ISBN 0–415–16712–4 (hbk)
ISBN 0–415–16713–2 (pbk)

TO UMA, JAY AND KIM

Henceforth, let the inhabitants of the world be divided into two classes – them as has seen the Taj Mahal; and them as hasn't.
Edward Lear, 1874

I'd rather go round an aeroplane works than visit the Taj Mahal.
Eduardo Paolozzi, sculptor

The Taj Mahal is only a typical illustration of how all historic buildings and townships from Kashmir to Cape Comorin, though of hoary Hindu origin, have been ascribed to this or that Muslim ruler or courtier.
Oak, 1979, 23

(The Taj) is representative of the amazing capacity of the Indian artisan to adapt himself to changed conditions and to assimilate the inspirations to which he is introduced from time to time.
Nath, 1972, 5

CONTENTS

List of illustrations viii
Acknowledgments ix

Introduction 1

1 Constructing tourist space 10

2 The regulation of tourist space 41

3 Narratives of the Taj Mahal 69

4 Walking, gazing, photographing and remembering at the Taj 105

5 Enclavic and heterogenous tourist spaces in Agra 149

6 Tourist plans for Agra and the Taj 181

7 Conclusion 200

Bibliography 205
Index 215

ILLUSTRATIONS

Figures

Frontispiece	Tourist posing on bench in front of Taj	x
3.1	Taj Mahal with European sightseers, 1815 (courtesy of British Library, London)	83
4.1	Tourist paths around the Taj Mahal	108
4.2	Local boys exercising on the banks of the River Jamuna	117
4.3	Boy holding up the Taj	134
4.4	Postcards from Taj Ganj	142
4.5	Model Taj Mahals on a stall in Agra	144
5.1	Siddharta Hotel, Taj Ganj	169
5.2	Treat Restaurant, Taj Ganj	170
6.1	Green Agra, Clean Agra	185

Table

5.1	Duration of stay in India	163

ACKNOWLEDGMENTS

I would like to thank the following people for their support and friendship in the creation of this book. First mention must go to people in India who helped and befriended me during my stay in Agra. The staff at the Park View Hotel were enormously helpful, especially Vishnu Srivastava whose good humour and kindness made my stay there full of fun. The discussions I had with Brijesh Chandra of Agra University were very stimulating as were the suggestions of Mr Srivastava at Agra Planning Department.

I must extend a particular debt of gratitude to Professor Sinha, who accompanied me on many trips to the Taj, supplied a constant source of advice and information, and helped me to carry out many interviews. Without his assistance, the study would have been considerably poorer. Equally, I would like to thank Ahmed Iftikhar and his brothers who helped me carry out some essential work and with whom I spent many hours of stimulating chat over innumerable cups of coffee.

John Urry and Chris Rojek gave invaluable guidance and all the staff and students of Cultural Studies at Staffordshire University have provided a friendly environment in which to explore ideas. Thanks are also due to the following friends with whom I have discussed this work: David Bell, Ged Brehony, Emma Crewe, Paul Davies, Mark Gutteridge, Azzedine Haddour, Paul Hepburn, Shirin Housee, Lopa Kothari, Shanti Kothari, Tara Kothari, Tina Kothari, Gordon McLeod, Alan Myers, Tony Stacey, Phil Woodhouse and Ruth Holliday.

Above all, I must thank Rosemary Williams and Uma Kothari for their support and love.

Tourist posing on bench in front of Taj

INTRODUCTION

The world's most famous tomb is situated next to the River Jamuna in the city of Agra, Uttar Pradesh. It is not a dominating feature of the skyline like the Statue of Liberty, the Eiffel Tower, or St Paul's Cathedral, but is usually approached unseen, and is dramatically revealed upon entering the site. The Taj Mahal was constructed on the orders of Shahjahan, a Moghul emperor, as a mausoleum for his wife Mumtaz Mahal, who had died in 1631, giving birth to their fourteenth child. The Taj was completed twenty-two years later and has been a magnet for tourists almost since its completion.

As one of the most famous buildings in the world and the most renowned and recognised icon of India, there have been innumerable symbolic and metaphoric ways in which the Taj has been exploited (see Pal, 1989, 9–13). The name has been appropriated by Donald Trump for his casino in Las Vegas, a five-star hotel in Bombay, a blues singer and countless Indian restaurants throughout the world. Its image is found on packets of frozen food and embodied by, and embossed upon, ornaments of every kind. As a signifier of quality and magnificence, the site continues to be used in a host of metaphorical ways. After the death of Diana, Princess of Wales, images were recycled of the princess sitting alone in front of the Taj, a lovelorn figure, neglected by her royal partner. The symbolic juxtaposition of the romantic qualities embodied in the Taj and a lonely woman proved irresistible to newspaper editors. Such representational practices have rendered the building something of a cliché, signifying quintessential luxury, quality, romance and splendour.

The impressions gained during my first visit to the Taj Mahal in 1987 are now a blur, swamped by the numerous accounts of the site I have heard since and by visiting the site for most days over a six-month period as a researcher. Backpacking around northern India, I had caught the 'Taj Express' from Delhi and joined a coach tour which culminated at the Taj Mahal by way of Fatehpur Sikra and Agra Fort, two impressive nearby attractions eclipsed by the fame of the Taj. Like most tourists, I entered the monument after a brief security check, stood on the platform below the central gateway, and composed the familiar image of water-course, mausoleum and sky through my camera lens, aiming for maximum symmetry. Click. There was but half an hour to explore the site, and so I briskly walked towards the mausoleum, effusing about the building's beauty along with my travelling companions.

Since this time, I have become intimately acquainted with the attraction through carrying out research at the site in 1993, 1994 and 1997, interviewing hundreds of visitors and workers at the Taj and in Agra, and spending many days watching tourists. My attempt to make sense of this research is the subject of this book. My interest in the sociology of tourism and dissatisfaction with theories in this literature motivated me to carry out an exploration of what tourists do and think at symbolic sites, and the Taj suggested itself as a site where there might be a proliferation of contesting touristic notions and practices.

This is a narrative based on ethnography; as a researcher based in a Western academic institution carrying out work in India, I was mindful of the notion that 'colonialism, ethnography and tourism are forms of intervention and expansion that inhabit the space cleared by the reach of Western power' (Little, 1991, 159). Like colonisers and tourists, ethnographers tend to objectify and spectacularise what they find through the mobilisation of particular techniques. Moreover, all three are often relatively wealthy and powerful. Also like colonisers and tourists, I was arriving with a host of preconceptions, a predisposition to gaze in a particular way and a situated and institutionalised form of knowledge.

In recognising that all forms of knowledge are situated, and in order to create a narrative without closure, I have incorporated a diverse range of stories, although of course, the final selection of narrative is my responsibility. Hopefully the voices in this book create a 'messy text' wherein multiple perspectives are conducive to the production of a 'communitarian moral ethic' (Denzin, 1997, xiv–xv) which informs the best ethnographies. This of course, is diametrically opposed to colonial knowledge, which erases the voice of the colonised and authoritatively enunciates objective facts about the space and culture it surveys.

Crick has recognised some of the parallels between tourists and ethnographers, especially insofar as they both reproduce conventional representations and discourses which codify how difference can be understood. Both also follow instrumental strategies whereby they may acquire experience and tangible rewards; tourists gain souvenirs and photographs whilst ethnographers, like myself, collect material for publication (Crick, 1991, 16). In recognition of some of the parallels between tourists and ethnographers, and in order to put myself in the picture as a performer in tourist space, I have, where appropriate, attempted to summarise the ways in which I narrated the Taj, walked around the site and gazed at objects of interest to me.

There has been a recent profusion of writing on the inevitable situatedness of research and theory within the social sciences which has acted to focus concern upon the extremely ethnocentric approaches of many Western ethnographers (Clifford and Marcus, 1986). These have been brought to book for failing to locate their ontological and epistemological framework within a particular culture. This emphasis has highlighted the necessity of locating the self in any

INTRODUCTION

ethnographic research. Despite the best intentions of the researcher, the elimination of ethnocentric bias cannot be completely expunged and it is as well to admit that any ethnography is bound to be affected by the culturally specific responses of the researcher. A careful reflexivity about the likelihood of making situated assumptions is advisable.

There were means of reflecting upon my early preconceptions by discussing my research with traders and tour guides in Agra, several of whom became good friends. Most of these people were interested in my project, partly because it related to their livelihood, but also out of curiosity. These dialogues helped me reject any wild assumptions I might make, and often helped me contextualise certain observations and responses from interviewees.

Studies of tourism have tended to highlight certain practices and subjects in particular (Western) settings and generalise about them to produce meta-theories about tourism and tourists. Accordingly, non-Western tourists and tourism in non-Western locations may not fit in with these theories and models. Paradoxically, over-general theorising about tourism tends to pre-empt an examination of the specific genealogies of the relationship between visitors and sites. But tourism cannot be typified by one type of motivation, societal function or social condition. Rather, it consists of a range of practices and epistemologies which emerge out of particular cultural locations. Before outlining my own approach, I will briefly critique some influential theories of tourism.

Probably the most well-known theory about tourism is that expounded by MacCannell, who considers tourism to be a search for a vanished 'authenticity', no longer to be found in the tourist's home and everyday life (MacCannell, 1976). Yet this quest is doomed for tourists only experience 'staged authenticity' by the tourist industry. This explanation however, only concentrates on the specific practices of Western, middle-class tourists and their attempt to understand and categorise the 'other' (Graburn, 1983, 18), thus generalising about notions of a particular form of authenticity. For desires for 'authenticity' arise out of particular historical and geographical settings, and the power to authenticate emerges out of 'the political economy of taste and status discrimination' (Bruner, 1994, 408). For instance, the notion of an 'authentic, non-Western other' emerges out of colonial tropes of desire and classification. Rather than reifying authenticity, it ought to be conceived as dynamic and emergent, not an objective property but a negotiable quality open to subjective interpretation (see Bruner, 1994; Pearce and Moscardo, 1988). For instance, sites previously considered authentic are now regarded as false (see Edensor, 1997a). At symbolic sites there tend to be several, competing interpretations as to what constitutes its 'authentic' attributes.

MacCannell also contends that tourists are contemporary pilgrims, compulsive collectors of supposedly important objects and places. The drawing of this parallel between tourism and pilgrimage usefully highlights the touristic pursuit wherein 'world sights' become 'must-sees' and tours and itineraries are

INTRODUCTION

organised accordingly. However, MacCannell ignores other notions of the sacred that may be imputed to specific sites by tourists, notably those from non-Western cultures whose consumption of sites as religious pilgrims may be of an intensity and reverence that is qualitatively different from the Western consumption of 'sights' and souvenirs.

Certain tourist sites attract competing forms of pilgrimage that may either be contested between different religious groups, such as Jerusalem (Rinschede, 1992, 58), or are the site of religious and secular tourism. Eade and Sallnow consider pilgrimage to be a 'realm of competing discourses' and argue that rather than generalising about what typifies pilgrimage, the category as a whole should be deconstructed and culturally specific meanings identified (1991). For instance, the Vatican City and St Peters Cathedral in Rome are important religious centres and are also fixtures on the itinerary of many tourists visiting Italy (Nolan and Nolan, 1992, 72). On the other hand, popular pilgrimage sites may not attract significant numbers of secular tourists. Furthermore, pilgrimage to religious sites and secular tourist visits often constitute separate parts of a single itinerary, wherein different activities are combined.

The variety of secular and religious practices played out at particularly symbolic attractions only serves to blur the distinction between tourism and pilgrimage, and they appear as 'a continuum of inseparable elements' (Graburn, 1983, 16) Indeed, it has become impossible to conceive of a pure, hermetically sealed process of pilgrimage which is unsullied by contemporary tourist images. For instance, pilgrimage sites in India are stocked with souvenir shops and guides tout for business.

Another influential account considers tourism to be a form of ritual inversion wherein individuals escape the routine of everyday life in special spaces (Cohen, 1988, 38–41; Graburn, 1983, 11–17). Pre-modern activities, such as medieval carnivals, inverted the order of everyday life and took place within 'liminal' spaces in which the usual hierarchies were temporarily dissolved or reversed, producing a sense of communitas. These rituals are alleged to have a parallel in contemporary tourism, although rather than producing liminality by reversing the usual order of things, contemporary tourist spaces are distinguished by a paler, 'liminoid' effect wherein discipline and order co-exist alongside a more calculated design which merely *suggests* a transgression or transcendence of the usual disciplinary bounds (Turner and Turner, 1973).

Problematically, the process is conceived as having three stages, namely 'separation from the normal', the experience of 'liminality and inversion', and 'reintegration'. Thus, the touristic ritual of leaving the everyday for a short time has a functionalist social purpose which results in the reintegration of the traveller with his/her society upon returning, often with an enhanced social status. The assumption that tourism is a function of the social need for integration seems to suggest that the actions and meanings of tourists merely act to reinforce social cohesion.

The generalisation that foregrounds tourism as an archetypal activity through which people escape from the social conventions ignores the diversity of 'escape attempts' from what Cohen and Taylor call the 'paramount reality' of modernity (1992). And by generalising about tourism per se, the specific, situated historical and spatial relationships between particular tourists and the distinctive type of experiences they seek in especial places is neglected. We are therefore unable to comprehend, 'why particular behaviours are suspended' or why certain tourist groups follow specific forms of inversion (Graburn, 1983, 21).

The theory of ritual inversion is useful, however, in highlighting the ways in which most contemporary tourism occurs in specifiable and constricted settings which are subject to what Featherstone calls a 'controlled de-control' (1991). Most tourism is not an unfettered excursion into the realm of the senses and it is important to recognise the extent to which the search for liminality is conditioned by the ordering of experience through the circumscribing of particular practices which (re)construct tourist spaces. However, tourist spaces and routes to 'escape' are structured differently and later I will examine the ways in which tourists' experience is shaped by the temporal and spatial contingencies of their tour.

Finally, Boorstin argues that modern tourists typically travel in an air-conditioned bubble on a superficial quest to consume 'pseudo-events' (1964). This account echoes the later concerns of theorists of postmodernity about the consumption of 'depthless signs', simulation and simulacra (Baudrillard, 1981), the schizophrenia engendered by a placeless, timeless existence (Jameson, 1991), and the production of 'hyperreality' (Eco, 1986). Again, these sorts of assumptions identify tourism as exemplifying particular social processes or structures; in this case, a postmodern condition.

Several authors have located a postmodern tourism within late-twentieth-century capitalism wherein economic restructuring, the intensive search for new areas to commodify and the increasingly global operation of capital has led to a proliferation of images and signs (Lash and Urry, 1994), 'time/space compression' (Harvey, 1989), the integration of aesthetic production and commodity production (Featherstone, 1991) and an intensifying of local, regional and national instability. Corporations and state organisations marketplaces, attractions, people, customs, landscapes and histories, intensifying competition between localities for investment as they attempt to reconstruct themselves as tourist spaces (Britton, 1991, 465).

The resulting proliferation of tourist sites provides spaces for postmodern tourists to consume the depthless markers, images and soundbites which offer 'transitory fulfilment, sensations, fleeting attainment of styles, and elevation and confirmation of taste' (Britton, 1991, 465–6. This suggests that tourism has blended into a melange of consuming activities, typified by a structure of feeling which is instantaneous, depthless, affective and fragmented, a condition which apparently thwarts an enduring sense of identity.

It is notable that postmodern accounts of tourism tend to focus on particular Western sites such as the Disney theme parks (Zukin, 1992), shopping centres such as West Edmonton Mall (Shields, 1992) and heritage sites stocked with simulated events and simulacra. This is compounded by a concentration on the package tourism of whistle-stop tours, 'environmental bubbles' and soundbites. Whilst it is important to recognise that forms of postmodern tourism exist, they are best conceived as part of a 'specific regime of signification in which particular objects are produced, circulated and received', usually in a Western context (Urry, 1990, 83). However, tourist sites are consumed and interpreted in other ways that do not correspond with 'postmodern' modes of signifying.

Although I have criticised the ethnocentricity in some accounts of postmodernism, postmodernist theory more generally has proposed that the demise of modern meta-narratives has enabled other stories to contest imperialising forms of knowledge (Lyotard, 1984). There are also useful post-colonial theories which stress the same theme, highlighting the situated assumptions of Western ideas and revealing the subaltern voices which contest them (Said, 1978; Spivak, 1990; Bhabha, 1994). Both theoretical perspectives demonstrate that the authoritative voice of the bourgeois, Western male has been stifled, his cultural texts de-legitimated and his representational practices scrutinised. Such accounts recognise the gendered, class and racialised operation of power and, with regard to tourism, there certainly remain dominant narratives and practices at sites. However, these are subject to challenge.

The accounts of tourism critiqued above over-generalise and fail to investigate what different tourists actually feel, understand and practise. And, as symbolic sites, tourist attractions may engender a deep level of engagement amongst groups of people to whom the site is nationally, religiously or politically significant. Certain sites are so 'full' of meaning that they cannot be rendered superficial through their commodification.

My approach in this study has been informed by Neumann's contention that:

> Tourist sites are an appropriate place for locating the broad debate over self and society. . . . Tourism is a metaphor for our struggle to make sense of our self and world within a highly differentiated culture . . . it directs us to sites where people are at work making meaning, situating themselves in relation to public spectacle and making a biography that provides some coherency between self and world.
>
> (1988, 22)

Renowned tourist sites such as the Taj Mahal are places where visitors are engaged in constructing and reproducing meaning and carrying out particular performances. As a global site, a destination for people who follow journeys of different scale, from the Western tourists to local visitors, these meanings vary greatly, are contested, and are articulated by different narratives and practices. As Urry says, sites are

INTRODUCTION

constructed through multiple texts which combine to produce a particular tourist text, albeit one whose meanings are shifting, unstable and contested. At the same time it is important to recognise that texts themselves are part of larger frameworks of signification, of narratives, concepts, ideologies, metaphors, practices.

(1994, 238)

My aim is to identify the major ways in which different tourists make sense of the Taj Mahal, and also how they perform a diverse range of enactions at the site. In order to carry out this objective, I will look at the construction of tourist space, and then move to consider how tourists can be conceived as performers in tourist space. This book is thus framed by the following theoretical approaches.

Firstly, contemporary tourist processes produce distinct forms of tourist space on a global stage. Tourist space is liable to be commodified in particular ways, and its organisation provides a distinctive material character, replete with hotels, highways, tours and other infrastructural facilities, which often contrasts with adjacent, non-tourist space. There are therefore dominant ways in which tourist space is represented as a commodified entity. However, symbolic tourist spaces and places are diversely represented, with contesting notions about what they mean being articulated by different groups of people. For instance, tourist sites provide a space where political, spiritual, cultural or national identities can be imagined and expressed. In addition, and this is crucial to my analysis, particular tourist spaces are regulated differently. The admission or exclusion of certain people may prevail, or they may be subject to various forms of surveillance and policing; spaces may be subordinate to distinct forms of aesthetic control; and stringent norms about which activities are considered appropriate may be externally or self-monitored. These distinctions are brought out in my identification of the contrasting features of enclavic and heterogeneous tourist spaces.

Secondly, in order to situate the symbolic qualities of tourist sites in a wider context, I highlight the ways in which attractions are diversely incorporated into 'imagined geographies'. The inclusion of places into wider spatial frameworks signifies specific relationships between visitor and site which articulate geographical identities of varying scale, be they local, national or transnational. This illuminates the influence of cultural preconceptions on tourists and the continuity of touristic traditions that are mobilised at particular sites. This incorporation of places within diverse larger spatial networks will be explored in this work to advance a 'progressive sense of place' (Massey, 1993), which identifies the numerous ways in which locales and sites are constituted by these intermeshing processes and refutes notions that places have some sort of 'essence'. This also raises questions about the ways in which spaces and identities are being produced in a globalising economy. While assumptions about the production of cultural and spatial homogeneity often seem to be borne out by the production of serialised monotony in spatial forms and touristic organisation, a simple correlation between globalisation and homogeneity appears to founder upon the proliferation of narratives and practices at globally famous symbolic sites. I will examine these contradictions throughout the book.

Thirdly, in order to specify the (changing) practices which tourists carry out, I have chosen to develop the metaphor of tourist performances. I consider performance to be useful conceptually since the constraints and opportunities that influence tourist's actions and experiences are important. I have noted that tourist spaces are differently regulated. If we consider these tourist spaces to be performative spaces, or 'stages', it is clear that certain types of performance are constrained by carefully managed stages, whereas less overtly controlled stages potentially permit wider scope for improvisation. Similarly, tours are organised according to distinct spatio-temporal imperatives where restrictions on performance might be imposed by tour personnel, or conversely, individual travellers may be unsupervised. Thus, I will explore the relationship between different forms of tourist space and tour management, and tourist performance, specifically around narration, walking, gazing and photographing, and remembering, activities which continually reconstitute tourist space.

To summarise: rather than attempting an overarching definition, I emphasise the different and ever-changing processes of tourism and also stress that tourist sites are themselves not static entities. Their material shape, symbolic importance and the ways in which they are perceived, represented and narrated change over time. The Taj Mahal is a suitable site to exemplify these processes in view of its global fame, the large numbers of domestic and foreign tourists who visit, the colonial origins of tourism to the Taj, and the profusion of written accounts in travel and tourist literature. There are a proliferation of meanings and practices that circulate around the site.

In Chapter 1, I briefly discuss the increasingly global marketing and commodification of tourist space before moving on to look at the forms of hegemonic and subaltern representations which surround tourist sites. I conclude by identifying the characteristics of the three most pertinent imagined geographies in this study, namely colonial, sacred and national space. Chapter 2 focuses on the regulation of tourist space and here I contrast 'enclavic' with 'heterogeneous' tourist space. This provides a basis for my subsequent argument which proposes that tourism is appropriately considered as a range of performances.

In Chapter 3, I look at the different and competing narratives which are written about, and performed at, the Taj Mahal. Following on from the identification of symbolic spatial frameworks, I distinguish between Western accounts which have their roots in colonial discourses, religious narratives which value the Taj as a sacred site, and stories of the nation which use the Taj as a signifying metaphor of contesting national qualities. Chapter 4 dwells on the most consistent modalities of the other variants of tourist performance, those organised around walking, gazing, photography and remembering. In Chapter 5, I move away from the Taj to examine the distinctive tourist spaces in Agra, the enclavic

INTRODUCTION

Agra Cantonment and heterogeneous Taj Ganj. I distinguish between the ways in which they are regulated, show how they are the sites of particular social activities, discuss whether they encourage or discourage tourists to meet locals, and identify the ways in which they constitute sensual spaces. In Chapter 6, I concentrate on the plans to further commodify, regulate and conserve tourist space in Agra, how these schemes testify to the globalisation of ways of producing tourist space, and the unequal contestations such proposals generate.

1

CONSTRUCTING TOURIST SPACE

The Taj Mahal is one of the most familar tourist sites in the world, and certainly one of the best-known global icons. Accordingly, any discussion of the Taj requires an investigation into the ways in which tourist space comes to be represented in particular ways. In order to contextualise this examination, it is necessary to appreciate how the contemporary production of tourism involves the commodification of particular spaces and cultures. Thus the chapter begins with a brief survey of the expansion of global tourism.

After this brief discussion of the ways in which capital, bureaucratic and political power is embodied in forms of tourist space, I will explore how this material production has been accompanied by a proliferation of globally transmitted images which are likewise inscribed by hegemonic suppositions about how symbolic sites should be represented. However, I will show how these power-laden representations of symbolic space may be interpreted in a multitude of ways and be subject to competition from alternative representational practices. I will then focus on the ways in which modes of representation are closely linked to a situated way of understanding place and space. The ubiquity of widely disseminated pictures disguises their origins. Finally, as a prelude to looking at the myriad ways in which the Taj Mahal is conceived and portrayed, I will contextualise the traditions whereby the site is represented by examining colonial, sacred and national space. For particularly significant sites are symbolically and practically incorporated into wider spatial constructs, which specify the relationship between visitor and site.

Tourist space in a global frame

In a globalising capitalist economy, the predominant material production of space involves the organisation of built environments that facilitate the flow of profit, goods, money, labour, communication and information; the construction of powerful administrative centres; and the division of space into distinct functional zones. There is an intensifying search by increasingly footloose capital to seek out new spaces for investment, and reconfigure old spaces in new productive ways. One of the processes this has generated is 'time-space compression'

(Harvey, 1989, 240–2) whereby distances in space and time become diminished through technologies of communication, information and travel. Thus, ever more flexible regimes of accumulation traverse and exploit space, demolishing spatial barriers and embracing new spaces.

Tourism is an increasingly important part of this economic drive to reorder space. As Britton stresses:

> (Tourism is) a predominantly capitalistically organised activity driven by the inherent and defining social dynamics of that system ... an analysis of how the tourism production system markets and packages places and people is a lesson in the political economy of the social construction of 'reality' and social construction of place.
>
> (1991, 475)

Increasingly, places and spaces are subject to intense pressures to market and commodify themselves in order to maximise opportunities to attract international capital and tourists. Consequently, there has been a global proliferation of tourist space.

However, the production of tourist space is not only recent but can be partly understood as an expansion of inscribing power through the materialisation of bourgeois ideologies since the nineteenth century. For instance, the contemporary imposition of planning techniques and styles, and the commodification of the environment by the tourist industry extend the nineteenth-century drives to market local culture and aestheticise capital accumulation (Kearns and Philo, 1993, 12). Likewise, concerns about surveillance, public order and aesthetic regulation from tourist managers also enlarge this bourgeois project of rational recreation and orderly leisure pursuits. However, the processes of blending culture and capital have become increasingly disembedded from localities and become the provenance of an international class, who displace the paternalistic, moral control exercised by local agents. Accordingly, places are now conceived not as nuclei of cultural belonging, 'foci of attachment or concern', but as

> bundles of social and economic opportunity competing against one another in the open market for a share of the capital investment cake.
> (Kearns and Philo, 1993, 12)

Paradoxically, this more recent exploitative marketing of local specificities makes us 'more sensitised to what the world's spaces contain' (Harvey, 1989, 294). But whilst bureaucrats and entrepreneurs try to manufacture uniqueness and stress spatial distinctiveness, they usually only succeed in producing 'a "recursive" and "serial" monotony, producing from already known patterns or moulds places almost identical in ambience from city to city' (Harvey, 1989, 295).

In some ways, it seems as if the outcome of these global processes is a sort of 'universal cultural space', since the increase 'of postmodern shopping malls, leisure centres and supermarkets provides the same aesthetic and spatial references wherever one is in the world' (Rojek, 1995, 146), whereby similar buildings and design codes are constructed. Similarly, heritage centres, hotel landscapes, resorts, interpretative and information facilities, conference centres, souvenir and craft emporia, hi-tech transportation and communication, and a host of supplementary amenities, along with the aforementioned malls and supermarkets, are the typical ingredients of a serially produced tourist space. Britton has further elaborated upon this power to envelop specificity that capitalist and administrative powers wield in producing tourist space:

> tourism incorporates unfamiliar and conventional cultures, peoples, places, sights, behaviour, and settings into a commercial and institutionalised system constructed to satisfy demand for these experiences.
> (1991, 454)

This tourist 'product' must conform to a set of regular forms that can be efficiently produced and marketed and easily consumed by tourists:

> To transform travel and tourist experiences into commodities they must be standardised and rendered amenable to capitalist production techniques. A tourist industry has evolved which simultaneously enables tourist experiences to occur, encourages tourists to anticipate their experience and the expected social returns, and convinces tourists they have had the requisite experiences.
> (*ibid.* 1991, 454–5)

The spatial organisation of package tourism facilitates consumption in restricted periods of time. Thus, the touristic production of recognisable and 'bite-sized' images and narratives conforms to a structure of feeling that is induced by much modern consumption with its preoccupation with ephemerality, soundbites and a sense of distracted involvement.

Through place-marketing and the construction of tourist attractions, potted historical narratives are produced, only certain features of attractions and tourist space are highlighted, and the movement and time of tourists must fit in with this packaging. Accordingly, as places become locked into this international tourist system, increasingly controlled by fewer and larger concerns, the spatio-temporal organisation of tours, the form of holiday, and the standards required appear to conform to particular notions of convenience, comfort and consumability.

Yet these characterisations of tourist development are only partially convincing. Whilst they trace the imperatives of capitalist and administrative power, however dominant these processes seem, forms of tourist space can never merely conform to a homogeneous pattern. In fact, the strategies of different commercial interests and forms of commodification may be in opposition, and goals to commodify places may contrast with administrative and political objectives. These tensions are played out on local stages. In Chapter 6, I will trace some of the contestations over tourist spaces between different fractions of capital, and also highlight the competing globalising discourses organised around intensified tourist investment and conservation which inform plans about the development of tourism at the Taj and in Agra.

Equally however, whilst tourist space is represented and regulated in hegemonic ways, and is constructed through the incorporation of themed sites in common-sense itineraries, critical and subaltern representations, alternative symbolic geographies and tourist performances escape the normative narratives and rituals referred to above. The Taj Mahal is a useful site at which to examine the serial production of tourist space and normative tourist practices. Yet the Taj has many meanings and the tourists who flock there are inspired by a multitude of stories and carry out a wide range of practices.

The differently scaled economic, political and discursive processes that meet at the Taj Mahal and Agra are the subject of this book. Emerging out of distinct genealogies and histories, these influences contest the meaning of the Taj, and are mobilised in putting forward proposals and completing different, often contesting, tourist developments. I will try to show how these uneven touristic patterns epitomise the uneven, heterogeneous processes of globalisation.

Representations of space and place

Representations are integral to tourism and the tourist industry. Symbols, images, signs, phrases and narratives provide the ideas that fuel the commodification and consumption of tourist sites. Representations are disseminated by souvenirs, travel guides, postcards, travel accounts, photography, guidebooks, travel programmes and in a host of popular cultural forms including televised and cinematic drama, news bulletins and lifestyle magazines. These textual and visual forms reproduce discourses of 'otherness', luxury and escape and also reconfirm notions about travel destinations by plundering texts and images from each other as well as from older sources.

Besides promoting particular tourist locations, such representations are part of a technology of enframing sights and cultures which forms the epistemological apparatus through which tourists see and interpret difference. The culturally located ways of framing sights and arranging narratives is a selective process that usually reproduces the predictable; the already said, written and photographed. Thus travel brochures use dependable techniques of titillation based around familiar signs of exotica, bodily relaxation and discovery, and guidebooks preselect objects of interest and interpret them to minimise perplexity. Meaning is further consolidated when professionals such as tour operators and tour guides recite phrases and point out scenes. Thus the urge to consume signs that connote cultural qualities and induce the semiotic practices of tourists (Culler,

1981) are catered for by the directing and contextualising techniques mobilised by the tourist industry.

These techniques not only stimulate tourists to travel and organise the ways in which they look at and interpret sights and cultures, they also form the basis for tourists' own production of images and texts through photography and their orally transmitted and written travel narratives. The process of representing tourist space is continual, constituting a hermeneutic circuit in which tourists contingently (re)produce representations of tourist space as well as consuming them (Little, 1991). And the proliferation of tourists, tourist sites and the representations that frame these expanding cultural spaces contribute to the explosive 'economy of signs' that typifies postmodern, post-industrial production (Lash and Urry, 1994).

The construction of place and the global marketing of tourist sites rely on familiar codes to excite tourists. This division of tourist space into, for instance, areas that specialise in sex, the 'sacred', the 'exotic' and the strange, is firmly located in a Western imaginary which projects assumed qualities onto places and maps increasingly mobile desires and fantasies onto the globe. In non-Western tourist destinations the framing of commodified 'otherness' relies on themes of the 'exotic', suggestions of sexual adventure, the 'sublime' and 'beautiful', 'exploration' and 'discovery', 'timelessness' and 'authenticity', amongst others. Moreover, within particular countries there are specialised areas where international tourists can explore particular experiences.

Through their electronic and printed transmission in brochures, magazines, TV programmes and films, these representations are devoured and incorporated into global 'mediascapes', which provide repertoires of images and narratives to prospective tourists (and to a vast majority who can only fantasise about travel) throughout the world. According to Appadurai, these mediascapes typically valorise the qualities of a reified 'other', thereby stimulating 'the desire for acquisition and movement' (1990, 299). This global transmission of conventional representations of tourist space contributes to a network of mediatised signs, images and symbols which codify sights and render them intelligible (Rojek, 1997, 53). And increasingly, forms such as films and television programmes inspire the creation of tourist attractions, having already represented them fictionally. In addition, in proliferating tourist destinations such as malls, festival marketplaces and hotel landscapes, environmental symbolism increasingly derives from the popular culture produced in global mediascapes, recycling representations from films, television, pop music and magazines. This limited range of themes is identified by Gottdiener as 'tropical paradise', the 'Wild West', 'classical' civilisation, nostalgic portrayals of the 1920s and 30s, 'Arabian fantasies', the 'pedestrian city', and 'modernism' and 'hi-tech' (1997, 144–51).

Globalisation theorist Roland Robertson has described international tourism as 'one of the most conspicuous sites for the contemporary production of the local and the different' (1992, 173). This captures the commodifying processes cited above, but it also suggests that the production of representation and meaning may be carried out at a local level as well. Although Giddens (1991) argues that local production – and the production of the local – is now 'disembedded', shaped by distant influences, such global forces are not all-encompassing and often co-exist with continuously developing local practices. Indeed, as Hall maintains, global processes must be worked 'in, and through, specificity' (1991, 28–9) – through local capital, classes and politics amongst others.

For however much global capitalism commodifies sites, cultures and spectacles, despite the production of reified accounts and pictures in international tourism, neither interpretations of global attractions nor tourist practices can be delimited. The shifting processes of identity formation and the making of meaning in tourist space are complex. Subaltern and vernacular interpretations of symbolic sites contest commodified versions and inhabitants often resist any 'manipulation of culture and history' which contradicts local understandings (Kearns and Philo, 1993, 25). And images from global mediascapes are liable to be interpreted from local standpoints and can even be appropriated to enchant political campaigns (see Edensor, 1997b).

It is necessary to locate the historical and geographical traces in narratives and images of tourist spaces and places. However, rather than portraying a cacophony of equivalent interpretations, it is essential to identify which representations are inscribed with dominant ideologies. The uncovering of the interests, assumptions and desires inscribed within these representations, the traces of class, gender, racial, ethnic, political and colonial power, must be undertaken before alternative and subaltern portrayals are examined.

Characterisations of difference continue to be dominated by Eurocentric conventions and techniques of representation. These procedures are ingrained with an epistemology which relies on the 'illusion of realism', which is apparently affirmed by the existence of material spatiality. Keith and Pile point out the effects of these attempts to fix common-sense understanding: 'Conceptually squashed into the frame of reference as an artifact, space is always in danger of losing its plastic, multifaceted character' (1993, 24). Western empirically based thought has maintained that modes of representing the world can mimetically reflect the reality that they confront (Lefebvre, 1991, 30). Accordingly, the 'transparent reality' of spaces and places can be captured by a text, picture or photograph. And the mind's eye can accurately capture the essence of the scene if the correct words are skilfully chosen, since they:

> are felt to link up with their thoughts or objects in essentially right and incontrovertible ways: the word becomes the only proper way of viewing this object or experiencing that thought.
> (Eagleton, 1983, 134)

Accordingly, particular forms of representation such as landscape painting, cartography and scientific discourse proclaimed their accurate portrayal of spatial reality. For instance, linear perspective not only 'organised represented objects in relation to each other' in two-dimensional form but also posited a

> fixed relationship between object and subject, locating the viewer outside of the picture, and outside of the relationships being depicted. The viewer is therefore rendered transcendental, outside of history.
> (Thomas, 1994, 21–2)

The politics of looking constructed by this form of representation expresses a privileging of vision, the distanced authority of the onlooker and the consequent passivity of the scene under view, a disposition which informs the visual practice of tourists on tour, who 'are never left without a place from which to look and record' (Little, 1991, 153). The rise to prominence of this 'ego-centred landscape' (Bender, 1993, 1) coincided with the rise of 'abstract space', quantifiable, capable of being authoritatively represented and apportioned, and sold and commodified both as material space and cultural object. These ways of representing the world are deeply implicated in imperialist expansion and the construction of colonial space – and contemporary tourism.

Although Western tourist sensibilities continue to be provoked in reliable ways by repetitive images, themes and phrases which continue to ignore local interpretations, the imperialist notion that there is a place of overview from which to analyse and 'objectively' report the world has been contested. Arguments against this monologic authority have recognised that representations of space and place are multiple, interweave and mutate and are formulated on a moving earth. Universalist, realist projects that seek to capture and impose the 'essential' characteristics of space and place have been decentred by the diverse claims that have come into representation. There can be no system of representation that finally fixes space. As Mitchell says, 'the innocent eye is blind' for 'the world is already clothed in our systems of representation' (1986, 38).

Thus, touristic narrative and visual practices such as travel writing, fiction, poetry, painting and photography are inevitably located within a particular situated set of classificatory tendencies, aesthetic rules and sensibilities, myths, affections and ideologies. These touristic forms of representation are marked by their emanation from situated ways of thinking. As Bruner illustrates in his discussion of Western tourists visiting New Guinea: 'the only way to explore the real is through one's own symbolic system' (1991, 242). For travel experience not only involves a journey through space but also through 'an internal landscape which is sculptured by internal influence and cultural influences' (Rojek, 1997, 53). Rojek similarly argues that tourist representations are chained to cultural habits:

> We are drawn to the exotic in fashion and amusement. However, we confront these attractions as members of a particular class, race, nation and civilisation. And were we able truly to abandon these identity

values we could not function. Our escape attempts... are encoded activities within structural parameters.

(1993, 212)

Hegemonic forms of representation disguise their parochial origins by placing sites within a generalised spatial entity such as the nation or the empire. Yet by circumscribing the subjectivity of their addressee, they reveal their situatedness. More specifically, interpretations of space and place interpellate certain subjects – for example, those belonging to a particular race, class, religion, nation or gender – as the inheritors of particular heritage, thus situating them in a temporal and spatial frame, specifying their relationship with a particular history and geography. These dominant forms of representation interpellate 'insiders' and can surpress their individual interpretations and experiences (Shields, 1991, 262).

The power to shape meaning is instantiated in the production of enduring forms of representation. And power is manifest in the global circulation of commodified representations by the tourist industry. The normative themes in such representations occlude other images and narratives about racism, unequal trade relations, fiscal constraints imposed upon already impoverished economies, local and international oppressions, political insurgency and subaltern social movements, the historical legacies of colonialism, and contemporary neo-colonialism. Instead, they mobilise a way of looking at places and cultures that romanticises and objectifies. The stimulation of dispositions and practices regarded as proper and appropriate in touristic contexts bespeaks of the normalisation of meanings and practice through power over representation.

However, as I have remarked, hegemonic representations of space are contested by alternative narratives and images. The decline in the authority of dominant forms of spatial representation has been accompanied by the proliferation of other stories and pictures about space and place which have contested the pseudo-objective universality of the former. Narratives and images wrought by women, ethnic groups, religious minorities, and the previously colonised have claimed and reinterpreted spaces in their own ways. Local, oral and subaltern histories of place have challenged 'official' and commodified versions, artists from minority traditions have inscribed themselves into space, and both famous and alternative symbolic sites have been reclaimed by dissenting traditions.

There are other, non-Western ways of imagining and representing the landscape where, for instance, 'what lies above the surface or below, may be as or more important' (Bender, 1993, 1), or where place is represented 'less in terms of outward appearance than as impression, feel, significance or meaning' (Thomas, 1994, 21). I will discuss the ways in which sacred landscapes are read shortly. Besides these situated meanings and practices, visitors to sites are differently disposed to consume and reproduce dominant representations. The fixing of meaning and the framing of sights can give way to more fluid practices which are stimulated by critical visions and ironic approaches, or alternatively, webs of representation can be untangled by chance occurrences, strange juxtapositions, unusual things in obscure corners, producing ambiguity and dissonance in the most over-represented domain. In fact, most representations, for instance those produced during colonial times, are ambivalent and ambiguous, suggesting both attraction and repulsion, order and fantasy, violence and desire, and a shift in modes of looking or reading can produce a disturbance in the apparent fixity of meaning.

One aim of this book is to examine the limits of dominant representations of, and ways of representing, tourist sites. I examine the extent to which a dialogic interpretation of places is possible, and whether meaning can be constructed out of a multiplicity of different representations. I also concentrate on the ways in which the different spatial and temporal regulation of tourists are conducive to the rejection of the dominant meaning of places or their substitution with other interpretations. For instance, I will explore how forms of tourist performance, such as walking and gazing, lead to this supplanting, and how different environments are too variegated to be fixed by representation. I will also suggest that other sensual stimuli such as sound, movement, touch and smell can decentre the visual imperialism which places and categorises environments (see Howes, 1991). Representation often seems inept, indeed may reach its limits in attempts to articulate atmospheres, scents and emotions.

There has been some anthropological work on the cultural situatedness of modes of smelling, tasting, touching, hearing and seeing which purports to demonstrate that the senses are not only 'means of apprehending physical phenomena, but also avenues for the transmission of cultural values' (Classen, 1997). Whilst to an extent, the sensual world of others is unknowable, certain attempts can be made to understand elements of sensual epistemologies (Howes, 1991; Stoller, 1989) which highlight the ways in which space can be experienced. Although tourism has been typified by the visual practices of gazing and photography, the diverse sensual qualities of the spaces that tourists move through are rarely considered. Thus an ocularcentric approach tends to ignore at least the potential for a wider range of sensual experience which occasionally might disrupt modes of repatriating the observed back into conventional systems of representation.

Representations and discourses that incorporate symbolic sites articulate with, transform and are transformed by texts from other conceptual frameworks (Barnes and Duncan, 1992, 7). Thus representations of place, although often persistent, are constantly in the process of transformation and may articulate with other representational modes, remain monologic, or be appropriated to signify new meanings. Discourses may be synthesised, but they can just as well exclude each other, even be unaware of each other. This means that sites are compendia of intersubjective meanings despite attempts to fix their meaning.

The increasing plurality of representations in the 'economy of signs' is nowhere more obvious than in global tourist settings, which as well as being appropriated by commercial, 'official' and colonial powers, also contain the histories and continued presence of men and women, diverse ethnic groups and classes, and are symbolised in contesting ways by religious and political movements. Thus, international tourist sites epitomise conflicts over spatial representation. I argue that given this proliferation of representations and the distinct forms of touristic practice that surround such sites, experience cannot always be recapitulated back into predictable and commodified discursive forms and systems of representation.

Place and spatial networks

To develop an exploration of ways of representing space and place, I will now examine the ways in which symbolic sites are represented as synedoches or metaphors for larger spaces, or are mapped onto an intertextual spatial system comprising a host of interlinked places which epitomise particular themes. The large symbolic reference points that are relevant in the context of this study are colonial, sacred and national spaces, which I discuss below. These spatial contexts are fashioned by the representations which connect places and are evoked at them. They are also practically constituted by the itineraries which tourists follow.

I have discussed the ways in which representations of places circulate through production and consumption in tourism. This picture is complicated by the consideration that landscapes and places, as ordered assemblages of objects and features, are *also* texts: their material organisation is intended to communicate meaning. This semiotic transmission of meaning operates in an intertextual way by utilising particular representational conventions about the style, architecture and decoration of sites and the arrangement of forms in the landscape to produce a linked set of signs (Edensor, 1997a).

The hermeneutic process whereby places are constructed and reconstructed is captured by Barnes and Duncan:

> Places are intertextual sites because various texts and discursive practices based on previous texts are deeply inscribed in their landscapes and institutions. We construct both the world and our actions towards it from texts that speak of who we are or wish to be. Such 'texts in the world' then recursively act back on the previous texts that shaped them.
>
> (1992, 7–8)

Consequently, the incorporation of symbolic tourist sites into particular discursive and mythical frameworks means that they always intertextually refer to other places and landscapes whether through popular representations about them or through architectural language. The references that are communicated by and about these related places aggregate into larger symbolic spaces, particular 'imagined' geographies in which key sites reinforce cognitive and affective meanings. Such spatial frameworks include the 'nation', ethnic and racial 'homelands', empires, realms of 'otherness' or sacrality. Moreover, tourist itineraries also join places together and construct symbolic routes which are themed according to exotic, historical, spiritual and communal qualities.

Thus conceptual frameworks inform spatial practices as well, since, as Rodman observes, 'places come into being through praxis, not just narratives' (1992, 642). These practical tourist networks constitute an assemblage of objects, places and people that are bound into a relationship. Thus, the discursive and representational forms which order these connections are 'performed and embodied in the network of the social' (Law, 1994, 22), reproducing the meaning of places and people's relationship with them, and the wider space they are part of, but not necessarily through a reflexive or proactive process. Thus, symbolic tourist sites are embedded in networks which depend upon the enaction of techniques and incorporation within an itinerary.

By their emplacement in various spatial contexts, places are diversely distinguished from, and linked to, other places and imaginary geographies. The mix of diverse practices and interpretations are unique at any point in time but these constituents continually change. What I want to show here is the way in which a particular symbolic site is incorporated into different symbolic and practical frameworks.

An identification of these various spatial networks through which places become diversely constituted advances a progressive notion where places are conceived as 'processes' rather than 'essences'. Places have multiple identities, are situated points at which a variety of activities occur and a diverse range of people pass through on different routes. The connections people make with places 'physically, by phone or by post, or in memory and imagination' (Massey, 1993, 65) vary enormously. Whilst places are unique they are not the result of some 'long internalised history' but are

> constructed out of a particular constellation of relations articulated together at a particular locus [comprising] . . . particular interactions and mutual articulations of social relations, social processes, experiences and understandings, in a situation of co-presence . . .
> (Massey, 1993, 66)

This recognition that the epistemological and representative frameworks and practical networks within which places are situated are constructed on a larger scale over time militates against the withdrawal into introverted and defensive reifications. Moreover, as social relations are (increasingly) stretched out over space, identification of the networks that operate in and through place can advance a global sense of place, through the recognition that social relations and spatial concepts are constituted at different scales, from the local to the global.

Places are constantly reconstituted by practices that occur in and around them but in conditions that are culturally and historically shaped. Shields has pointed out the ways in which spatial practices act to preserve dominant conceptions of space:

> an overarching order of social spatialisation is reproduced in concrete forms as a practice upon the world. It restates as well as reproduces 'discourses of space' which constitute it.
>
> (1991, 65)

Thus the ways in which different people experience and perform *in situ* relate to the institutional power relations that control which people gain access to the spaces and activities they are permitted to engage in once they have entered (Pred, 1990, 12). Several questions arise from this proliferation of practices and interpretations: Which are the dominant voices? Do dialogues occur between tourists from different cultural locations and, if so, do they produce mediated or hybrid practices or fierce contestation?

Especially pertinent here are the different ways in which people are situated within a local–global nexus, how they are located within global processes for instance, as international bourgeoisie or transnational capitalists; as religious conservatives or 'fundamentalists'; as package tourists from the West; as cultural intermediaries who interpret global and local forms of knowledge; as local traders; as nationalists or locals expressing a 'recursive' sense of place. International tourist sites are meeting points for people from different cultural locations, centres of domestic and foreign investment, and places where diverse forms of consumption and identification occur.

The theme and scale of tourist itineraries which intersect at a particular site can reveal the various ways in which visitors make sense of the route they follow, or highlight the significance or status of the site in the journey as a whole. The contemporary tourist may incorporate sites into a global framework (for instance, as 'wonders of the world'), a national context (for instance, a patriotic site such as a royal residence) or at local level (a fair). The construction of all itineraries signifies an approach to travel which embodies particular cultural concerns and priorities, based upon genealogies of spatial interpretation.

In the next chapter I will look at specific forms of tourist space which are constituted through the ways in which the different destinations are sewn together by tourists and travel agents thematically and intertextually. Next, however, I want to examine the most prominent symbolic spatial frameworks into which the Taj is incorporated in order to contextualise this study. The first symbolic realm into which the Taj was incorporated was the Moghul realm. The site symbolised Moghul imperial power and Islam (which I will discuss in greater detail in Chapter 3) in that an Islamic cosmology is represented in its architecture and design. Subsequently, the intensification of investment in developing tourist space has meant that the Taj has been discursively incorporated into global narratives which assign the significance of sites on a world scale, producing hierarchical assumptions about the symbolic geography of the world. Yet as an integral destination in different itineraries, diverse tourists incorporate the Taj into distinct symbolic realms. In order to both exemplify the formation of symbolic spaces and the ways in which tourist praxis reinscribes them, I will examine colonial, sacred and national forms. These realms are themselves marked by contestation over meaning and whilst there are dominant representations and practices in each formation, this contestation renders the site, and hence the wider symbolic realms of which it is part, unstable and in continual process.

Colonial space

Tourism continues to be strongly influenced by the longing to experience 'otherness', a desire which developed during the colonial era. Tourist and colonial development accompanied each other. During the era of British imperial expansion, travel writers were an advance party that formulated ways of knowing and writing about the 'other'. Once colonial administrations were established, the desire to travel through this newly accessible, decoded realm inspired numerous nineteenth-century travel accounts.

Although colonial powers asserted different cultural, economic and administrative priorities, they pursued the common goal of bringing hitherto unexploited spaces into production, transforming them into profit-maximising systems. Europeans came to assume that they had a right to divide and apportion the world, imposing their laws of property, exchange and production on other spaces. This giant colonial project employed the 'dual motion' of deterritorialisation, and then, reterritorialisation (Noyes, 1992, 114). Natural resources were deemed to belong 'rightfully to "civilisation" and "mankind" rather then to the indigenous peoples who inhabited those lands' (Spurr, 1993, 28). In a neo-colonial process, it is often imagined that it is the right of the wealthy contemporary tourist to travel the world in search of difference – parts of the world are colonised by tourists (with their enclaves and colonies) and their distinctive tourist infrastructures and technologies.

The ways in which contemporary tourism is typified by a technology of representation whereby objective and authoritative description can capture 'reality' has its roots in colonialism. In order to justify the violence and exploitation inherent in the colonial adventure (to themselves and metropolitan subordinate classes), the colonised had to be constructed as something other than, or opposite to, the colonisers. Since the colonised realm could not be 'othered' by adopting its own systems of knowledge, it had to be incorporated into European ways of understanding, absorbed within 'an accepted grid for filtering through the oriental into Western consciousness' (Said, 1978, 6). The rationalising, classifying force of science, and metropolitan notions of historical progress and civilised behaviour were used to distinguish the space of the colonising self and the space of the colonised 'other'. This binary construction offered a sense of ontological and epistemological security when dealing with and entering the realm of this 'other', confining the threat of alterity (ibid., 167).

The project to incorporate this otherness, 'its odd calendars, its exotic spatial configurations, its hopelessly strange languages, its seemingly perverse morality' (ibid., 166) involved

> regulatory codes, classifications, specimen cases, periodical reviews, dictionaries, grammars, commentaries, editions, translations, all of which together formed a simulacrum of the Orient and reproduced it materially in the West.
>
> (ibid., 166)

This situated way of seeing and knowing the 'other' is exemplified by the way in which certain Western practices of pictorially representing places in the colonised realm often entailed the writing out of people from the landscape. In this way, the scene could be surveyed and understood according to criteria that ignored local presence, aesthetics and knowledge. This commanding gaze conveys a sense of mastery over landscapes and bodies whilst conforming to European norms of the picturesque. A set of signs epitomising difference were integrated into signifying systems out of which emergent representations stimulated the search for 'landscapes to admire' (Tillotson, 1993, 142) whilst tempering their exoticism by making them conform to a set of supposedly universal aesthetic values.

Local forms of representation were rarely considered. Because of the presumed 'inability' of the colonised to represent and understand their own space, the 'expertise' of the coloniser was required. Kabbani captures this well in describing how the space of the other

> is caught in a state of timelessness, crammed full of incidents remarkable for their curiosity or eroticism, hushed into silence by its own mysteries, incapable of self-expression, mute until the western observer lends it his voice.
>
> (1986, 73)

Again, there are parallels in the way in which 'official' guides and tour personnel ignore local knowledge and representations and decode the exotic for tourists according to conventions of the picturesque and the classificatory.

With the 'discovery' of the rest of the world, the curiosities of 'others' were represented for consumption as a spectacle, a *tableau vivant*. Colonial authorities reassembled, framed and defined the 'otherness' of colonised space, producing the world as exhibition, actualised in the great nineteenth-century world expositions, the growth in museums and encyclopaedias of 'mankind' in the West. Colonial powers put the 'other' on show, marvelled at its strangeness, yet domesticated and rendered it intelligible, further easing passage through colonised space. With the rapid increase in global travel, 'other' cultures 'on display' can now be sought in their indigenous contexts; the whole world becomes a tableau where key features are highlighted and practices are staged (McClintock, 1994).

As the foremost exponents of European ways of feeling and describing the (space of the) 'other', travel writers were 'the seeing eye, and the recounting voice' (Kabbani, 1986, 6). Travel writing was embedded in the objectivist ethics of the new sciences of anthropology, archaeology, geography, map-making and planning. Exponents often saw themselves as heroes 'rescuing the Orient from the obscurity, alienation and strangeness which [they themselves] had properly distinguished' (Said, 1978, 121). For instance, the foremost 'Indianist' of the late eighteenth century, Sir William Jones, stated that his aim was to know India better than anyone else (Keay, 1989, 19–38).

European travel writers devised itineraries in which particular fetishised sites were stages upon which the 'other' could be imagined; they become exotic attractions epitomising global high points of cultural difference and splendour. Once encoded, subsequent travellers minimised any personal fragmentation, and could consume reliable signs of otherness:

> certain images, once codified in language, become static and final . . . travellers depended on each other's testimony in forging their narrative; the place became the place they had read about; the natives functioned as the traveller imagined they would do.
>
> (Kabbani, 1986, 114)

As we will see, contemporary tours and guidebooks pursue, often almost to the letter, the obsessions and foci of colonial accounts about sites and cultures, and follow similar codes by which difference is incorporated. Moreover, the ranking of sites/sights during colonialism which are held to embody difference continues to inform the shaping of tourist itineraries.

Colonial administrators also introduced an ethics of conservation whereby romantic ideas about particular sites were subject to 'the criteria of the colonial power' to decide which buildings were considered to be of architectural and historic importance (King, 1990, 56). As I will demonstrate in the final chapter, the development of global tourism has given this priority extra impetus, as attractions become graded as to their importance and are conceived of as belonging to the world, not merely the specific culture in which they are situated.

In constructing a colonial space in India, pre-colonial travellers first imagined 'an entire series of European institutions on the natural landscape' (Spurr, 1993, 30) and then colonisers imposed them. Thus the work of domestication was underway in the pre-colonial imagination, envisioning European agriculture, rustic scenes and churches. Subsequently, European notions of space were materially transmitted to colonial space by architects, planners and agents of surveillance. This created a particular geography incorporating urban nodes, newly designed regions, transport networks, military and administrative installations, and disciplinary institutions such as schools, prisons and hospitals.

Colonial cities were the 'nerve centres' of colonial exploitation, linking metropolitan and colonised economies and cultures by serving as administrative centres, nodes in communications networks, military centres, locations where indigenous and colonising residents inhabited different spaces, and places which were remodelled according to Western aesthetics and principles (King, 1990, 17–19). The foundation of institutions was later followed by the building of separate residential European quarters with their distinctive housing and leisure facilities. This new spatial order was governed by military, political and cultural customs and laws which controlled and excluded particular residents. In this dual city, the prescription of who should reside, and which activities were appropriate, was stringently regulated.

Many Indian cities contained a cantonment area where military and administrative functions were carried out and European residents lived, which was in marked contrast to the 'native quarter'. In the former, a disciplinary regime of order was physically evoked by the geometric pattern and enforced exclusivity, and a British visual order was maintained through the construction of wide avenues, gardens, and cultivated verges. Mixing between the 'races' was limited to organising the work of the local servants who were generally forbidden to reside in the cantonment. In this white enclave, styles and activities conformed to an imagined Englishness. English adaptations of indigenous styles, such as the bungalow, or the importation of selective features of English provinciality, such as Gothic churches, typified the colonisers' public space. This was compounded by the introduction of European institutions such as the golf and tennis club, the colonial bar and the park. Plants and flowers that reminded the British of home were also brought in. However, rather than constituting a wholesale importation of Englishness, the codes that informed the organisation of the cantonment were hybrid in that they utilised and adapted local features to conform to their own taste.

In this book, I address the ways in which contemporary tourism duplicates some of these conditions. Firstly, in the next chapter, I discuss how the producers of tourist enclaves similarly produce a spatial order. The enforcement of a distinct separation from the local population suggests a neo-colonial relationship between tourists and inhabitants. Secondly, these enclaves themselves, and the wider system of enclaves with which they are linked, contain design features, and points of familiarity, such as global eating and drinking outlets and shops, to make tourists feel 'at home'. Thirdly, the exclusive medical, transport, information and recreational facilities available for tourists often contrasts profoundly with their local equivalents.

The relationship between the regimented, domesticated European enclave and the 'other' space, that of the indigenous population, was complex, mirroring the ambivalence Europeans felt for colonised space and its inhabitants. For the colonisers, the 'native quarter' was:

> the out-of-bounds city where the living and the dead intermingle . . . the carnivalesque world of the bazaar city where nothing is delineated but everything exists in a chaotic state of intermingling: a carnival of night and a landscape of darkness, noise, offensive smells and obscenities.
>
> (Parry, 1993, 245)

At one level, the perceived chaos evinced by physical proximity and contact, disease, the lack of an obvious demarcation between public and private, and the multiplicity of movements and types of people provoked a disorientation amongst the colonisers, a constant fear that the structures of power and order might become contaminated, brought down or seduced by too close an association with the 'other'. At another level, however, the colonial fantasies discussed above could be reimagined in this space, played out in brothels and performed during festivals.

Although the dominant tropes of colonial representation asserted that the West was more advanced, enlightened and at a higher evolutionary stage than the colonies, the flip side of this was that such spaces were also conceived of as realms of 'lost innocence' where a more 'authentic' culture was being replaced by the tragic inevitability of European 'progress', an 'imperialist nostalgia' (Rosaldo, 1993) which continues to stimulate travel to the non-West and reflects contemporary anxieties about a loss of cultural authenticity.

These fantasies and desires about colonised subjects and space constitute shared imaginary repertoires (Stallybrass and White, 1986, 5) which persist in international tourism. For example, India is aestheticised, 'reified under western eyes as a frieze or a pageant, and romanticised as an object of sensuous and voluptuous pleasure' (Parry, 1993, 299) as well as being depicted as the negation of moral order and sanity. The common link between the tropes is power, which is both driven by desire, and the urge to possess and control. The creation of these desirable mythic realms emanated out of the suppressed fantasies of the colonisers and provided a 'malleable theatrical space' for 'self-dramatisation and differentness' (Kabbani, 1986, 11). During the colonial era, the essentialising discourse of science was always echoed by fantasies (Low, 1993, 199). With the decline of modernist rationality, these submerged desires have emerged, exemplified by the qualities of 'otherness' which tourist brochures commodify.

Ultimately, contemporary representations of the space of the 'other', like representations of colonial space, reflect what Said has called 'flexible positional superiority' (Said, 1985, 7), the power to contingently define, order, and describe. Their ambivalence shows that the perceptions and practices of the powerful can be disaggregated, but since they have an interest in a common project, it becomes apparent that 'discursive strategies' (Thomas, 1994) are mobilised to incorporate their various interests.

Having drawn several parallels with the material and imaginary construction of colonised space, I argue that a spatial conception conceived during the colonial era structures the experience of most Western tourists to India, both in terms of the representations they consume and reproduce, and the ways in which the construction of tourist space follows colonial imperatives.

Almost all package tours to India include what is popularly termed the 'Golden Triangle', the circuit linking visits to Delhi, Agra and Jaipur, where certain attractions are visited. In all these places there are palaces, forts or religious buildings, mostly originating from the Moghul and medieval period of Indian history. This emphasis on the past reinforces the idea that India is trapped in the past since few aspects of contemporary India are addressed in the tour.

Most package tourists interviewed were fulsome in their praise of the historical attractions and the standard of service. However, when it came to discussing contemporary India, many recited a litany of those themes by which the 'Third World' is imagined in the West, notably over-population, poverty, begging, disorder, filth and the lack of self-help. The evaluations as to what constitutes 'civilised behaviour', 'abuse', 'self-help' and the like emerge out of a particular set of unmediated Western experiences with roots in colonialism:

> Eric *(American professional, late 20s travelling on a 'round the world ticket' with his friend)*: Ever since we left Australia we've been experiencing Third World poverty and we're sick of being in places that are less civilised than we're used to. India stinks. The Taj is kinda nice but I'm sick of seeing people defecating and expectorating everywhere. Who needs to see that?

> John *(49, office manager from Southampton, UK, with his partner on a three-week package tour)*: You've seen them here, pissing and shitting anywhere, and spitting, chucking things in the street. They are dirty, there's no doubt. And the trouble is they take their habits with them and it causes friction when they migrate to live in England.

> Fiona *(29, solicitor from London, taking a 17-day package tour for the first time with her partner)*: It does bring home to you that it's population control that's the biggest problem here – the millions and millions of people everywhere – and I don't think they know how to solve it.

> Bess *(62, retired head teacher, travelling with her friend on a two-week package tour)*: The impression has been that there's tremendous poverty, more than I expected, and I've been amazed at the dirt. It's the whole fabric of the country. They can't escape it can they, the dryness and the dust.

These impressions are especially notable because the tours undertaken by these tourists were structured precisely to shield them from local life. Nevertheless, the glimpses of non-enclavic, non-heritage space snatched on the way to attractions, hotels and emporia are sufficient to disturb many tourists and seem to confirm their neo-colonialist, unmediated preconceptions.

A different imaginary India is that expressed by non-package Western tourists, or backpackers. The common themes on their 'alternative' travel circuit focus on particular types of experience based upon the 'mystical', the 'sacred' and the drug-induced. The establishment of 'freak' centres such as Goa, Pushkar, Dharamsala and Manali; and spiritual centres and ashrams at, for example, Pune and Rishikesh mean that these are incorporated into backpacker itineraries. The themes of exploration based around drugs, mysticism and the allure of the non-Western testify to a neo-colonial construction of the exotic, where India becomes a magical space in which self-realisation can be accomplished.

Sacred space

An exploration of the forms of sacred space is particularly important for this study since by far the commonest form of tourism in India is for pilgrimage. The landscape of India is already saturated with representations of sacrality since:

> The work of the puranas and other scriptures was to superimpose a complex, psychologically profound body of myth on the surface of place rooted sanctity. It provided a mythic geographic structure on a grand scale, limining a subcontinent.
>
> (Sopher, 1987, 14)

Many tourist sites are symbolic sacred locations and centres of religious practice and at local and national scale, landscapes are saturated with places, routes and regions designated as sacred. The widespread assumption that earthly space reflects, symbolises and is a constituent of the sacred realm, and the sheer profusion of places that are deemed sacred, considerably influences the experience and perception of space in India.

I have emphasised that there are multiple interpretations of place, and similarly, the sacred characteristics of places, areas and paths can be variously configured into wider spatial schemes of sacrality, or incorporated into certain religious traditions and geographies. Such multiplicity is especially apparent in India with its diversity of religions, sects and cults, each paying adherence to specific sacred centres and networks, and often the same sites in different ways. These overlapping conceptual and practical spatial frameworks make generalisation about sacred landscapes, routes and sites difficult, but in order to establish the basic characteristics of sacred space, I will identify certain commonalities.

Any discussion of the religious geography of India needs to recognise the different scales at which geographies of the sacred are constructed. Most evidently, India is inscribed as Hindu and is widely conceived as synonymous with Hinduism, the religion adhered to by 85 per cent of India's inhabitants. This notion of 'Mother India' as the sacred spatial container for its children has tended to naturalise the Hindus as the 'proper' historical subjects, although this may also include religions that are held to have emerged from within the Hindu tradition such as Sikhism and Jainism. As will be discussed, the attempts of post-independence 'secular' nationalists to construct the heritage of the Indian nation as constituted by all the various religious traditions that are included within its boundaries has come under severe attack from Hindu fundamentalist nationalists who emphasise the Hindu essentials of India's spatial and historical dimensions.

In contrast to this Hindu sense of dwelling in a spiritual homeland, Muslims orientate themselves towards Mecca, specifically facing the *Kaaba,* during daily prayer as is indicated by the *mihrab* (niche) at all mosques. Whilst there are numerous Islamic sites within India, Mecca is emotionally and geographically conceived by Muslims as the 'navel of the world', symbolically linking heaven and earth (Schimmel, 1991, 175). The *Kaaba* mirrors its rectangular counterpart in the realm of heaven, and terrestrially, its four corners are imagined to point towards 'all spatial relations in the world' (Schimmel, 1991, 175). This orientation to a supra-national point again causes Hindu fundamentalists to question the loyalty of Muslims to India and emphasise their essential foreignness.

The Hindu sacred geography of India is differently constituted at local, regional and national scales. At village level, sacred features mark everyday living and working space:

> In the village, at its portals, within its core, on its boundary, along nearby streams and on hills within its view, some mark of the sacred will be found. At this scale, sacred places may be taken to be ubiquitous in the Hindu ecumene.
>
> (Sopher, 1987, 6)

Most Indian villages are planned according to religious symbolism. Temples are sited in auspicious places, banyan trees planted to please deities, small shrines mark sites of ritual activity, and areas within villages are demarcated according to caste, itself a manifestation of a divine order (Park, 1994, 227). Beyond village level, there are shrines, sacred sites and temples that are the focus of annual or more frequent visits from those residing within a region. The density of widely recognised sacred places varies and some regional clusters of sites have attained national significance. Although particular sects have sites of central importance, at the national level there is a generally recognised hierarchy that enshrines seven places as particularly sacred and worthy of visiting as a pilgrim. These are Dwarka, Ayodhya, Mathura, Varanasi, Ujjain, Hardiwar and Kachipuram. The importance of these holy sites is ontologically and practically underlined through the undertaking of pilgrimages which 'promise more general, more esoteric and more salvational results than the small shrines of regional importance' (Jash, 1990, 9).

The nationwide distribution of these sites is widely believed to have promoted the awareness of a shared nationality as well as a common religious heritage despite the complex differences in culture and language between Indians. Pilgrimage to these super-sites, according to Srivastava,

> serves the purpose of disseminating the manners, customs and values of different regions and cultures of India . . . and acts as an agent of India's age old vision of unity in diversity.
>
> (1990, 86)

This is believed to be particularly so since special conditions pertain at such sites, for instance, the rules of caste and untouchability are suspended, engendering a feeling of shared experience and belonging.

Stoddard conceives of sacred space as having three dimensions, namely points (places), lines (routes) and areas (regions) (1987, 96). Intensifying their sacrality, the most holy places tend to be regional agglomerations of sacred points which are interconnected by symbolic paths. In many cases these routes connecting sites are circumambulated many times as a mark of devotion by the pilgrim. In general, Hinduism perceives there to be no division between sacred and profane space as in other religions since the earth and all that is contained within it are deemed to be holy. However, important pilgrimage sites are set off 'from the broader religious fabric by the practice of a more condensed and higher intensity version of that known and practised elsewhere' (Morinis, 1984, 231). The sacred geography of such sites is imbued with paths of intense sacredness. For instance, at Varanasi, the following of one path is described by Stoddard as 'moving through a tunnel of sanctified space connecting 108 shrines' (1987, 99).

The sheer scale of religious pilgrimage in India, where it is a common part of everyday life, must be stressed. Pilgrimage itineraries often include a number of sacred places as well as secular sites. As I have discussed, the parallels between pilgrimage and tourism have frequently been drawn, but in an Indian context, secular and sacred sites seem to be the focus of separate practices and feelings.

At the largest scale is the Kumbh Mela which occurs every three years, consecutively occurring at four holy places. The gathering at Allahabad in 1989 numbered fifteen million pilgrims (Finlay et al., 1993). However, there are also numerous regional and local processions and marches for various sects and commemorations, constituting an extraordinary diversity of religious sites and pilgrims. Hindu pilgrims principally visit Saivite and Vaisnavite shrines, but there are numerous other centres for sects and followers of particular deities and gurus. Sacred sites are often invested with particular significance by different groups, and accordingly are the focus of multiple meanings and practices.

For instance, in Uttar Pradesh there are particularly important shrines dedicated to Sufi saints at Fatehpur Sikri and Ajmer. Although they are part of the Islamic pilgrimage tradition in India, these sites also attract large numbers of Hindu pilgrims. Besides arguing that people go on pilgrimage for innumerable reasons, Bhardwaj argues that such sites are multi-religious especially if they are purported to possess some healing or wish-fulfilling properties (1987a), emphasising the rather earthly, pragmatic concerns for divine assistance that impel much pilgrimage.

Geographically, the most important centres of pilgrimage for Hindus are *tirthas*, river-crossing places, and all rivers in India possess a sacred and purifying character. There are also many holy lakes, mountains and other natural features which are woven into sacred myths, and imprint landscapes with layers of sacred meaning.

The physical fabric of the main pilgrimage centres and routes is complexly woven into diverse cosmological narratives and meanings by the spatial practices of the visiting pilgrims. The embodied sacred symbolism of the geographies of such centres and religious performance have been explored by scholars, particularly in the case of Varanasi or Kashi, often considered to be the pre-eminent Hindu site. Sacred and symbolic ritual paths within the city proliferate, and the traversing of these routes integrates 'cosmogonic, mythic and experienced times' (Singh, 1987). The sacred symbol of *mandala* which integrates the cosmos and human being is superimposed upon the form of Varanasi, and enacted through the pilgrim's ritual passage, constituting what Singh terms a 'faithscape' (1990, 141). The affective, mnemonic significance of these rituals reinscribed religious subjectivity in space.

Remarkably, Varanasi also includes within its own sacred geography all the other *tirthas* in India, and all the sacred places are symbolically present here, encoded onto actual physical sites. Transposed onto Varanasi's geography are other pre-eminent cities cited above, the 'four abodes of the Gods' located at the north, south, west and east of India, and the twelve *lingas* of light, besides many other India-wide sacred places. Cosmologically then, 'Kashi is the paradigm of the sacred place', and symbolically embodies the whole of India: 'Kashi is a cosmopolis – a city that is a world' (Eck, 1991, 138).

The complex facets of sacred space in India can also be illustrated by another example, that of Prayaga, or Allahabad, the point where the holy rivers Jamuna, Ganges and Saraswati meet. The triangular piece of land in between the rivers is commonly perceived as 'the *mons veneris* of the goddess Earth, and Prayaga is regarded as its generative organ' (Dubey, 1987, 135), a geo-cosmological allusion that inscribes the site as the centre of creation, an intersection of human and earthly geographies and the space of the heavens. Temporally, the past, present and future flow into one another, so that this corresponds to 'the ultimate sense of sacrality related to space and time' (Dubey, 1990, 117).

This demonstrates the ways in which landscape and place are constructed out of sacred cosmologies and practices. In India, ways of looking at and experiencing the landscape are highly influenced by the sacred places, routes and regions that proliferate and are thereby differentiated from European practices and affective responses. For pilgrims, the sacred destinations of their journeys, although they may be in 'picturesque' settings, are more important for their spiritual properties than any aesthetic qualities. Notions of the cosmological and metaphorical significance of landscapes and places generally predominate over the aesthetics of the romantic picturesque. Thus, a voyage through local countryside, or more extensive travels, are marked by passing a host of sacred features and sites.

For instance, in the cosmological scheme of Hindu thought, *tirthas* are conceived of as being located in the earthly realm, or *loka*, of the universe, but are also imagined as fords between universal *lokas*, points 'of intersection of heaven and earth, the divine and human' (Morinis, 1984, 278). These 'nodes in a sacred geography' defy notions of a 'genius loci' for 'most of them lack the distinctive attributes of place that might be seen and sensed on the ground' (Sopher, 1987, 8). During pilgrimages, the window to divine power reveals that earthly perceptions of place are illusory. The terrestrial intertextual reference points that conjoin places become 'replaced by sacred nodes and geography itself becomes a sacred geometry' (Sopher, 1987, 14).

Besides the already evident sacred imprint on landscape, architecture and planning has attempted to represent the sacred by devising and dividing spaces to correlate with a wider spiritual realm, inscribing a textual quality. Hindu architecture follows the ancient *vastu-canons*, wherein buildings and towns are constructed according to layouts which reflect a cosmological spatial significance. Hindu temples are suffused with imagery and symbols representing sacred realms. On a larger scale, town-planning is also carried out according to a sense of the cosmological (see Bohle, 1987, 280–89). Similarly, in Islamic architecture, cosmological symbolism is part of the structure. For instance, as at the Taj Mahal, funerary gardens are divided into four parts so that they point to all parts of the earth and the canals that divide these parts symbolise paradise in which four rivers are believed to flow (Schimmel, 1991, 178).

Following this general discussion of the characteristics of sacred space, I want to concentrate on the ways in which the Taj Mahal is incorporated into this symbolic spatial conception. In fact, roughly half of domestic visitors to the Taj are on pilgrimage and decide to stop off on the way to their sacred destination. For Hindu pilgrims, the Taj is not the principle purpose of their tour and thus forms part of the itinerary, although it does not fit into the sacred landscape which their journey reconstructs. The subordinate position of the Taj in these religious routes was stressed by several interviewees:

Jadhav *(59, schoolteacher from Mahrashtra, one of a party of eight)*: The reason we are here is because we are on a pilgrimage to Kashi and Mathura. As Agra is near Mathura, we thought we would come and look at this historical place as we had a bit of spare time, otherwise we wouldn't have come.

Anil *(38, architect from Mumbai with a family party of eight)*: Yes, we enjoy ourselves at the Taj but chiefly we are away from our homes for one thing, to visit Mathura, of great importance to us who follow the Lord Krishna.

The area around the Taj contains plenty of locally notable sites, and Uttar Pradesh is full of important Hindu sites. The holy rivers, the Ganges and the Jamuna, pass through the state and the sacred Himalayas slope into its northern reaches. Varanasi, Mathura, Allahabad, Kanpur, Ayodhya, Rishikesh, Hardwar, Badrinath and Gangotri are the main spiritual centres and this is reflected in the itineraries of domestic visitors. More locally, the headquarters of the Radah Soami sect is on the outskirts of Agra and attracts many devotees who pack in a visit to the Taj.

The Taj Mahal is in its own right a sacred site and symbol for many Indian Muslims, a dimension I shall look at in more detail in subsequent chapters. Tens of thousands of Muslims flock to the Taj during the annual pilgrimage to Ajmer to visit the tomb of a renowned sufi saint, also shared by Hindus as a holy site, and it is often conceived as part of the pilgrimage:

> Mohammed *(58, shopkeeper and part-time priest from Bangalore en route to Ajmer with family party of seven)*: This was built by a son of Jehangir, a great Moghul and a great Muslim. Every year I come to Ajmer for the annual *Urs* and I always visit the Taj at the same time.

At nearby Fatehpur Sikra lies the tomb of the sufi Saint, Shaikh Salim Chisti, also popular with both Muslims and Hindus, particularly for childless women who desire a son.

Although Vaisnites are the most numerous pilgrims who visit the Taj, due to the proximity of Mathura, there are also Shaivites and followers of diverse Hindu sects and gurus, Jains and Sikhs. Also, there are a number of important Buddhist sites relatively near Agra, notably Sarnath and Sanchi, and Buddhist pilgrims from within and outside India also visit the Taj en route.

These pilgrimages usually entail a minimum of sightseeing since most time is spent in sacred centres, or in travelling, which, for some, is considerable. In general, large groups of pilgrims travel together from all over India and commonly charter a coach. At the Taj Mahal, many village groups of forty or fifty quickly walk round the site before rejoining their bus to continue their journey to Ajmer or Mathura.

The Mathura–Vrindaban–Gokul complex is only fifty-seven kilometres from Agra and is the most popular attraction for pilgrims passing through the city and visiting the Taj. Over 75 per cent of the Hindu pilgrims I interviewed at the Taj intended to stay in pilgrims' lodges and guest houses for a few days carrying out religious acts and visiting the temples. Popularly known as Braj Bhoomi, the area is a centre of pilgrimage for Vaishnavites since it was in Mathura that Lord Krishna, the incarnation of Vishnu, was born and his heroic exploits and adventures with the *gopis* (shepherd girls) are believed to have taken place in the area. There are several thousand temples in Mathura and Vrindaban and many bathing *ghats* on the banks of the Jamuna.

At most pilgrimage centres such as Braj Bhoomi, the calendar is divided up into different pilgrimage seasons, auspicious periods and commemorative occasions when visits may be undertaken for specific purposes and to celebrate specific events and deities. During these religious festivals, especially from August to October, the area is extremely crowded with pilgrims visiting the many places of worship, bathing in the *ghats* and buying religious souvenirs and symbols. The surrounding landscape is thoroughly suffused with the divine. This is best exemplified by a popular map sold for three rupees to pilgrims which points out the chief places of sacred importance along with accompanying images of Krishna's legendary deeds.

The map highlights the density of sacred spots connected with the life of Krishna. These events are often woven into the landscape. For instance, at Goverdhan, Krishna held aloft the Giriraj hill on one finger for seven days to protect the populace from the rainstorm sent down by the rain deity, Indra; and at Barsana, according to a brochure, 'the four prominent hill peaks, symbolic of four faced divinity, are adorned by temples in reverence of Ladliji' (the latter being Radhika, Krishna's lover) ('Mathura – Vrindaban', UP Tourism, Lucknow). Besides mountains and water-tanks, the most important physical feature is the River Jamuna along which Krishna watered his cows and sported with the *gopis* (shepherdesses). On the map, moreover, the landscape is portrayed as replete with icons of Hindu sacrality: cows, temples, *ghats* and banyan trees. This sacred landscape is not merely gazed upon but is space upon which pilgrims practise particular bodily acts of devotion. They swim in the bathing *ghats*, meditate by the river and complete the devotional act of *parikaama*, a fifty-kilometer circular walk around the most venerated sites.

At a pilgrimage site such as Mathura, the distinction between secular and religious tourists in terms of experience of the site and inspiration for undertaking the journey is apparent. There are certainly aspects of secular tourism in the practices of pilgrims to Mathura, for instance, a visit to the Taj. Furthermore, the mass buying and selling of souvenirs in Mathura and Vrindaban and the urge to see all the important sites are activities that many visitors are engaged in. However, the central purposes of the pilgrim's visit – to gain religious status, to worship and celebrate the heavenly, to seek special divine favours, to witness and experience the power of the divine – are not comparable to secular tourism which, for all its urgent search for the symbolic and romantic, does not approach the intensity and involvement of the pilgrim's experience of sacred space and place.

In Braj Bhoomi, the devotion and emotional response to (images of) Krishna at some of the important temples, and the identification and self inscription through religious ritual activity involves a deep personal relationship with the sights beheld and a figural and bodily engagement that is qualitatively distinct from secular tourist awe in the presence of the famous or spectacular. The force of the experience in confronting the longed-for sacred site, undertaken often with considerable hardship by poor pilgrims, although superficially akin to the secular tourist quest to visit the globally renowned, is usually an experience that strikes much deeper into the notion of the self and emotional life. Thus the gasps of joy and immersion in the experience of witnessing the sacred, or the serene absorption in meditation of the holy, is the culmination of a spiritual journey which depends upon a different construction of symbolic space to secular conceptions. The Western touristic experience of India is typified by a distance between the self and the observed, that of the visitor in the realm of the 'other', whereas pilgrimage depends more on the absolute identification with place, self destiny and history.

The notion that the specific symbolic sites I have discussed are incorporated within a larger sacred realm, namely India itself – the spiritual and geographical homeland of a religious community, usually taken to refer to Hindus and associated faiths – brings us to the symbolic geography of the nation.

National space

Geertz has commented on the 'conceptual ambiguity' and 'theoretical eclecticism' which have bedevilled attempts at defining the 'nation' (1963, 107–8), a problem exacerbated by the manifold forms that 'nations' have assumed. This mutability highlights the flexibility of the nation as concept and the concomitant propensity for nationalism to be allied to a diverse range of projects, aspirations and ideologies. Chameleon-like, nationalism has conjoined with class, religious, ethnic and racial articulations of identity and become subsumed within fascist, communist, democratic and monarchist movements.

There has been much debate over which pre-eminent features define the nation, notably between conceptions that emphasise the political, territorial entity demarcating the rule of particular laws, citizens and government, and the cultural dimensions which express the ethnic and traditional constituents of the national subjects, their birthright and their cultural heritage. My emphasis here is upon the spatial characteristics of the nation and nationalism but rather than focusing upon the nation as a bounded 'power container' (Giddens, 1985), upon the political dimensions of territoriality, I am more particularly concerned with the cultural representation of the nation as a space with distinct qualities and the diverse ways in which this is imagined. What follows is an examination of the processes by which nations are culturally constructed, the ways in which national subjects are inscribed in the national space, and the importance of especial symbolic national sites which signify (aspects of) the nation as a whole. Rather than comprising a set of reified notions however, these constituents of national space are continually subject to external and internal contestation.

Smith considers that the nation has been the dominant modern spatial division. As the 'most inclusive community' and the most effective 'limit for distinguishing the outsider' (Smith, 1991, 44), it has served the modern quest for the ontological and emotional security of a place in history and in the world. It is often asserted that in a world of 'expanding horizons and dissolving boundaries' (Morley and Robins, 1992, 5), through the proliferation of information flows and mass migration, the affective and cognitive staying power of the nation is being replaced by more fluid, hybrid spaces and selves. However, in the face of such rapid social and economic change, the recursive comforts of the 'homeland' can offer a familiar, circumscribed space of identity which provides a defence against the very loss of situatedness in time and space that globalising processes threaten.

These contradictory global processes have produced tensions between identification with the nation and with other spaces: larger (the Indian diaspora, Asia, the community of nations), smaller (Kashmir, the village) and also virtual and imaginative spaces (cyberspace, a future Indian/Hindu empire). These tensions find their expression in the continuing national political discourses about control over the economy, the erosion of cultural values, and campaigns for self-determination for subaltern groups. Whilst the nation as concept is in a state of flux, national identity continues to offer ontological and epistemological security.

As a cultural construction, the nation consists of a 'definite social space within which members must live and work'. Moreover, it demarcates 'an historic territory that locates a community in time and space', within which anniversaries, rituals and religious occasions are collectively celebrated. The notion of national space is consolidated by symbolic sites, national landscapes, and the existence of supposedly archetypal objects and scenes which populate national space. These scenes and artefacts are repeatedly represented and circulated throughout the nation and beyond, are frequently celebrated by writers and poets, photographed and portrayed by artists. Official historic accounts and literary canons are transmitted via national education systems, which, along with the system of government, law and religion, constitute the institutions which govern national life and have their own symbolic centres. Finally, these themes and images of the nation are continually discursively reproduced via the national and international media, and in the burgeoning tourist industry, and constitute the images and narratives by which tourists imagine 'other' cultures.

However, the symbolic ingredients of the nation are continually fought over, defended and undermined. For most nations contain groups who attempt to circumscribe nationhood, to posit exclusive versions of national identity, and those who adopt more inclusive discourses. For instance, the nation usually has a well-defined territory with clear boundaries, a demarcated space which is often represented as a definitive 'homeland', a historic land,

> where terrain and people have exerted mutual, and beneficial, influence over several generations . . . (and have produced) a repository of

historic memories and associations, the place where 'our' sages, saints and heroes worked, prayed and fought.

(Smith, 1991, 9)

Exclusive versions assert that only bona-fide members of this homeland, the 'true nationals' can respond to common memories, myths, symbols and traditions. This consolidates the idea that there is a 'national genius', an indigenous character unique to this national space, signifying a political 'super family', a 'community of history and destiny' (Smith, 1991, 161) wherein traditions, history and genes mythically continue. Within this family, different roles are allotted on the basis of class and gender (Edensor and Kothari, 1994; Yuval-Davies, 1997). Moreover, representatives of this naturalised and 'authentic' community attempt to define national belonging, labelling those who do not follow 'national' traditions and ceremonies, myths and 'official' histories, and national religions as 'invaders', 'foreigners' or 'enemies within'.

Exclusive representations of the national subject embody specific ethnic, racial, religious and sexual attributes. Frequently, the 'rediscovery' of national authenticity and purity posits a particular 'authentic' national subject who symbolically embodies the pre-lapsarian ideal, and is represented as the true heir to the national space. Immigrants, colonisers, racial, religious and ethnic minorities whose antecedents are supposed to have come to dwell in national space after the 'Golden Age' may not share purified notions of the national culture and heritage, and this makes them subject to suspicion regarding their national loyalty.

However, within the national space there are a multiplicity of shared memories, heroes, myths and histories. Monolithic assertions of nationality are always difficult to sustain and this has particularly been exemplified by the proliferation of challenges to 'official' histories by subaltern groups who have 'rewritten' themselves into history and decentre the established versions and symbols of national subjectivity. Similarly, national sites, ceremonies and landscapes are subject to contestation. These contestations may be perpetrated by groups who either wish to proffer alternative interpretations of these cultural elements, or replace them with other symbolic entities.

'National landscapes' and the selection of elements utilised to represent national character are equally subject to contestation, an issue particularly pertinent to this study. For example, the English National Trust is criticised for the importance it places on restoring and preserving country houses at the expense of the countryside, reinforcing the notion that they symbolise a pre-modern, ideal national rural order (Wright, 1985; Hewison, 1987). Moreover, through tourist marketing and films, the representation of the English countryside is often held to be biased towards a southern (non-existent) rural idyll. Similarly, Pawson has shown how the landscape of New Zealand is remembered and represented in contrasting ways by European descendants and Maoris (1992, 15–33).

The meaning of particular national symbolic sites changes over time and is continually subject to contestation. National monuments have been particularly subject to the vicissitudes of politics. In Eastern Europe, the mass removal of statuary commemorating communist leaders and heroes is the most recent dramatic example of a change in the arrangement of national symbols in the landscape.

Attempts to fix national memory and identity, to 'map history onto territory', are integral to the ideological rhetoric of nationalism (Boyarin, 1994, 16). The idea of the nation as 'imagined community' (Anderson, 1983) presupposes a demarcated space which incorporates particularly symbolic landscapes and sites. Revealing the 'uniqueness of the nation's moral geography' (Smith, 1991, 16), these 'sacred centres' are repositories of common memories, myths and traditions and the sites for a range of collective and individual performances of ritual and pilgrimage. In most nations there is an ongoing attempt to identify 'national landscape ideologies' (Short, 1991) which incorporate valorised rural realms and symbolic sites. Statues of key historical figures and epic national monuments are situated at locations around which public life is organised. Johnson has argued that the power of these structures lies in their status as 'points of physical and ideological orientation' and together they constitute materialised 'circuits of memory' (1995, 63) around which performances and everyday life are organised.

Typically, nations contain an amalgam of significant sites which are considered to be of especial national importance. In England, for instance, these are sites symbolically central to 'official' national histories and political power, namely Buckingham Palace (royalty), Westminster Abbey (dead royalty, poets and statesmen), the Tower of London (the Crown Jewels), the Houses of Parliament (democracy) and Trafalgar Square (a paramount national hero). A network of sites consolidates national attributes and history. Intertextually linked by themes of glory, majesty and patriotism, they are the nuclei or framework of national geographies, form part of the 'national environment ideology' and are the most popular stops on typical tourist itineraries.

Hetherington has described how the important English national site of Stonehenge is the focus for many conflictual and contested meanings. The dominant interpretation is that Stonehenge is a key site of Englishness, an important encapsulation of English heritage. However, this is challenged by the rival notion that it is a place for carnival, a pagan site suitable for the festive celebration of 'New Age' values (Hetherington, 1996). I have also looked at how Bannockburn and the Wallace Monument in Stirling are similarly subject to competing forms of remembrance (Edensor, 1997a). Similarly, Game discusses the fluid and contested meanings attributed to one of Australia's most symbolic sites of national identity, Bondi Beach (1991, 166–85). These divergent meanings of place are not merely reflected in the narratives about places but are encoded in the diverse activities which different visitors enact.

In a fascinating discussion exemplifying changes in the dominant meanings of symbolic places over time, Duncan focuses upon Kandy, in Sri Lanka (1989, 185–200). He elaborates upon the cosmological design of pre-colonial, pre-national Kandy, the sacred ceremonies that took place there and the hierarchy of power enshrined in the loci of temples and palace which mythically transformed the power of the earthly rulers. The power of the God-king was deeply inscribed upon the landscape. This landscape then became transformed with the onset of British colonial rule. By both co-opting and replacing the symbols of kingly power with their own, the British reinscribed the landscape. The government agent came to reside in the palace, streets were renamed, and a huge pavilion which dwarfed the king's palace was erected. The central areas of symbolic power were colonised by a jail, a church, police courts, a Protestant school, statues and sports facilities. Other areas were left to decay. The landscape was reshaped to reflect aesthetic ideals so that the town resembled 'a romanticised image of pre-industrial England' (Duncan, 1989, 192). Thus was Kandy redesigned to facilitate British movement, cater to British tastes, and reflect British power. With independence, the effaced symbols of Sinhalese power became revitalised. As a place that held out against imperialist threats long after most other areas, Kandy has also become a site of national importance. Changes in the landscape have been effected, statues have been removed, street names changed once more, and the palace turned into a museum.

Where nations come into being after centuries of foreign dominance or colonisation, there is a widespread tendency for nationalists to restore 'authentic' national customs, knowledge and belief. The knowledge systems of the West, ideas of rational governance and citizenship are contrasted with the 'superior mystical organic bond between peasant, land and community' (Hutchinson, 1994, 19).

Bernard Cohn has pointed out the growing reflexivity about Indian identity during the later colonial period and after independence:

> What had previously been embedded in a whole matrix of custom, ritual, religious symbol, a textually transmitted tradition has now become something different. What had been unconscious to some extent becomes conscious.
>
> (1984, 29)

Familiarity with European modes of defining and dividing space facilitated a critical disposition, enabling Indians to objectify their culture and hitherto unformulated questions about what actually constitutes national culture become serious issues in the attempt to overthrow the colonisers and establish a national project.

Yet from the outset, these notions of 'Indianness' and nationhood were contested and at present, historical veracity and interpretation are debated with great intensity in India, reflecting a crisis over how the nation should be represented. The ideologies of secular nationalism perpetrated by what are often decried as a 'Westernised elite' are coming under increasing challenge. This eroding secular hegemony has been subject to prolonged attack from the rising force of 'Hindu fundamentalism'. Intense debates about Indian identity, what constitutes the Indian nation, and the 'Westernisation' of governance fill the pages of newspapers and academic journals, and rage at meeting places from dinner parties to street corners.

In addition to these contestations over what constitutes the authentic history of India are concerns about national space. Both secular and 'fundamentalist' accounts are part of what Krishna calls the current 'cartographic anxiety' in India (literally, worry over the national map) which is 'suspended in the space between the "former colony" and "not-yet-nation"' (Krishna, 1994, 508). This cartographic anxiety is exercised with maintaining the borders and boundaries of the nation, preventing infiltration from abroad, and controlling internal secessionist movements. Crucially, Krishna claims that, 'as the physical map of India gains ubiquity as an iconic representation of the body politic, it becomes the terrain for competing efforts to define, and possess, the self' (1994, 510).

Partly, this concern focuses on the meaning of national symbolic sites, reconsidering the histories and myths which surround them. As we will see, the fears about the national integrity of India, which are so apparent in political and popular discourses about where the nation has come from and where it is going, are articulated in the contesting narratives which identity the significance of the Taj Mahal.

Above, I have discussed the particular post-colonial, national and sacred symbolic spaces which are pertinent to a discussion of this globally famous tourist site. These frameworks provide imagined geographies through which such a site is represented and also influence and shape the form of tourist itineraries. The production of these spatial frameworks, emerging out of particular times and places, is an ongoing process and in Chapter 3, I will highlight the ways in which the Taj Mahal is incorporated into larger symbolic geographies in popular narratives. In this chapter, I have been principally concerned with the ways in which tourist space is produced through representation. The operation of power through such discourses is acknowledged but there are a multitude of ways in which symbolic sites are represented. The theme of power in the production of tourist space is continued in the next chapter, where I move to consider the regulation of tourist space. This will complete the theoretical context within which I shall examine tourism at the Taj Mahal.

2

THE REGULATION OF TOURIST SPACE

In this chapter, I focus on the regulation of tourist space, whether in the form of policing and surveillance, the inculcation of ways of behaving and the development of forms of self-surveillance that monitor the practices of bodies in space. I will begin with an overview of the theoretical concepts which I use in this analysis, and then I will go on to distinguish between enclavic and heterogeneous tourist space, particularly concerning how they are regulated, the range of activities which occur within them, the forms of movement through them, and the ways in which they provoke and delimit sensual experience. The final section will consider the merits of using the metaphor of performance for an examination of tourist practices.

In any analysis of power and space, it is necessary to examine the mix of regulatory processes in different settings. Certain areas such as the prison and the school are more densely regulated by external power than other spaces such as the home. Many commercial and residential spaces in the West have become progressively less policed by the immediate community and more incorporated into wider networks of surveillance. Centralised planning and the commodification of places have extended their reach with the consequence that public space has increasingly become aesthetically regulated. Also, coinciding with and implicated in this heightened control has been a retreat by individuals into private space and the exclusion of certain people from other spaces. It is my contention that an important characteristic of globally proliferating tourist spaces has been the intensified regulation exercised over them.

Foucault's theories about the way in which power dominates space have been extremely influential. He commenced with an analysis of genealogies of discourses concerning the modern technologies by which particular spaces were disciplined: the hospital, prison and workhouse were total institutions which regulated space by unending, remorseless surveillance through panoptical visual monitoring (1977). Later, however, Foucault showed how bureaucratic 'carceral networks' were superseded by discursive techniques of self-discipline over bodies, beliefs and activities (Foucault, 1978; 1988; Martin *et al.*, 1988). However, external surveilling techniques have far from disappeared and tend to co-exist with other forms of monitoring. In modern spaces, one's behaviour, movement and presence may be regulated by a combination of advanced policing methods, the gaze of others and a reflexive self-awareness.

To differentiate between exclusionary and inclusionary spatial demarcation, Sibley distinguishes between 'purified' spaces which are strongly circumscribed and framed, wherein conformity to rules and adherence to centralised regulation hold sway, and weakly classified, heterogeneous spaces with blurred boundaries, in which activities and people mingle, allowing a wide range of encounters and greater self-governance and expressiveness (1988, 412).

The delineation of a purified space tacitly identifies the 'outsider', the stranger or the 'other', as 'out of place' (see Cresswell, 1996), both regulating their movements and presence and constructing spaces which are assigned to these 'others', typically represented as disorderly, chaotic and dirty, the antithesis of 'purified' space. These 'other' spaces are feared and avoided but paradoxically, are also fantasised and imagined as realms of desire, permitting of interconnection, hybridity and possibility by virtue of their 'weak framing'.

This notion of weak framing is suggestive of Foucault's concept of 'heterotopia', which he describes as 'the juxtaposing in a single real place (of) several spaces, several sites that are in themselves incompatible' (1986, 25). Whilst rather vague, several writers have used academic licence in interpreting this richly suggestive notion (Siebers, 1994; Soja, 1995; Genocchio, 1995; Hetherington, 1996). Indeed, Lees has remarked that the concept is 'open to a variety of quite different readings' (1997, 327) and it is this fluidity which has encouraged its recent popularity. I want to use the notion of heterotopia to identify two forms of contrasting space. Firstly, Foucault describes spaces into which everything is not only accumulated but organised and classified by an ordering regime which places and contextualises all difference. This systematic and 'rational' regime, which seeks 'to impose a univocal mode of ordering' (Hetherington, 1996, 160) has typically thought to be epitomised by museums and libraries (Bennett, 1995). I suggest that contemporary commodified spaces, with their careful arrangements of exotic and everyday consumables, also constitute an ordering process. Moreover, heritage landscapes which situate symbolic forms in the landscape and draw attention to architectural and vernacular features are also partially constructed by ordering imperatives.

Secondly, Foucault cites the fairground as another form of heterotopia which teem with 'stands, displays, heteroclite objects, wrestlers, snake-women, fortune-tellers and so forth' (Foucault, 1986, 26). The conglomeration of objects here is not composed to form an ordered whole but is placed together arbitrarily, and is unfixed, in flux. As Bennett points out, these scenes have been largely rearranged by a regulatory, ordering regimes; these forms of heterotopia have been replaced by those which order and contextualise difference. For instance, museums replaced individual collections and cabinets of curiosity and theme parks replaced fairgrounds (Bennett, 1995).

These unfixed heterotopias resist definition, epitomise fluidity of purpose, and are characterised by a shifting panoply of occupants and passers-by, and an ever-changing medley of activity, stimuli and movement. Moreover, they merge the routine and the unpredictable, the public and private, the profane and the sacred and consequently thwart any attempt to fix meaning. To return to the theme of the previous chapter, these heterotopias are not easily absorbed into conventions of representation.

These heterotopias offer the possibility of resistance to dominant spatial regulation, with their confusing and heterogeneous mix of familiarity and otherness. Passage through this heterotopic space defies attempts at definition because of the contradictions, anomalies and surprises that confront the bystander or passer-by. Since they subvert dominant practices and meanings, they frequently serve as refuges, homes or destinations for those who consider themselves, or are labelled, marginal or transgressive. For such people, these heterotopic spaces are places for exploration and self-expression.

The concepts of strongly and weakly classified space put de Certeau's notion of pedestrian 'tactics' into perspective. Refuting the idea of an all-powerful panopticonism, de Certeau foregrounds 'tactics', practices by which 'users reappropriate the space organised by sociocultural production' (1984, xiii) and escape the constraints of carceral networks. These 'tactics' contrast with 'strategies', the rational practices of the powerful which (re)construct 'technocratically constructed, written and functionalised space' (ibid., xviii).

De Certeau describes the improvisational, unpredictable nature of 'tactics' whose 'trajectories trace out the ruses of other interests and desires that are neither determined nor captured by the systems in which they develop' (ibid., xviii). He privileges walking as a particularly inventive spatial activity through which pedestrians construct narratives by 'weaving places together'. Moreover, at a more affective level, he maintains that childish sentiments and formative imaginings are stimulated by journeying through streets filled with desires and memories:

> To practice space is thus to repeat the joyful and silent experience of childhood; it is, in a place, to be other and to move toward the other.
> (de Certeau, 1984, 110)

Although he offers a useful critique of techno-spatial determinism, de Certeau seems to elevate pedestrians to an heroic level by suggesting that they avoid the ubiquitous material and symbolic presence of capital and bureaucracy. Constantly unmasking and subverting the workings of power through fantasising, they retain a sense of freedom and mobility. Furthermore, there seems to be no subjective notion of class, gender, racial or any other identities which are attributable both to the specific form of power exercised over space or the identity of pedestrians. This seems to render de Certeau's contentions somewhat ahistoric and asocial, and this is compounded by the rather uncontextualising focus on the 'immediate interaction experience' (Rojek, 1995, 107) of pedestrians. Whilst de Certeau does capture some aspects of spatial practice, the places he considers seem to exist within an overarching spatial order. But what is especially important about his account is that he points out that the conventional strategies which regulate places are merely techniques which order the ambiguities, juxtapositions and peculiarities contained within these places. In reality, they are heterotopic. If the logic of these codes is unpacked and unpicked, the play of incommensurable differences, usually obscured by the presentation of materials as commodities, becomes apparent. Pedestrian tactics escape into a more individual and idiosyncratic realm of imagination but they occur within the context of a purified space. Such ruses must be fleeting, and whilst they may occasionally reveal the artifice of regulation, a code of normativity remains embodied in the buildings, their design, the placing of objects and the techniques of control.

By contrast, weakly classified space, since it is not under the sway of some overarching convention of ordering, seems to make available a wider range of opportunities for the sort of experiences suggested by de Certeau's tactics. I do not want to suggest that forms of regulation do not operate in these spaces, but the decentred and contingent operation of this power diverges from the systematic and disinterested technocratic procedures of strongly classified space. My aim is to identify the ways in which these weakly classified heterotopic spaces have the potential to facilitate imaginings, epistemological dislocations and memories better than others.

The distinctions between strongly and weakly classified spaces also suggests the modern tensions between Apollonian and Dionysian tendencies. Whereas Apollonian culture affirms 'structure, order and self discipline', Dionysian culture represents 'sensuality, abandon and intoxication' (Rojek, 1995, 80). These tensions are highlighted by the proclivities of people, on the one hand, to demand and impose epistemological, social and spatial order, and on the other, to long for disorder, transgression and sensuality. The dominant tendency in modernity is to seek refuge in regimes of order in the face of continual change. In spatial terms, it appears that in the West, the balance between strongly and weakly classified space has shifted decisively towards the production of the former. Yet the desire to transcend regulated minds, bodies and environments, what Cohen and Taylor term 'paramount reality', constantly bubbles below the disciplined surface of everyday life and finds various outlets (Cohen and Taylor, 1992). And this desire for transgression is particularly mapped onto, and sought in, distinct forms of tourist space.

The medieval carnival culture formerly served as the occasion for the transformation of the everyday, invoking Dionysian celebration, transgression, symbolic inversions of order and hierarchy, and untrammelled emotional and bodily exhibition. However, the currently dominant Apollonian tendency in modernity has ensured that these carnivalesque elements have been 'pruned and replanted at the margins of society' (Rojek, 1995, 86). This spatial relocation, or dislocation, is part of the ongoing production of 'otherness' in 'places on the margin' that Shields describes (1991). It is also typified by neo-colonial regimes of spatial production which marginalise the space of the 'other'.

Stallybrass and White have convincingly conveyed the contradictions of the tendency wherein modernity

> continually defined and redefined itself through the exclusion of what it marked out as 'low' – dirty, repulsive, noisy, contaminating. Yet . . . Disgust always bears the imprint of desire. These low domains apparently expelled as 'other' return as the object of nostalgia, longing and desire.
>
> (1986, 191)

Colonialism is the modern example par excellence of the incongruous, simultaneous production of ordered space and spaces of desire. The projection of fantasies onto colonial space emerged out of the denial of desire in calcified disciplinary regimes. A more contemporary tendency is for commercial interests to attempt to satiate the desire for sensuality, providing 'the dream stuff for exercises in imagined otherness' (Rojek, 1995, 89). Such fantasy material is widely circulated by the flows of international tourism.

Oppermans has usefully identified the co-existence of informal and formal sectors in tourist space. Correctly pointing out the bias in research towards international 'package tourism' which has tended to reify 'the tourist' as of this type, Oppermans suggests that different types of tourist are accommodated and served in different spaces, particularly in developing countries (also see Crick, 1992). Whereas package tourists remain in the 'formal' sector, domestic and backpacker tourists tend to spend time in the 'informal sector' (Oppermans, 1993). I have identified two contrasting forms of heterotopic space above and, with this is mind, I have distinguished between 'enclavic' and 'heterogeneous' tourist spaces. Their marked differentiation befits my examination of the contrasting tourist spaces in Agra to which these two concepts are applied. However, some of the other spaces that I look at, most pertinently the Taj Mahal itself, are a mixture of characteristics which seem neither to constitute an enclave nor a heterogeneous tourist space. I will now identify the distinguishing features of these distinct tourist spaces.

Enclavic tourist space

'Organised' tourist spaces (especially in developing countries) are typified by their 'enclavic' character. Here, tourists are characteristically cut off from social contact with the local populace and are shielded from potentially offensive sights, sounds and smells.

Such spaces are typified by the following: high capital investment and the provision of 'international' tourist standards with an infrastructure that generally includes hotels of a 'suitable' standard; large retail outlets, usually selling crafts that are subject to some form of 'quality control'; restaurants serving Western-style food and adapted versions of local dishes; car hire facilities; travel guide services; air-conditioning; and trained staff who are tutored in responding to tourists in the 'appropriate' manner. This complex of facilities, frequently owned by large national and international corporations, provides a self-contained environment where tourists are encouraged (or intimidated) into spending as much money as possible. To this end, aside from visiting celebrated local sites, entertainment is usually provided by in-house recreational facilities, craft displays and frequently by 'exotic' shows and simulations which celebrate stereotypical, fantastic aspects of local culture.

Often proclaimed as prestigious development projects, these enclavic tourist spaces receive funding from international business and aid agencies as well as from the national and local state. The local state, usually in conjunction with bodies that represent the conglomeration of tourist enterprises, imposes a regime that attempts to maintain 'Western' standards of service and a range of disciplinary measures over the enclave. Locals who are not employed in the enclave are often barred, and workers from the informal sector are denied the opportunity of approaching tourists to sell their wares or services (see Wood, 1994). Sales inside the enclave are conducted in a manner that tries to eliminate discomfort amongst tourists, for instance, by fixing prices. These comparatively high prices deter many domestic tourists and backpackers from staying and purchasing in the enclave. The environmental aesthetics of the enclave are strictly maintained by landscaping and watering, and anything considered to be an 'eyesore' is removed. Similarly, the internal spaces of the enclave, the restaurants, hotels and emporia, have a monitored aesthetic, whereby ideals of cleanliness and just a hint of the 'exotic' concoct the requisite combination of high standards and strangeness (Ayala, 1991).

In economic terms, many of the businesses in organised tourist space organise reciprocal arrangements whereby, for instance, hotels and emporia will reward tour companies and guides with commission for directing tourists into their premises. The effect is to create a spatial, economic and cultural circuit. Tourists move between hotels, emporia, entertainment centres and restaurants to the exclusion of other local commercial enterprises. Subsequently, tourist dollars circulate within the enclave and small businesses in the informal sector are denied the opportunity to attract custom because, unlike entrepreneurs in the enclave, they are unable to afford the rates of commission charged by guides. Using an enclavic resort in Luperon in the Dominican Republic as an example, Freitag argues that such tourism is a form of dependent development and acts to reduce cultural and economic links at local and regional level. Enclaves, characterised by inclusiveness, 'create and control a cultural as well as a physical environment' (Freitag, 1994, 541).

Local people have an ambivalent relationship with organised tourist space. Although more homogeneous and intensely regulated than most other local spaces, tourist enclaves provide economic and employment opportunities. Yet they provide neither facilities available for locals' use, nor spaces in which they may wander, socialise or linger. Locals may spend their work-time here, but rarely their leisure time.

Colonialist practice in dividing public and private realms in distinct ways was affronted by the ways in which Indians used open space: 'People washed, changed, slept, and even urinated and defecated out in the open' (Chakrabarty, 1991, 16). This perceived 'Indian chaos' was contrasted with the

> immaculate 'order' of the European quarters, where 'pleasant squares', 'white buildings with their pillared verandahs', and 'graceful foliage' lent, to European eyes, 'a fairy-like loveliness to "the whole scene"'.
>
> (ibid., 17)

Ironically, in many post-colonial settings, organised tourist space takes over the old colonial quarters, reproducing the old distinction between Western colonialists and 'natives' and circumscribing appropriate spaces for each. Weightman describes Indian tourist enclaves, suggesting that:

> perhaps the wide avenues and rational geometry of (post-colonial Indian cities), at one time symbolic of social order and control, soothe the nerves of those who confound confusion with danger in their perceived disarray of the maze-like indigenous city.
>
> (1987, 235)

Although the production of highly regulated, commercial and enclavic space is a globally uneven process, according to Chakrabarty, Western notions of 'civic consciousness' and 'an order of aesthetics', of health and hygiene, have become part of a globalising discourse. In India, he argues that increasingly 'the thrills of the bazaar are traded in for the conveniences of the sterile supermarket' (Chakrabarty, 1991, 16).

More generally, the production of enclavic tourist space is part of a wider process whereby space, particularly in the West, is becoming more regulated, commodified and privatised. Multi-functional, hybrid spaces, weakly defined and inclusive, are being replaced by single-function spaces, bounded to assert distinction and sharpen definition. The imperatives of modernist planning and consumer capitalism have tended to transform space so that it maximises consumption and facilitates transit. In industry, business parks and industrial estates stand boldly separate from residential spaces, which in gated communities (Judd, 1995) and private retirement homes increasingly typify the extension of suburban desires for a clear spatial distinction from the urban (Fishman, 1987). A battery of concepts and metaphors has been developed to account for these transformations. Sennett refers to the growth in 'dead public spaces' (1994), Augé has coined the phrase 'non-place' (1995), and

Mitchell uses the term 'pseudo-public space' (1995) to account for these forms of space.

In the more specific context of leisure spaces, theme parks, shopping malls and festival marketplaces are designed to exclude the quotidian worlds of work and home, although ironically, they are familiar enough by virtue of their design codes, spatial organisation and the themes which connote familiar mediatised images and qualities consumed in the home.

Sites of pleasure and carnival such as fairs, amusement parks, music halls and seaside resorts have been superseded by enclavic spaces marked by technological surveillance, the marketing of the exotic and *commodified* difference. Whilst these commodified landscapes appear to promise a cornucopia of infinite variety, this is a manufactured and 'controlled diversity' rather than a realm of 'unconstrained social differences' (Mitchell, 1995, 119).

Accordingly, whereas leisure spaces were previously symbolic spaces for the production and transmission of local identity, their reconstruction or disappearance has resulted in the erasure of much social, sensual and rhythmic diversity, and the provision of safe, familiar, well-regulated environments minimises the discomfort – and excitement – provoked by confrontation with alterity and inversion. The grotesque and unexpected features of heterotopia are replaced by pale suggestions of 'otherness'.

Contemporary Apollonian and Dionysian tensions are played out in the field of leisure with the production of 'spaces of eros' (Wang, 1996, 126). Dionysian desires for the irrational, erotic and chaotic are co-opted by advertising and marketing strategists. However, the production of contemporary leisure spaces that attempt to arouse the imagery and ambience of the carnival can serve as no more than 'sites of ordered disorder' (Featherstone, 1991, 82). Such a spatial containment and commodification encourages a 'controlled de-control of the emotions' (ibid., 78), a desire toned down by a self-regulating of the body and the passions that seems a culmination of the modern 'civilising process' (Elias, 1978, 1982). The range of objects of desire and transgressive practices is reduced and, unlike earlier carnivalesque spaces, these spaces are *designed* to stimulate desires: to escape, to meet 'others' and to transgress, whilst ironically in such controlled environments, the possibilities for transgressing, experiencing sensual richness and confronting difference are sharply delimited by the ordering processes that dominate.

The quality of this 'ordered disorder' testifies to the regulated lifeworld which such leisure spaces promise temporary escape from. Suppressed desires must be content with moderate pleasures such as 'the chance meeting of an acquaintance, the tactile but not too physical interaction with a crowd, the sense . . . of something happening beyond the close world of oneself' (Shields, 1992, 102). Conversely, they often also promise realms of sociality for strolling in which suggest the previously convivial spaces of city centres, except that they are crime-free, uncluttered and clean, and contain no 'anti-social' elements (Gottdiener, 1997, 112).

These 'themed milieus' are designed according to a limited range of motifs derived from media cultures to constitute what Barber terms 'McWorlds' (1995). The theming of enclavic space, the application of 'sceneography' (Gottdiener, 1997, 73), is designed to maximise consumption by providing a pleasurable environment in which to purchase.

I will now identify the social activities, modes of regulation, forms of movement and sensual stimuli which are produced in enclavic tourist space.

Social activities

In a sense, enclavic spaces seem to accord with the 'non-places' described by Augé. Instead of being 'relational, historical and concerned with identity' (Augé, 1995, 107), these are realms of 'transit' as opposed to 'dwelling', sites of 'interchange' rather than a meeting place or 'crossroads', where 'communication (with its codes, images and strategies)' is practised rather than affective and convivial language (ibid., 107–8).

In enclavic tourist space, activities are monitored through surveillance and by what is considered 'appropriate' in dominant tourist discourses and by tour personnel. Uncontrolled social practices such as congregating, sleeping, 'hanging out' and lounging on the pavement are all deterred. Moreover, the range of commercial activities is restricted by the dominance of large corporate retail outlets who control the management of space and refuse entry to smaller stalls, peddlers and mobile services. This also reduces the relations of barter and vocal enquiry in the process of consumption, mechanising and speeding up the relations of exchange. Most activity in the enclave is devoted to its maintenance and smooth-running, or features tourists being moved, marshalled, sold articles, served or informed. Where gaps in the tour programme occur, tourists must organise their own activity, which usually revolves around browsing in retail outlets or eating.

Regulation

Enclaves resemble 'total institutions' in which a group of people 'cut off from the wider society for an appreciable period of time, together lead an enclosed, formally administered round of life' (Goffman, 1961; cited in Ritzer and Liska, 1997, 106). Lefebvre argues that tourist spaces are controlled and managed by regimes that impose their own 'rituals and gestures . . . discursive forms . . . and even models and modulations of space (hotels, chalets)' (1991, 384). Despite the rhetoric of freedom, he maintains that such spaces 'are planned with the greatest care: centralised, organised, hierarchised, symbolised and programmed to the nth degree' (ibid., 59). To minimise tourist disorientation, the tourist industry works hard to interpret (and package) these limited number of attractions. As Neumann declares:

> Tourists are rarely left to draw their own conclusions about objects or places before them. Instead, they more often confront a body of public discourse – signs, maps, guides and guide books – that repeatedly mark the boundaries of significance and value at tourist sites.
>
> (1988, 24)

Shields argues that instead of providing zones of freedom and escape, enclavic realms are 'controlled limen zones of permitted, legitimated leisure still very much within the grid of social control' (1992, 8). This 'soft control' (Ritzer and Liska, 1997, 106) both constitutes a range of external controls such as security guards and CCTV cameras who exclude 'undesirable elements', and internalised rules about what comprises an 'appropriate' tourist disposition in these spaces concerning factors such as bodily posture, dress, voice modulation and the like.

Tactics which test the patience of the guards or transgress the codes of tourist behaviour are evident in small acts of theft and extrovert performance by tourists and locals alike, but the control over activity compels these would-be subversives to adopt more covert strategies. Transgression depends upon the temporary seizure and transformation of public space in order to transmit alternative symbolic meanings. Whilst the presence of 'mall rats', beggars and shoplifters testifies to certain forms of resistance to normative codes and expectations in pseudo-public space, such opposition seems fleeting and gestural in the face of intensive surveillance.

Movement

Themed spaces are organised to facilitate directional movement by both pedestrians and traffic by reducing points of entry and exit, and minimising idiosyncratic distractions. Access between the facilities and attractions in enclavic tourist space must be as seamless and efficient as possible to maximise the quest for commodities and experiences. Sites within enclavic space serve as stations through which people are relayed. If movement is supervised, for instance on a guided tour, the tempo of tourist pedestrians takes on the character of a brisk march to reach the destination, interspersed with periods in which information is transmitted, photographs taken and souvenirs purchased, to constitute a segmented stop–start collective performance. This impulse to move rapidly from one spectacular site to the next seems to conjure up the contemporary lust for pure velocity described by Virilio (1991). The sequence of tourist sites merely gives shape to this craving for detached stimulation. The bombardment of the senses which this organised tourism produces diminishes the capacity for tourists romantically to consume places at leisure, according to Kracauer (1995).

Coverage of space is highly selective. Tours objectify 'selected landscapes inclusive of their inhabitants' and pass over disenchanting local features

(Weightman, 1987, 236). Only certain key tourist attractions are visited; the consumption of particular cultures, sights and souvenirs are encouraged; activity is group-oriented and tourists are dissuaded from individual exploration; all factors which minimise spatial exploration. Moreover, such tours are also impressed by the task of managing large groups of people and minimising risk. To this end, many tour operators are at pains to emphasise that they cannot be held responsible should the tourist venture out of organised tourist space and they inculcate fear to curtail such movement, a strategy which may resonate with the tourists' desire for safety. Whilst local spaces promise transgression and mystery, fear usually conquers curiosity and tourists remain in the enclave.

Where tourists enter periods of 'free time', the purified design of the enclave which generally restricts attractions to retail and dining outlets is conducive to the browsing typical of large retail spaces in the West, the passing of shops 'in review'. The rhythms and choreographies of enclavic space are characterised by purposive, directed movements which follow a limited number of strongly demarcated paths, usually designed to maximise selling possibilities.

Additionally, although my principle focus is on distinctively located spaces, a feature of tourist travel is that such enclaves are also mobile. By this I mean that passage from attraction to attraction, or from enclave to enclave, exists in an air-conditioned vacuum of travel buses, planes and trains in which contact with, and bodily experience of, external conditions, such as temperature, humidity and dust, are eliminated as they are at the hotels and restaurants of fixed tourist space. Weightman argues that package tours are typified by 'directedness', 'encapsulation' and 'outsideness'. The latter two characteristics are produced by tourists' confinement in the 'environmental bubble' (Cohen, 1972, 166), the mobile enclave in which they travel which enables confrontation with the other at a safe distance. Environmentally isolated from noise and smells, and cut off from interaction with locals, such tours can result in the 'perpetuation of stereotypes and . . . prejudices' (Weightman, 1987, 228).

Sensual experience

The structure and regulation of themed enclaves powerfully influences the sensual experience of tourists. Often, the very commodity promised to tourists in the promotional literature of the holiday-makers is that they will undergo a memorable, sensual experience. But rather than the multi-sensual, complex and more immediate sensation of the 'outside world' this is a mediated and simulated sensual experience (Rodaway, 1994, 173).

Above all the tourist enclave is designed for gazing. Theming imposes a visual order; a predictable spectacle of few surprises, generated by the need for the large retail outlets to capture the attention of consumers. Accordingly, the pedestrian's gaze is directed to large window displays and slogans and away from the outside of the enclave. This accords with the wider pattern of tourist spatialisation where certain sites are 'sacred landmarks in the mental maps of tourists'.

They crystallise a sense of place by excluding 'extraneous chaotic elements', reducing 'visual and functional forms to a few key images' (Rojek, 1995, 62). The homology with other cultural spheres extends with the consideration that for the effective maximisation of consumption, tourist environments require a degree of homogeneity which echoes the 'well ordered, pristine and pure' imaginary worlds fostered through advertising (Sibley, 1988, 415). Thus the spheres of tourism, advertising, design and film combine to produce environments which are saturated by processes of mediatisation. Ironically, they reduce unfamiliarity by reproducing the commodified and leisure spaces of the tourists' origin, providing a familiar spatial context for exploring otherness.

The imperatives to commodify or conserve historic features within tourist enclaves generates an aesthetic control in which characteristic features are *contextualised* for visitors as being of historic significance by tourist guides, books and information boards. Acting as signifiers of the past, these markers specify what is to be gazed upon, and this is reinforced by the professional interpreters of 'customised excursions' (Craik, 1995, 6). This aesthetic policing and the imposition of design codes produces a somewhat homogenised, international landscape which disguises its predictability by the incorporation of local features, which, however, are always staged to appear remarkable rather than being a part of space around which everyday activities revolve. The tourist gaze is structured by a repertoire of design codes which provide a soupçon of exotica and a few key images. This marketing of 'exotic otherness' occurs within a safe and familiar, 'McDonaldised' (see Ritzer and Liska, 1997, 99–100) environment which minimises the disruption and excitement provoked by confrontation with difference.

Tourist enclaves are comprehensively deodorised, and sometimes reodorised with commodified smells. This ordering of smell accompanies the process of removing perceived dirt and clutter to clear 'surplus' stimuli and redirect attention towards products in the themed shopping environment. Likewise, the raucous cries of traders, political speakers and recorded or performed music are banned or kept at appropriate volume, reducing the soundscape to muzak or a similar series of rhythms emanating from boutiques. Also, the narrow scope for improvised or contingent movement minimises bodily contact and the smooth continuity of the internal and external flooring texture regulates the sense of touch, 'weakening the sense of tactile reality and pacifying the body' (Sennett, 1994, 17). The tourist enclave is a rather unsensual space.

Whilst enclavic tourist spaces are governed by a system of ordering that materialises an ideology of consumption and regulates the performance of tourists, this acts to mask the heterotopic ambiguities and incongruities present. Materials, meanings and practices are organised according to predictable codes but these elements could be alternatively ordered in innumerable different ways. As Klugman (1995) has shown in her 'alternative ride' around Disneyworld, odd angles, unusual sights and cracks in the fabric are always present, and can be experienced by shifting perspective. Emphatically then, I do not want to deny any agency and suggest that the experiences of tourists in enclavic space are seamlessly produced by the tourist industry and entirely predictable.

Lefebvre holds out the possibility that tourist space can serve as a sort of counter space to the constraints imposed by power-in-spacing. By virtue of the temporary escape of the body from its usual surrounds, and the search for sensual pleasure and exuberance, the usual quotidian order is at least partly undermined (Lefebvre, 1991, 385). The idea is that a disruption of the usual routines and responsibilities constitute an aporia which can lead to a critical appraisal of the compulsions of work and home. In such temporal and spatial gaps tourists may realise the contradictions of their existence and unmask the ideologies which constrain them. However, as bounded and regulated communities, tourist enclaves masquerade as temporary utopian havens where visitors can 'get away from it all', but it is difficult for them to get away from the temporal and spatial constraints provided by the tour package.

I do not wish to deny the potential for transforming the self within enclavic space. Indeed, as I will show, tourists often experience frustration in enclavic tourist space and become irritated by spatio-temporal restrictions. As I have maintained, the contemporary pursuit of leisure is characterised by a search for transcendence, albeit usually within a commodified, regulated framework and, frequently, a desire to further transcend this 'ordered disorder' and enter the realms of the unknowable and random.

However, questions about the possibilities for oppositional tourist interpretations, narratives and practices in enclavic tourist space, and the limits of post-tourist subversive decoding need to be raised. Whilst such faculties and 'tactics' may be stimulated by the temporal and spatial break, it is surely essential to consider the characteristics of the space that tourists operate within.

Heterogeneous tourist space

The tensions between logos and eros are increasingly played out in the West in ever more commodified and regulated leisure spaces. Recently, there has been an upsurge in escape attempts to establish liminal places and occasions: e.g. rave events (see Thornton, 1995; Saunders, 1995), music festivals, alternative rituals and political demonstrations, often based around new social movements and New Age beliefs (see McKay, 1996; Hetherington, 1996), and car boot sales (Gregson and Crewe, 1997). These realms permit a conditional exploration whereby 'alternative' forms of play are enacted and a wider range of expressive practices and meanings are stimulated. However, these spaces are in all cases transitory and the wallowing in heterogeneity must always come to an end. There is another escape option: to travel outside the West in search of difference, fluidity and irregularity. In non-Western destinations where tourism has often emerged in an unplanned and contingent process, there is a profusion of heterogeneous tourist spaces, frequently situated adjacent to the large enclavic spaces described above.

Heterogeneous tourist spaces accommodate tourism as one economic activity but are not dominated by it. Tourist facilities co-exist with local small businesses, shops, street vendors, public and private institutions and domestic housing. There can be no question of keeping certain people out of the area on the grounds of maintaining a cultivated appearance, and tourists and locals mingle and go about their separate business. There is often a lack of distinction between private and public with domestic tasks being performed in the street, and houses co-existing with commercial establishments. Temporary shelters, such as pavement dwellings, are not subject to intense policing, indicating regimes of regulation which contrast sharply with the ordered confines of organised tourist space. Animals, small children and mendicants traverse heterogeneous tourist space and there is no urgency to remove rubbish and repair unkempt roads and buildings, let alone maintain verges, gardens and roundabouts. Weightman has described how a typical Western interpretation of such space might conclude that there is 'a seeming lack of care for urban facades, the juxtaposition of antagonistic structures and styles, and the ill fitting superimposition of Western forms' (1987, 232).

The tourist economy of heterogeneous tourist space is labour-intensive, often typified by small family-run concerns. These businesses – budget hotels, small cafés and restaurants, souvenir and craft shops, independent transport operators and unofficial guides – are unable to provide the 'international' standards that are mandatory in tourist enclaves. Hotels are usually small and cheap with facilities such as hot water, central heating and air-conditioning unreliable or non-existent, and they rarely operate exclusion policies. Restaurants offer a restricted range of local dishes with only a few concessions to Western tastes and pursue standards of hygiene and cleanliness that are less subject to bureaucratic constraints. Again, they are habitually shared by locals and visitors. Often operating close to the margins of viability, these smaller ventures may be crucially dependent upon enterprises in organised tourist space, for instance, by supplementing their income by transporting tourists to the enclave and thereby gaining commission, by providing the large craft retailers with some of their products, and by working part-time as hotel waiters, tour guides and the like.

I will now identify the social activities, modes of regulation, forms of movement and sensual stimuli which are produced in heterogeneous tourist space.

Social activities

Heterogeneous tourist spaces are usually located within market or bazaar areas in developing countries. These spatial complexes comprising streets, bazaars and fairs constitute an unenclosed realm which provides a 'meeting point of several communities' (Chakrabarty, 1991, 23). Organised as a cellular structure with numerous openings and passages, the flow of different bodies and vehicles crisscross the street in multi-directional patterns, veering into courtyards, alleys and cul-de-sacs.

As the sites for multiple activities, of 'recreation, social interaction, transport and economic activity' (King, 1976, 56), the main arteries of this spatial network are never merely 'machines for shopping'. Hotels co-exist with work places, schools, eating places, transport termini, bathing points, political headquarters, offices, administrative centres, places of worship and temporary and permanent dwellings. The multi-functional structure of heterogeneous tourist space provides an admixture of overlapping spaces that to Western eyes seem to merge public and private, work and leisure, and holy and profane activities. This diversity contains a host of micro spaces: corners and niches, awnings and offshoots.

In the bazaar a sense of familiarity is maintained through particular modes of address, types of economic exchange and the maintenance of formalised and convivial obligations. These strategies for dealing with the unfamiliar contribute to the formation of a gregarious environment which privileges speech and removes barriers between backstage and frontstage so that visual and verbal enquiry is facilitated. This provides a congenial environment for economic exchange, typified by barter, which, as Buie describes, is a sensual as well as economic activity; an 'art' a 'ritual' and a 'dance of exchange' (1996, 227).

Most tourist services tout for business on the street and, especially in poor seasons and at unprofitable times of the year, this causes a certain amount of 'hassle' for tourists, and vendors characteristically negotiate and haggle over prices. These enterprises are generally run and staffed by people from the quarter. Unlike in organised tourist space there is little descent into deference, and as tourists and locals must mingle with each other, the opportunities for meeting locals are part of the tourist experience.

The proliferation of spaces provides contexts for various social practices that range from the commercial to the recreational, and from the industrial to the ritual. The streets are 'centres of social life, of communication, of political and judicial activity, of cultural and religious events and places for the exchange of news, information and gossip' (Buie, 1996, 277).

As a commercial realm, heterogeneous tourist space is occupied by diverse enterprises, organised according to a variety of time–space constraints. Whilst there are fixed shops, the streets may also be the work place of mobile providers of services of all kinds. Moreover, the open fronts of most workshops mean that the activities of artisans spill out onto the side of the street, further blurring frontstage and backstage realms and activities.

As well as being a social space for transactions of news and gossip, particularly organised around particular micro-spaces such as transport termini and tea stalls, heterogeneous tourist space is a site for announcement, and is host to adverts and political broadcasts transmitted visually or by loudspeaker. Demonstrations by political parties, and religious processions, theatrically transform the street into a channel of embodied transmission, and striking workers hold meetings and occupy spaces. The street thus becomes a temporary stage where political dramas and religious observances are played out.

As a site for entertainment, children make their own amusement, playing sports and other games, whilst adults play cards or other local games. Moreover, travelling entertainers such as musicians, lottery sellers and magicians set up stall and attract crowds. Besides these travellers, there are disparate hawkers and beggars as well as bands of religious adherents. There is thus a constant stream of temporary pleasurable activities, entertainments and transactions. But there are also more mundane social activities such as loitering with friends, sitting and observing, and meeting people that also form distinct points of congregation.

Dwellings may be located at the side of the street, which consequently becomes a site for domestic activities such as collecting water, washing clothes, cooking and childminding. For pavement dwellers, streets may also serve as a temporary home, necessitating the public carrying out of bodily maintenance such as washing. Such temporary sites and activities dissolve preconceived notions of ownership and question the distinction between private and public (Chandhoke, 1993, 69).

The tourist temporarily dwells in and moves through this protean space. The range of social activities tends to deny the tourist the option of seeking refuge in a distanced disposition; the social immersion that such an environment demands disrupts any lofty detachment.

Regulation

Heterogeneous tourist spaces are typified by more contingent and local forms of planning, regulation and surveillance. Rather than security guards, video surveillance and policing, local power-holders exercise policies of exclusion and control. Overall, however, surveillance is rather low level. Whilst there are formal traffic rules, the various species of vehicles pay little heed to them as they jostle for position. Street performers, beggars and touts are rarely advised to 'move on' and the mentally and physically handicapped are not confined to institutions. The domestic, stray and wild animals that share the streets with people may be subject to cruelty but there are few systematic attempts at controlling their movements or numbers.

Furthermore, heterogeneous tourist space is rarely subject to aesthetic control or theming. On the contrary, an unplanned bricolage of structures is infested with ad hoc signs, contingent and personalised embellishments and crumbling masonry. This is not to argue that the politics of power is not played out in heterogeneous tourist space. There may be a gendered distinction between private and public, with most of the shopkeepers and artisans in the public realm male, and women confined to backstage or domestic realms. Moreover, other local forms of power may be exerted unbeknown to the tourist. For instance, in Indian heterogeneous tourist space there may be ethnic, caste and religious power struggles over space. Power also works its way onto the street in less obvious ways. Bribes and favours may be needed to secure commercial sites and violence may be held in reserve to prevent minorities from occupying particular domestic and work areas. Even in the most seemingly chaotic spaces of the 'shanty town', slum lords may wield control (Chandhoke, 1993, 70).

But the 'unintended city' of the 'shanty town' insistently projects into and subverts 'planned urban spaces', challenging the spatial ordering of cities and hence, the social order. Chandhoke argues that the 'urban poor make and remake space . . . seize spaces and reshape in this way the entire urban form':

> They intrude into individual consciousness at traffic crossings . . . they inform us that cities are unequally constructed and maintained . . . (they) disrupt the coherence of the planned urban landscape, they retaliate and talk back to history and geography by making the homelessness of these people dramatically visible.
>
> (1993, 64)

Whilst norms of movement, activity and appearance exist and are mediated by local power-holders, the elastic attitudes to regulation diverge from the bureaucratic disciplining of enclavic tourist space. However, the bureaucrats and entrepreneurs who produce and represent enclavic tourist space and wish to extend it frequently order clampdowns on the range of social activities and the appearance of heterogeneous tourist space. Restrictions on the commercial practices and concerns of small traders mean that livelihoods are often put at risk by such disciplinary projects. Given the disparities in economic and political power between opponents, the extension of control over these spaces and resistance to such control is usually an unequal struggle as we shall see.

Movement

In heterogeneous tourist space it is often difficult to move in a straight line. The pedestrian has to weave a path by negotiating obstacles underfoot or in front, avoiding hassle and teasing, and remaining alert about the hazards presented by vehicles and animals such as monkeys, cows, pigs and dogs. Walking cannot be a seamless, uninterrupted journey but is rather a sequence of interruptions and encounters that disrupt smooth passage.

The abundant simultaneous cross-cutting journeys mean that purposive travel towards an objective must take account of others who will cross one's path. Rapid progress is usually frustrated. A variety of activities is enacted at different speeds. Some participants linger or lounge, others gather in groups for long spells, adding to the host of differently constituted time–space paths. A miscellaneous collection of vehicles and other diverse forms of transport all move at different speeds as they manoeuvre for space, providing an ever-changing dance of traffic, which contrasts with the controlled flow and pace of traffic movement on thoroughfares in enclaves.

Thus passage is marked by disruption and distraction, not only by the exigencies of avoidance and the physical collision with others, but also by the distractions and diversions offered by heterogeneous activities and sights. The choreographies of the street, with intersecting movements differing in direction and tempo, and constituted by humans, vehicles and animals, continually change, incorporating the necessarily contingent character of the pedestrian's dance.

At a larger scale, another aspect of the regulation of movement is the extent to which people are able to travel without external constraint. India, for instance, is a country of diverse forms of mass movement and migration. The notion of strictly controlling movement is unrealistic since pilgrimage is an important cultural practice and complex migratory patterns criss-cross the country. This contrasts with Britain where the introduction of the Criminal Justice Bill in 1994 (an amalgam of policies introduced by the Conservative Government to 'improve' public order, which amongst other measures restricted the right of groups of people to travel and assemble together) has placed draconian curbs on the right of travellers to move around the country and thwarted their search for an alternative lifestyle. The scale of India, and the potential it offers for moving through a vast space unrestricted by temporal constraints, offers a temporary opportunity for the Western tourist to move through differently regulated space.

Sensual experience

I particularly want to bring out the rich sensual encounter of the Western tourist moving through heterogeneous tourist space. The relationship between sensual experience, and spatial form and practice, has been barely touched upon and represents a rich field for further exploration (although see Porteous, 1990; Rodaway, 1994). Distinctive material spaces are surely more likely to stimulate sense and feeling (although not in any mechanical, Pavlovian way), and are themselves produced out of local social practices and meanings, including those which account for the senses. It is my contention that the pedestrian enjoys a more vivid and varied sensual experience in heterogeneous tourist space, and one which is not purely centred upon visual pleasures, although there is no evident way of reading cultural epistemological and ontological conventions from the physical and sensual nature of environments. For instance, the fragmentation of separate realms within the bourgeois Western house for different activities which produced different sensory effects has acted to fragment the sensorium (Howes and Classen, 1991). In heterogeneous tourist space, the co-existence of these activities in an undemarcated social space produces an intermingling of sensations.

I have discussed the divergencies of movement in heterogeneous tourist space, the cross-cutting interplay of bodies and machines in motion. This panoply of beings and machines in motion against a backdrop of randomly arranged buildings and objects produces an ever shifting series of juxtapositions. Unforeseen assemblages of diverse static and moving elements provide surprising and unique scenes. Such haphazard features and events dis-order the tourist gaze. The flow of distracting sights negates scopic surveillance and easy visual consumption as the eye continuously shifts, alighting on changing episodes to the left and right, far ahead and close at hand. The norms of pleasurably jostling in the crowd, moreover, engender a haptic geography wherein there is continuous touching of others and weaving between and amongst bodies. The different textures brushed against and underfoot, and the heating of one's skin from nearby stoves, render the body aware of diverse tactile sensations which interrupt concentrated gazing.

The centrality of vision is also denied by the powerful combination of other stimuli. The 'smellscapes' of heterogeneous tourist space are rich and varied. The jumbled mix of pungent aromas – sweet, sour, acrid and savoury – produces intense 'olfactory geographies'. Equally diverse is the soundscape which combines the noises generated by numerous human activities, animals, forms of transport and performed and recorded music, to produce a changing symphony of diverse pitches, volumes, rhythms and tones.

By looking at the experience of, and negotiation with, modes of activity, movement, regulation and sensual experience, it seems that the sensual and social body passing through heterogeneous tourist space is continually imposed upon and challenged by diverse activities, sensations and sights which render a state at variance with the restrained and distanced distraction of the tourist enclave. The senses are excited by a more variegated set of stimuli – sights, smells, noises, movements – which do not accord with mass-produced tourist imagery. The imaginative, improvisational predilections of the pedestrian are stimulated into unexpected flights of fancy, and the passage through the street is rhizomic rather than linear. Through haggling and repudiating advances, tourists must interact with the local population in shops and restaurants, with beggars and touts, and with people interested in sharing ideas and information. Thus, opportunities for dialogue and exchange are encouraged. The power-laden processes of classifying, spectacularising and commodifying difference in the disciplined space of tourist enclaves contrast with the changing juxtapositions of difference found in the heterogeneous tourist space. Rather than being a distanced spectator of manufactured spectacle, the pedestrian is part of this heteroglossia of 'otherness'. Enmeshed in its sensuality it may be difficult to maintain an imperialist subjectivity. The ability to remain shielded from local life in heterogeneous tourist space is not possible, but in any case, it is these streets that are sought by backpackers in search of 'authenticity' and the thrill of encountering the 'other'.

Chakrabarty captures the ambivalence of such a space, the sense of risk and unpredictability which contributes to its allure:

> The bazaar or the street expresses through its own theatre the juxtaposition of pleasure and danger that constitutes the 'outside' or the open, unenclosed space. The street is where one has interesting, and some-

times marvellous, encounters. They do not always eventuate but the place is pregnant with the possibility.

(1991, 26)

However much heterogeneous tourist space is reclaimed within dominant systems of (post) colonial representation, tourists who gravitate towards them experience different forms of sensory experience, social interaction, regulation and movement that seem to be unrepresentable. The seeking out of such experiences attests to the contemporary need to reinstate desire and unpredictability into life. Symbolically then, heterogeneous tourist spaces provide an escape route, or labyrinth, an alternative system of spatial (dis)ordering where transitional identities may be sought, sensual and imaginative experimentation indulged, and the Western hegemonic power/knowledge axis bewildered and challenged. In a sense, such a pursuit seems close to the activities of the early modern flaneur (see Edensor, 1998). Although critics have attempted to democratise the originally elitist notion by suggesting that the contemporary consumer or tourist in themed space is a contemporary version of the flaneur (see Smart, 1994, 162), in such commodified spaces haphazard diversity has been 'liquidised into the lubricant of profit-making contraptions' (Bauman, 1994, 151) and the freedom to loiter, so critical to witnessing the momentary passing scenes, is denied by the policing of activity and the velocity of movement. Such commentators fail to acknowledge that flaneurie is typified by wallowing in flux, witnessing the transitory, observing unique juxtapositions and incidental meetings; in short, being at home 'in the ebb and flow, the bustle, the fleeting and the infinite' (Baudelaire, 1972, 399).

Whilst I have constructed them as separate realms, heterogeneous and enclavic tourist spaces are usually clearly separated by a zone of transition, usually a space where medium-range tourists stay, where standards and facilities fall somewhere between budget and international, where some, generally more affluent, locals dwell and where the roads and surroundings become less populated and spacious. Additionally, the relationship between these two forms of space is often complex. Denizens of heterogeneous tourist space may service or supply larger concerns, or work in enclavic tourist space. As I have already indicated, enclavic spaces are more thoroughly penetrated by bureaucratic and capitalist power, and attempts are apt to be made by entrepreneurs, politicians and administrators to extend and deepen this power in heterogeneous tourist space. Nevertheless, since my scheme relies upon a binary conception, it is important to point out that while the spaces that I examine seem to sustain the dichotomy, much tourist space is more hybrid than might be apparent, and many tourist spaces are typified by an interpenetration of enclavic and heterogeneous elements (as is the Taj itself).[1]

Tourist performances

In Chapter 1, I discussed representations of tourist space and the imagined geographies to which they contribute. The production of tourist space is not only representational, however, for an over-concentration on discourse and representation can miss the fact that 'much of conceptualisation is "embodied" in the sense that it is structured by physical experience' (Palmer and Jankowiak, 1996, 253). As performers, tourists are informed by representations yet produce representations of their own. They 'affirm, reinforce, complete or complement images presented by others' and furthermore, 'by co-ordinating performances, they project collective images' (ibid., 1996, 245). In this section, I consider tourists as performers in distinct forms of space with reference to the discussion above, thus completing the theoretical foundations for my analysis of tourism at the Taj Mahal and Agra.

I have argued that theories of tourism have tended towards ethnocentrism, over-generalisation and functionalism. Thus certain tourists, places and activities have been identified as defining tourism per se. Additionally, much energy has been expended on drawing up tourist typologies (for instance, see Smith, 1989; Cohen, 1979). Whilst analyses of tourism are required to identify regularities, it is essential that these be understood as varieties of practice rather than types of people. Moreover, there is a danger that such categorisations become reified as immutable. On the contrary, I argue that tourism is a process which involves the ongoing (re)construction of tourist praxis through the generation of forms of knowledge and enaction. While there are certain regularities, dominant tourist conventions are open to challenge and are contingent upon historical and geographical contexts, and the spatio-temporal organisation of tours and itineraries.

It has been plausibly observed that it is increasingly difficult to separate tourist practices from everyday life, that 'people are much of the time tourists whether they like it or not' (Urry, 1990, 82). For instance, it is claimed that local sights have increasingly become subject to a tourist gaze. Such gazes are typically enacted in passing, are necessarily brief, and are interwoven with other everyday activities and goals. These fleeting and contingent touristic enactions, interspersed with everyday social actions based around home and work, differ from more prolonged gazing practices in that they are constrained by the spatio-temporal exigencies of duties and responsibilities. Thus, while there is a continuum and an overlap between the everyday and periods when one is a tourist, what distinguishes more extensive tourist practice is that it is informed by an ontology which is constructed according to distinct spatial and temporal parameters. For whilst there are these continuities and overlaps between everyday routines and tourist practices, tourism involves the adoption of distinct dispositions based on the understanding that tourism involves the displacement of everyday constraints, wherein quotidian time is differentiated from tourist time, and movement is directed towards and engineered through space that is understood as tourist space.

In order to examine these spatio-temporal conditions and conceptions of tourism, and the varieties and processes of tourist practices, I will use the metaphor of tourist performance to construct a theoretical metaphor to establish a basis for the examination of the diverse enactions that centre upon the Taj Mahal. These performances are shaped by the constraints and opportunities that tour structures produce and are informed by beliefs about the symbolic meaning of the site, and they vary from the rigid enaction of tourist rituals and 'duties' to attempts to construct and transmit alternative meanings. Performances are set apart in time and space, and this is particularly useful given my focus on the spatio-temporal organisation of tourism.

In a wider context, tourism is understood as a time of play, as opposed to work, and this sense of play suggests the liminal and fun-oriented nature of performance. Tourism occurs over a diverse range of time frames. Thus performances are of varied duration and this implies that the degree of control over play may be conditioned to fit into a limited time slot, or alternatively, expand into a longer spell.

Performances are also enacted in 'physically and symbolically bounded space' (Chaney, 1993, 18), which suggests that there are distinct tourist stages. I have discussed the material organisation of a distinct form of space which includes attractions, hotels, highways and restaurants for instance. The construction of tourist space involves the establishment of 'the meaningful settings that tourists consume and tourism employees help produce' (Crang, 1997, 143). Moreover, I have shown how competing representational practices also (re)construct symbolic sites. I have also examined the ways in which these symbolic stages are incorporated into multiple, overlapping spaces, and thus they are fluid entities whose meaning changes and is contested by performers. Accordingly, the sense of what sites symbolise may generate myriad forms of performance on a single tourist stage, in which different roles, scripts, choreographies, group formations, instructions and cues are followed. Indeed, the coherence of culturally specifiable performances depends on their being performed in specific 'theatres'. There are different onstage areas, which may be the focus of the enactment of distinct dramas, and signifying objects which, semiotised by their location on stage, may be moved around, played with or ignored by particular groups of actors. All these performative processes ceaselessly reconstitute the symbolic values of tourist sites and reproduce them as dramaturgical spaces. Clearly there is a relationship between performance and enclavic and heterogeneous tourist spaces. According to my conception, enclavic spaces are carefully staged and designed so that performance is somewhat prescriptive, whereas in heterogeneous spaces, stage boundaries are less clear and a wider range of improvisation is encouraged.

Certain writers (notably Geertz, 1993 and Goffman, 1959) state that social life is thoroughly dramaturgical, and that we are constantly playing roles according to the social contexts in which we find ourselves. Social action is inevitably 'mannered, stylish, aims to be coherent through time and aspires to be able to use the resources for signification at hand' (Chaney, 1993, 17). Yet, although it seems particularly apt, there have been few explorations of tourism as a set of performances. MacCannell (1976) has focused on the touristic search for backstage productions and Crang has examined how the tourist product may be performed by tourist personnel, showing how they are increasingly required to be 'cast members' or at the least, wear outfits that fit in with themed environments. Tourist workers are trained to enact roles that fit in with their institutional setting and express attributes such as deference, eagerness to please and friendliness (Crang, 1997). The most adventurous explication of tourism as performance has been attempted by Adler, who describes travel as 'performed art'. She details the historical emergence of tourist praxis by showing how travel accounts and guidebooks 'served as a means of preparation, aid, documentation and vicarious participation' by constructing tourism as a pursuit 'whose execution could be guided and publicly evaluated' (Adler, 1989b, 1,367–8).

She argues that tourists follow the 'norms, technologies, institutional arrangements and mythologies' (ibid., 1,371) that prevail at particular places and in the organisational imperatives of tours. Such practices are enframed and informed by different discourses about the meaning of symbolic sites which cultivate subject positions, specifying what actions should take place at particular places and times. Her description suggests the staged nature of tourism, the inscription of roles, and the following of appropriate techniques and directions. This captures the performance of the 'work' of tourism, the unreflexive enaction of common-sense practices and routine cultural maintenance. It does not, however, necessarily cover more creative and indeed critical tourist performances, which are usually more self-conscious. Moreover, it seems to evade the more ludic qualities of much tourist performance.

Nevertheless, normative practical orientations about which activities should be enacted at notable tourist sites express culturally coded patterns of behaviour that are located in particular places and at particular times. They express how performance is grounded in habitus and the dispositions that evolve around class, gender and ethnicity, to produce distinctive gaits, ways of speaking, dress and demeanour. As Chaney observes, 'the relations of dramatic performance articulate (a sense of) shared forms of perception and understanding' (1993, 4). As staged enactions, they embody culturally situated symbolic meanings which rely on representations of the tourist stage upon which they are played out. Thus, tourists look at symbolic attractions in distinctive styles, communicate and consume particular narrative interpretations and move through tourist spaces in specifiable ways. Such practices are situated in the relationship between performer and site that suggests a practical knowledge that is geographically and historically located.

The enaction of distinctive performances specifies the relationship between tourists and place. This interaction with the environment maps out individual and group identities, and as we will see, these performances allude to the wider spaces described in Chapter 1 which the stage is part of and symbolises. As I have suggested, the performing of identity by most tourists at the Taj cannot be divorced from colonial, sacred and national spatial conceptions. This introduces the relationship between power and performance.

Performances have been described as a 'discrete concretisation of cultural assumptions' (Carlson, 1996, 16). The codification of performances — what is appropriate, the order of action, who should participate — is frequently regulated by key personnel, who monitor and instruct participants and maintain key scripts. The cultural power to synthesise meaning and action and normalise performance exerts control over bodies, constructing a common-sense praxis and reaffirming cultural norms. The importance of performance as a communicative tool is recognised by authorities who inculcate embodied habits through ritualistic performance to reinforce and re-encode hegemonic meanings. To preserve the enaction of these established duties and roles, supervisors rehearse participants and measure their competence. As Geertz has shown, performances may articulate a meta-social commentary which reproduces the centrality of social norms and conventions (1993). Moreover, the mobilisation of performances in unfamiliar terrain can be strategies 'for encompassing a situation', which takes no account of local attitudes and focuses an imperialising disposition on the definition and subjectivity in space. However, as Schutz has asserted, social performances may bypass, or negotiate with, normative rituals, by organising a patchwork or bricolage of meanings and actions to generate new dramatic configurations (1964, 72–3). While dominant rules and principles organise many participants, performances vary enormously and depend upon the regulation of the stage and the players, and the relationship between the players. I now want to outline some of the constraining and enabling influences that shape the production of particular forms of tourist performance.

Having discussed the properties of enclavic and heterogeneous tourist spaces, it is clear that these distinct spaces organise different stagings for tourist performance. Thus, the nature of the tourist stage is important: whether it is carefully managed, facilitates transit, contains discretely situated objects around which performance may be organised, whether there are personnel on the stage to direct performers; or whether its boundaries are blurred, it is cluttered with other actors following incomprehensible scripts, is full of shifting scenes and random events or juxtapositions, and can be crossed from a range of angles.

Chaney remarks that as tourists 'we are above all else performers in our own dramas on stages the industry has provided' (1993, 164). However, the extent to which the participants are directed is a crucial determinant of tourist performance. Supervised choreographies and the monitoring and surveilling of actors may contrast with those performances where there is little or no supervision. However, at another level, performances need to be learnt and there are assumed to be degrees of competence and proficiency. Tourists may monitor themselves and are also subject to the monitoring gaze of co-participants and onlookers. Thus both surveilling and reflexive monitoring may restrict the scope for movement across the stage and limit the range of activities.

Besides external supervision, collective and communal group norms may be observed, which likewise constrain the actor. Conversely, where the tourist is alone, individual performances may be enacted without the censure of the group. This also raises the question about the intended audience for the performance. Since much social drama is a communicative attempt to transmit meaning and identity, the effect of performance is contingent upon an audience that understands the message the actors hope to convey. Although performances may be exclusive affairs, designed only to reinforce communal solidarity amongst the participants, it may be the case that onlookers, especially if they enact different forms of performance at the same site, either fail to understand the resonance of others' performance, or disparage their competence or the meanings they impart. Alternatively, solitary performances may be enacted for reasons that do not require a wider audience.

All these factors contribute to the degree to which tourist performers are self-reflexive: how much time is available for reflection; the extent to which performances are directed; the diversity of sights, stories, people and places encountered; the different pressures imposed by group-oriented activities and solitary pursuits; and the aims of the performers. The degree of reflexive awareness of the performer in turn, generates a detachment or immersion that limits or enables a distance from the role being played which conditions the possibility of mobilising a critical awareness.

Given the constraints and opportunities that influence tourist performances enumerated above, I now wish to consider four forms of tourist performance.

Firstly, there is a team performance, which follows the ritualistic conventions I have alluded to above. As a highly directed operation, with guides and tour managers acting as choreographers and directors, the performance is repetitive, specifiable in movement, and highly constrained by time. Besides acting out their own part in the drama by photographing, gazing and moving en masse according to well-worn precedent, the group also absorb the soliloquies of the central actors, the guides, who enact the same script at each performance. The rather over-determined stage upon which the performance occurs is regulated by stage managers, and scenery and props rarely change, constituting fixtures around which movement is organised. A good example is suggested by Bennett who discusses the development of the public museum, which he argues, 'provided a performative environment in which new forms of conduct and behaviour could be shaped and practised' (1995, 33).

Whilst the actors are often immersed in their roles, there is little room for reflexivity or improvisation given the narrow repertoire and the rigid script around which performance is organised, so participants generally remain typecast, occupying specified roles and enacting prescribed movements. The dispositions of such participants are dutiful, with a concern to perform efficiently in the 'appropriate' fashion, in compliance with group ideals and orthodoxy. Such performances are typical of religious and ceremonial rites performed at symbolic sites as well as the rituals of package tourism. In this instance, tourists collaborate 'in the production of the spectacle' (Chaney, 1993, 164).

Secondly, there are tourist performances which are partly improvised but nevertheless follow particular conventions and norms. Certain acts are commonly assumed to be integral to tourist performance such as photography and souvenir collection, and the organisation of itineraries which include symbolic places. While not necessarily participating in collective rituals, such performers select where to go, what to look at and how to behave from a menu of scripts and stage directions. Characteristically, they follow the looser instructions of a guidebook by which they organise their own performance and often consult with the script to measure whether their own experiences accord with the prescribed evocations. Less constrained by direction and spatio-temporal control, such tourists confront the unexpected. The travel manual only provides a rough guide after all, and cannot deal with many eventualities nor explain certain situations, forcing the tourist to improvise contingently. The stages moved across are likely to be a mixture of familiar, regulated spaces, and those to which tourists are unaccustomed. For instance there may be certain key sites such as hotels and cafés where tourists organise collective performances, but also unfamiliar areas which require some improvisation.

Where performances are more amorphous and open-ended, and scripts and actions are not tightly managed, 'there is scope for lying, creative ambiguity, deliberate misdirection . . . improvised codings of subversive messages' (Palmer and Jankowiak, 1996, 236). Thus another form of partially improvised tourist performance are those which have been identified as 'post-tourist' (Feifer, 1985; Urry, 1990). Acutely self-reflexive, and predisposed to distantiation from the codes of tourist performance, such actors play with normative scripts and roles, mocking the constructed and regulated nature of such performative codes whilst ironically intimating their awareness of the restrictions of the role. Such performances are rarely cynical, but are more typically playful, involving the production of farce and burlesque for the audience of fellow tourists. While participating in the ordered production of package tourism, at the same time they carve out an individual role for themselves that suggests a sophisticated performance which escapes the inscription of conventional roles and, as such, can be envisaged as a negotiated form of tourism.

Thirdly, a more complete form of improvisation takes place where tourists dispense with any sets of instructions and expand their repertoire to include an exploration of little-used spaces within the main tourist stage. Disavowing the conventions of much tourism by, for instance, photographing unusual angles and sights that do not reproduce conventional images, or even disavowing photography, improvised tourist performances include the enaction of a wide variety of collective and individual pursuits on tourist stages which seem to defy what common-sense notions dictate or officialdom decrees. Rejecting preordained scripts and ritualised behaviour, such performances often respond to chance meetings and contingent events, acting on the hoof, as it were. However, although much looser in organisation, in fact such forms of improvisation do often follow conventions, such as the production of status, for amongst some independent travellers, the escape from the perceived trappings of conventional tourism confers status and is a route to self-enlightenment. Whatever the delusions of such travellers, there is no doubt that through an attempted avoidance of regulated and normative conventions, such performances at least have the potential to create and transmit alternative meanings.

A pertinent example of such a performance is recounted by Klugman in her construction of an 'alternative tour' around Disneyland (1995). In order to escape the highly regulated nature of the stage and the normative expectations about what performances are appropriate, Klugman imagines her fellow visitors are actors whom she is directing. Through this subversion of conventional meaning and performance, the scene becomes saturated with otherness, is the site of the weird and fantastic. Moreover, simply by adopting a gaze askance to the norm, Klugman reveals the host of unpredictable oddities that abound in Disneyland. This improvisational, reflexive and contingent repertoire is enacted out of a desire to escape the routines of tourist performance yet is a response to a particular tourist stage and the conventions it embodies.

Fourthly, performances are not easily enacted in spaces where there are no directors or stage managers, and indeed little evidence of the circumscribed space that constitutes a stage. In heterogeneous tourist space, fluid events, activities and movements arise, random juxtapositions of objects and people occur, and there is a sensory and physical bombardment which precludes anything other than a contingent performance. The lack of any static or familiar reference points around which to orientate, or any obvious boundaries, further entrenches disorientation. This situation evokes the 'vertigo' described by Caillois (1961, 13) wherein perception is temporarily destabilised by a foregrounding of physical sensation and entry into an unregulated and indefinable space produces a truly liminal state. Unlike in regulated tourist space, appropriate performative codes are not known. This destabilisation may produce a state of acute self-awareness, brought on by the response of locals who perhaps regard the performance as involuntarily comedic or, on the contrary, is engendered through a condition of immersion in which each action is contingent and improvised. We are, of course, at the limits of performance here, but with a degree of social interaction with the denizens of such space, by observing the different codes and exigencies, a negotiated performance can be devised.

What makes tourist performance so interesting is the meeting and contestation on the same stage of different social roles, which embody questions of appropriateness and normativity, but which are all culturally located and express the power to define and inscribe naturalness and social reality through the active body. To summarise, tourist performances specify the relationship between people and the sites they visit. They are also constrained and enabled according to external constraints, peer-group pressure, conventions about what constitutes 'suitable' behaviour, the degree of reflexivity mobilised, the historic relationship between sites and visitors, and the parameters and management of the tourist stage on which performance occurs.

In this chapter, I have suggested that there is a relationship between the increased production of strongly classified space, particularly spaces of leisure and tourism, and the desire to escape the conventions that such regulation produces. The balance between enclavic and heterogeneous tourist space has been weighted decisively in favour of the former. I do not wish to suggest that there is any mechanical or deterministic inevitability that the organisational and commercial restraints in enclavic tourist space will produce entirely predictable performances, but rather, I want to emphasise that there is greater *potential* for tourists to improvise and reflect in heterogeneous tourist space. This will become apparent in Chapters 4 and 5, where the different performances and tourist spaces at the Taj, and in Agra, are examined.

Having outlined a theory of tourist performance, in the next two chapters I will identify particular forms of tourist practice and account for their diverse performative acts. In Chapter 3, I will explore the different narratives that are performed at and about the Taj Mahal, and in chapter 4, I will examine the different enactions of walking, gazing, photographing and remembering at the Taj.

Note

1 For an excellent example of a mixed space, which appears to simultaneously evince attributes of ordered difference and heterogeneity, see Lees, 1997.

3
NARRATIVES OF THE TAJ MAHAL

In the last chapter, I outlined how tourism can be conceived of as a set of performances. Here, I want to highlight narration, a form of performance especially pertinent to tourism. With narration, it is instructive to ask whether there are collaborative enactments which bring together different meanings and keep scripts open to change, or whether discrete groups act out their own exclusive narratives. Since I am looking at a global site here, the fame of the Taj might mean that hybrid improvisations which draw on 'recollected pasts' as well as the 'foreign media, symbols and languages' of global mediascapes (Clifford, 1988, 15) are prominent.

Of course, narration reproduces discursive representations of places, articulating the normative ways in which tourist sites are understood:

> (travel stories are) concerned with innovating or reaffirming norms of travel performance and with providing evidence that such norms had been honoured in practice.
>
> (Adler, 1989, 1367)

But whilst tourist narration involves the use of pre-existing resources and narrative conventions, the production of stories is also an ongoing process which may incorporate new elements and material from other narratives. Thus, 'participants in social events often choose to help write the script by verbalising scripts . . . by calling attention to potentially appropriate performances, and by inventing new scripts' (Palmer and Jankowiak, 1996, 250). Such contingent invention varies, for 'actors and audiences reinterpret the script, either incrementally or radically, with each performance' (ibid., 251). Here, I will examine the most popular stories about the Taj Mahal. These narratives re-present the Taj, often using well-established tropes, phrases and concepts, and the styles and contexts of their narration highlight particular traditions of story-telling.

Telling stories is an essential way of making sense of the world and transmitting identity. As Somers remarks, 'social life is itself storied and narrative is an ontological condition of social life' (1994, 613). This continual striving for coherent and consistent meaning is made more challenging with the acceleration of time–space compression. The persistent disruption of local and individual life-worlds has resulted in a contingent and flexible self-reflexivity which engenders the continuous revision of personal narratives (Giddens, 1991, 6). However, the latitude for story-telling is generally circumscribed by the necessity for identity to be located 'within a repertoire of emplotted stories' (Somers, 1994, 614) or codes which organise particular conventions of story-telling:

> people are guided to act in certain ways and not others on the basis of the projections, expectations and memories derived from a multiplicity but ultimately limited repertoire of available social, public and cultural narratives.
>
> (Somers, 1994, 614)

Somers explains that 'narrativity demands that we discern the meaning of any single event only in temporal and spatial relation to other events' (1994, 616). This process identifies the ways in which spatialising stories incorporate places and events into travel narratives as tourists 'sew' places together or have them linked by a travel organisation. The story of the tour is narrated continuously: ('We went there, then we came here, tomorrow we will go there'). Coherent links between places are reinforced by the logic of the journey and its prioritised foci, and may be narrated according to religious, political or national themes, for example. Travel stories are also recounted retrospectively, constructing a framed and selective account about what was encountered and seen.

Tourist narratives are often used biographically to mark episodes in personal life-stories. The moment of travel may thus be incorporated into a self-reflexive, serialised account of an individual's development. This is most obvious in particularly symbolic forms of tourism such as the honeymoon, the pilgrimage or the rites of passage associated with 'inter-railing' around Europe, or where certain symbolic sites are constructed as worthy of a 'once-in-a-lifetime-visit'.

The intersplicing of biographical and travel narratives is enacted at sites where subject positions are aligned with particular narratives, be they historical, political, nationalist, religious or colonial, and tourists inscribe themselves into the story of a place. Interpellating narratives of identity may be consumed in guidebooks or by the stories of guides, or they may be tales of belonging that groups tell themselves *in situ*. As Crang says, symbolic sites and objects 'become emplotted in affective tales that appeal in terms of the everyday – bringing abstract stories and everyday experience together' (1994, 345).

Thus, specific narratives of the self are performed at symbolic places. As I have emphasised, tourist sites are important locations where people attempt to make sense of themselves and the world in which they live, where they situate themselves in relation to the symbolic qualities associated with the site. Since tourists bring with them different cultural expectations, narrative forms and meanings, such sites are often the locus for a proliferation of stories. Narratives of place thus signify wider spatial and historical contexts.

The performance of tourist narratives suggests the construction and transmission of multifarious stories *in situ*, the reproduction of accounts in tourist guidebooks and travel literature, and the ongoing construction of travel tales on the move. The tourist industry is particularly concerned with packaging authoritative narratives which (re)present places, commodify old legends and structure tourist experience. But whilst 'official' narratives may be articulated by tour guides and communicated to members of tourist groups, individuals and small groups of tourists may reflexively negotiate the meanings of sites. The dominant versions about a place's history and significance may be eschewed and replaced by subaltern and minor accounts. Thus there may be considerable contestation amongst narrators to emphasise the veracity of their version of a site's significance.

In this chapter, I will explore the ways in which different narratives are constructed, transmitted and consumed at the Taj Mahal. As already mentioned, the fame of the Taj has been appropriated in numerous ways. Its metaphorical significance has been determined in a diverse range of contexts and in various locations. The adoption of the image of the Taj to enchant enterprises with reflected luxuriousness, romance and grandeur reinscribe the qualities conjured up in popular narratives of the site. However, representations of the Taj have a situated genealogy, emerging out of particular histories and traditions. I trace distinct narratives by examining old and contemporary texts and highlight how these stories persist in the enaction of narratives at the Taj.

At the Taj, as at most symbolic places, a great diversity of narratives proliferate and interweave, die or mutate. However, at any one time, particular strands are woven into distinct narratives that stand out as dominant themes by which the Taj is written and spoken about. As Samuel and Thompson declare, 'the powerful have a breathtaking ability to stamp their own meanings on the past' (1990, 18). The silences in particular accounts pinpoint the way in which discourses are mediated by power, and serve as a reminder that there are also many accounts that are rarely heard. My chief purpose here is to identify and outline the main contemporary narratives of the Taj, examining the circumstances out of which they arose and which subjects articulate them, and are interpellated by them. My aim is to highlight the genealogy of dominant, often commodified, narratives whilst exploring the ways in which other, less conventional accounts are proffered. These genealogies are traced both in written narratives of the Taj and in the contemporary accounts. There have obviously been some transformations in the ways stories have been told, especially in those oldest narrative traditions, yet as I will show, the continuities seem more evident than the changes.

Competing narrative formations about the Taj are of different vintage. The first narratives that I consider arose out of the aesthetics and political imperatives of nineteenth-century British colonialism, whereas the nationalist accounts I subsequently explore arose later, out of opposition to colonial oppression and through a growing sense of Indian nationhood. This means that there is a difference in the extent to which historical, written sources can be examined. For instance, there are numerous colonial travel accounts and contemporary guidebooks which contain narratives that are regurgitated by Western tourists and guides. While they are amongst the oldest narrative traditions, written Muslim narratives about the Taj are hard to locate and so a different approach was necessary which involved the examination of the Islamic semiotic inscription of the site and the Quranic text etched upon the buildings, in addition to the testimony of Muslim visitors to the site.

Colonial narratives of the Taj Mahal

Contemporary Western narratives about the Taj Mahal reproduce the phrases and themes of nineteenth-century accounts. The notion that the Taj Mahal is the supreme, romantic building of a fabulous, imaginary India emerged out of colonial classificatory schemes and fantasies. The Taj continues to serve as a theatre where such fantasies, embedded in the stories and descriptions that guides recount and guidebooks conjure up, are played out by Western tourists. This discursive repository is located in British representational practices from the late eighteenth to the early twentieth century. As Pal asserts, 'both the romance and the image of the Taj were largely a creation of the British in the last quarter of the eighteenth century' (1989, 199). He further contends that:

> significantly it is a romance that seems to have captured the Western imagination rather than the Indian . . . only in the last few decades have (Indian tourists) taken to the Taj with the same zeal as tourists from abroad . . . few eminent Indian artists have written about the Taj and still fewer eminent artists have painted it. The best known symbol of Indian civilisation is essentially a creation of Western enthusiasm.
> (Pal, 1989, 194)

During the period of British rule, the Taj Mahal evolved as a renowned tourist attraction, a must-see for British travellers and Anglo-Indians. The classifying imperative to rank civilisations, cultures and sites into those most worthy is echoed in Edward Lear's comment:

> Henceforth, let the inhabitants of the world be divided into two classes – them as has seen the Taj Mahal; and them as hasn't.

India has yet to be infected with the zeal for conservation found in the West and most historical monuments in India have not been carefully restored and maintained. Throughout India, there are crumbling palaces and forts, the preservation of which is almost entirely neglected, yet at the Taj, the gardens are immaculately maintained, and the site is policed. Cohn describes how, in the 1860s, an archaeological survey was established with Europeans selecting which monuments were important and worthy of preservation as legitimate parts of Indian 'heritage' (1984, 183). This highlights the colonial imperative which decreed the Taj as the site most worthy of preservation.

It is instructive to speculate what it was about the Taj, only one of innumerable large historical monuments and buildings in India, that so appealed to British colonial sensibilities. Pal suggests that the 'adulation' of the Taj by British visitors and artists at the end of the eighteenth century reflected a range of aesthetic preferences that emerged out of Orientalist fantasising. Nineteenth-century narratives of the Taj are infused with paeans to its attributes of proportion, sublimity and grandeur and it was the sort of structure that could be appreciated by a diverse range of dominant sensibilities:

> in the prevailing aesthetic attitudes of the time, the Taj could be placed in all categories. Its symmetry and geometric formalism, as well as the gleaming white marble, made it particularly appealing to those who admired the classical world. To those whose taste was for the sublime, the Taj was certainly capable of arousing strong emotional responses, a necessary ingredient of this particular 'mode of vision'. As to the romantic concern, what other monument in the world embodied such a tragic story. . . . For those who arrived in search of the romantic India, the Taj was the quintessential building by all standards.
> (Pal, 1989, 194)

Although the Taj has been continuously popular as the pre-eminent symbol of India, this is peculiar, since as Pal observes, it 'is a tomb built by a member of a minority community as an emblem of his love for his Persian wife'. This is despite the fact that, according to Pal, 'there are many older monuments in the country that are more impressive and more characteristic of India's older civilisation' (1989, 12).

Amongst the colonisers there were only a few adherents of Hindu architecture despite the proliferation of apparently impressive buildings. Still today, on a typical package tour to India, Moghul sites are the key points in the itinerary. The religions of Hinduism and Islam were both deemed inferior to the supposed illuminating power and civilising force of Christianity but they were reviled in different ways. Whilst Islam was typified as cruel, its monistic, liturgical and salvational parallels with Christianity made it at least comprehensible to the colonial mind. Hinduism, however, practically and philosophically, with its plethora of Gods, lack of central liturgy, and manifold sects, rituals and beliefs, seemed incomprehensible and threatening to Western moral and sensual order. Arguably, such colonial epistemological confusion in the face of a different dimension of sacred knowledge encouraged the British to classify Hinduism as evidence of primitivity in pre-colonial space (see Keay, 1989). Likewise, Hindu architecture was believed to reflect this chaotic, uncivilised character since it seemed to lack the aesthetic qualities of perspective and design that Eurocentric taste favoured, an outlook which permitted the colonisers to admire the Taj Mahal. This culturally situated discrimination about which sites are worthy of the tourist gaze percolates through contemporary tourist narratives.

British colonialism in India was inflected with a contorted ideological *mélange* which attempted to justify colonial exploitation and define colonised space. But the urges to extract wealth and devalue Indian culture co-existed and could be at loggerheads with the investment of desire, and a sense of responsibility to preserve certain historical sites and celebrate their qualities. This was the case with the Taj.

It is reputed that in the 1830s Lord Bentinck planned to dismember the Taj and ship the pieces to England where they could be sold. Furthermore, the grounds of the Taj were frequently used by British revellers who would chip out pieces of the marble inlay work as souvenirs (Carroll, 1972, 133). On the other hand, in the first decade of the twentieth century, the Viceroy of India, Lord Curzon, acted upon his strong feelings of imperial duty to preserve the Taj and renovate what he perceived as the unruly gardens (Pal, 1989, 86). Both the drive to conserve and the criteria by which such sites were classified and graded were located in particular nineteenth-century British scientific and aesthetic epistemologies. But at the same time looters, capitalists, military disciplinarians, scholars and scientists could compete to carry out different practices at the same and at different sites. Besides the colonial functionaries who followed imperatives to rule Indian colonial space and organise production efficiently, there were travellers, academics and artists who were consumed by 'capturing' India through representation and developing and producing knowledge. As far as the Taj was concerned, the preserving spirit within the British colonial regime won out and it became an essential site for travellers, artists and writers to visit.

Once visiting the Taj was institutionalised as a crucial part of a trip to India for the nineteenth-century traveller, the momentum that led to its construction as an unmissable sight was underway. To codify knowledge about their expanding empire, colonisers sought to classify and rank buildings on a world scale. Out of these debates, the Taj came to be commonly ranked as one of the finest buildings in the world. This process of ranking and debating its attributes became an essential part of tourist performance that reflected the sophisticated discernment of the onlooker:

> I decidedly think that this monument deserves much more to be numbered among the wonders of the world than the Pyramids of Egypt.
>
> (Bernier, in Arora, 1937, 6)

> With its purity of material and grace of form, the Taj may challenge comparison with any erection of the same sort in the world. Its beauty may not be of the highest class, but in its class it is unsurpassed.
>
> (Fergusson, in Arora, 1937, 5)

The continuing tourist search for superlatives and world-class attractions has created tourist itineraries that are shaped around their inclusion. This need to order, rank and consume the 'most' significant constitutes a central experience in much contemporary tourism. The Taj fulfils its role as the number one spectacle on a trip to India and continues to be broadcast as such by tour operators, guides and guidebooks. In contemporary guidebooks, the Taj is described as, 'the most magical building in the world . . . the most enduring symbol of human love' (Shearer, 1989, 279), 'the world's greatest monument to love' (Nicholson, 1989, 115), and 'the most accomplished monument the world has ever seen' (Kusy, 1989, 115).[1]

Besides this ranking perspective, the guidebooks also reinforce the notion that the Taj is the foremost symbol of India, describing it as, 'the supreme symbol of India' (Shearer, 1989, 279) and 'synonymous with India' (*Nelles*, 1990, 279). The *Lonely Planet Survival Kit* declares:

> If there's a building that represents a country – like the Eiffel Tower for France, the Sydney Opera House for Australia – then it has to be the Taj for India.
>
> (Finlay *et al.*, 1993, 337)

Most Western tourists articulate notions that the Taj is a symbol of India, and continue to rank it in global terms:

> Charles *(40, 'in property', from Bristol, UK, on a ten-day package trip)*: As a tourist I like to look at the most famous spots. It certainly compares well with some of the other man-made structures I've seen such as the Eiffel Tower and the Great Wall of China.

> Fiona *(31, solicitor, from London, UK, on a seventeen-day package tour with her partner)*: You couldn't come here without seeing the Taj, could you now? It's one of the great sights. It's like going to Egypt without seeing the Pyramids.

> John *(31, dentist, from Lincolnshire, UK, on a twelve-day package tour with his partner)*: As far as Westerners are concerned, it's India, isn't it? The Taj Mahal is India – a bit like the Eiffel Tower being Paris.

Besides these historical assumptions that continue to inform the Western modes of representing the site, the Taj also serves as a theatre in which Orientalist fantasies are articulated, as it has since colonial times. There are numerous travel accounts, poems and works of art which chronicle these colonial responses.[2] A common theme is the magnificence of the building, its sublimity, and its considerable effect upon the fine sensibilities of the onlooker. It is almost as if the intensity and stimulus provided by a visit to the Taj required the proclamation of deep personal sensations and refined tastes. These accounts first appear at a time when European tourism was expanding as a leisure activity and particular ways of interpreting and gazing upon the 'sublime' and 'romantic' were becoming normative.

The colonial encounter with different spiritual and cultural practices likewise produced an ambivalent response. Such exotic 'customs' were often typified as 'occult', anachronistic and superstitious, but Europeans were also attracted by the mystique and metaphysics they appeared to offer. This persists today with the appeal of the 'mystical East' in an increasingly secularised West. Part of this mystical appeal is reflected in the insubstantial, ethereal qualities assigned to colonial space. Moving into this disoriented or mesmeric state is often ambivalently presented 'as an entrance to an enchanted space of fulfilled desire, but from which the attempt to return can be fatal' (Spurr, 1993, 145). In contemporary tourism, movement into the space of the 'other' is frequently perceived as a quest for enlightenment or higher consciousness.

Pal observes of nineteenth-century accounts that, 'it is remarkable how visitor after visitor to the Taj commented on its ethereal insubstantiality' (1989, 211). The Taj was persistently described as a 'dream of celestial beauty' (Smith, in Arora, 1937, 6), 'a poem in stone', a 'sigh of love in marble' (Hamilton, 1937, 31), metaphors that continue to be evoked in contemporary guidebooks and by guides working at the Taj. These declarations of ethereality are conjured up by an Orientalist imagination which is unable to differentiate between distinct cultures within this fantastic generalised space:

> It is rather a fairy palace raised by some genie of the Arabian Nights Tales.
>
> (Arora, 1937, 5)

> Everything around you speaks of the Orient – you hear the whisper in the leaves and in the splash of the waters, you see the East mirrored in the marble fish ponds and in the silver spray of the fountains.
>
> (Hamilton, 1937, 13)

In the 1920s, a Hindu traveller, Bholanauth Chunder, mockingly remarked that at the Taj, 'many a visitor is moved to modest verse' (quoted in Alexander, 1987, 202). Indeed, the metaphors and vocabulary of the above effusions continue to saturate Western evocations of the Taj, and this way of perceiving and describing the site was echoed by many tourists:

> Paul *(32, computer programmer, from London, UK, on a two-week package tour with his partner)*: I thought it was almost ethereal. It was just sort of floating there. And I felt that if I closed my eyes it might have disappeared, like a mirage.

Other descriptions of the Taj from Western tourists included 'dreamlike', 'sublime', 'ineffable', 'from the land of fantasy', 'a total dream-world, not of this earth', 'magical', 'total perfection', 'sheer serenity', 'ethereal', 'like a mirage', 'like a floating castle', 'surreal'. The descriptive propensities of Western visitors to the Taj are still clearly shaped by these notions of insubstantiality which continues to spatialise the colonialist notion of Eastern mystery versus Western rationality. Thus the material, everyday space of the Western home contrasts with the dream space of the East.

Typically, the metropolitan evocation of the colonising figure was that of an adventurous male, travelling through, learning and finally mastering the colonised realm. Whether through scientific accounts, travel accounts or adventure stories for boys, these narratives inscribe their male subjects as coming into power, inheriting a patriarchal empire (Low, 1993, 196). Thus, a highly gendered mode of imagining colonial space interpellated the male European.

This gendered spatial imagery produced the Orient as a libidinous realm, safely distant from a mythical European sexual propriety. A common theme was that it was a space that was dangerous to European womenfolk because of the unbridled lust of the 'natives'. Protection by colonising men was necessary through the disciplining of colonised space and safety ensured by the construction of separate quarters for European populations. However, this construction of the space of the 'Other' as licentious, far removed from Europe provided a theatre upon which erotic fantasies could be displaced. European imaginations became captivated by images of Oriental unfettered lust and the body of the Oriental female became a site for fantasy, the object of the European male's gaze (see Phillips, 1997; Dawson, 1994). The art of Ingres and Delacroix, the 'scholarly' accounts of the harem divulged by male European travellers, and the popular themes of nineteenth-century pornography fuelled these projections (see Kabbani, 1986, 45–66).

Colonial narratives about sexuality combined warnings of the danger posed to European women by indigenous men with metaphors describing the desirability of penetrating and dominating a passive, feminised landscape. Indeed, colonial landscapes became thoroughly suffused with gendered metaphors about potential fecundity, made possible through the mastery of the coloniser. A particularly powerful trope is that where the land gradually reveals its secrets to their surveyors, submitting to their demand for transparency.

Many Victorian accounts of the Taj evoked an eroticised femininity, evoking contemporary obsessions with beauty and death. The examples below illustrate the sort of allusions to Oriental femininity that emerged out of this aesthetic:

> It is lovely beyond description but the loveliness is feminine. It awakens ideas of fair complexioned beauty; the soul is dead; the form, the charm, the grace of beauty are lingering there. The walls are like muslin

> dresses, radiant with flowers and jewels. The perforated marble gates are like lace veils.
>
> (J. Talboys Wheeler, in Hamilton, 1937, 7)

> (the minarets) white sentinels, each 137 feet high, standing guard over the Taj like men-at-arms, look defiant and rough, while the pale palace they watch is so fragile, so feminine and so queenly.
>
> (Hamilton, 1937, 12)

> The Taj . . . is Mumtaz Mahal herself, radiant in her youthful beauty, who still lingers on the banks of the shining Jamuna, at early morn, in the glowing mid-day sun, or in the silver moonlight. Or rather we should say, it conveys a more abstract thought: it is India's noble tribute to the grace of Indian womanhood – the Venus de Milo of the East.
>
> (Havel, in Crooke, 1906)

> (The Taj) symbolises some veiled eastern princess walking with bowed head and rhythmic footsteps . . . and the four watching minarets are the grave and kindly sentinels keeping guard over the beauty and tenderness, the modesty and charm which so often finds shelter behind the purdah screen of Indian womanhood.
>
> (Guide to Agra and Fatehpur Sikri, in Hamilton, 1937, 26)

> As a lovely woman, abuse her as you please, but the moment you come into her presence, you submit to her fascination.
>
> (unknown British artist, in M. Moin-ud-Din, 1924)

These quotes illustrate the kind of erotic fascination which the 'Orient' and colonial space held for the colonisers. The projection of a female, sexualised person onto the Taj, with its masculine 'sentinels' highlights the extent to which such fantasies of the 'other' find spatial expression in buildings, places and the landscape.

Interestingly, the ambivalence of the colonial adventure is highlighted by alternative narratives which conceived the supposedly gendered characteristics of the Taj as 'a weakness of femininity' (Crooke, 1906, 489) which constructed a gendered opposition between colonised spaces and subjects, and metropolitan space and colonisers:

> the masculine and practical brain will declare the Taj Mahal to be a much overrated monument.
>
> (Treves, in Hamilton, 1937, 34)

There is something slight and effeminate in the general design, which cannot be altogether obliterated or atoned for by the beauty of decoration.

(Crooke, 1906, 490)

These gendered representations of the Taj continue to be fulsomely evoked in contemporary guidebooks:

The Taj rises like a beautiful princess surrounded by four ladies-in-waiting . . . luminous and chaste (*Nelles Guide to Northern India*, 1990).

Furthermore, many guides at the Taj invoke such notions to the tourists they lead around the site:

Ahmed *(41, 'official' guide employed at the Taj)*: When we look at the Taj, we see feminine grace. Nowhere is it manly. The building appears like a bride – as if Mumtaz is smiling before us, a beautiful woman looking at us. If we compare it with Agra Fort, what is that? It is huge and manly, but the Taj is feminine.

Chagan *(35, employed by one of the large hotels)*: See when you go inside, it's like a woman. The gateway is a veil, and then the Taj is revealed – a beautiful and feminine form.

These narrative conventions delivered by guides sustain the colonial notion that the Taj is a feminine space. The fact that the mausoleum celebrates an Indian woman has given licence to fantasies about 'Oriental femininity' that constitute a hegemonic gendering of the site that is articulated by both Western visitors and guides.

Colonial fantasies about sexuality and femininity are more complex than a simple idealisation of the 'Oriental' woman. Mixed up with these romantic constructions are fantasies organised around violence and cruelty. Despotism served to contrast government in the 'civilised' West with the vagaries of a barbaric and decadent system of rule in the non-West, partly justifying the colonial mission. However, the numerous lurid descriptions of casual sadism, arbitrary execution and deranged cruelty reveal European prurience and desire. Although most guides know that they are apocryphal, there are stories, originating and related in most nineteenth-century British travel accounts and guidebooks, that they consistently recount during tours around the Taj. One of these myths emphasises Oriental despotism, in the shape of the cruel Shahjahan. The account given by Kalyan, an experienced guide of 55, is a version of a ubiquitous episode on guided tours which relates to the cruelty of the Moghuls:

> After the Taj was completed, Shahjahan cut off the hands of all the workers and craftsmen, all twenty-two thousand of them, so that no other building of such beauty could ever be built again – they could never work again, all those craftsmen.

Whilst some Hindu guides relate this tale to discredit the Moghuls (see below), it seems to sustain colonial notions that emerged out of the need to represent previous native rulers as casually sadistic and hence uncivilised, and the desire for fantasies of barbarism. A different, equally ubiquitous fictitious tale, is that Shahjahan intended to build a 'Black Taj', to mirror the original, on the opposite side of the Jamuna. When I asked a group of seven guides why they continued to relate these stories when they knew them to be fictional, Ahmed, the oldest of the group, spoke with the agreement of all:

> These tourists, they do not want the truth but they do want to be entertained. They like these stories. Why should we spoil this enjoyment for them?

If Ahmed is right, it can be argued that the tourists like to be entertained in reliable ways, that is, they like to be titillated with tales which satisfy their desire for a vision of the Taj and India which follows 'Orientalist' themes. As I have discussed, the imaginary 'Orient' constituted a baroque assemblage of stereotypical characteristics: despotism, cruelty, debasement, deviant and unbridled sexuality, opulence, moral and social disorder, and the mystical and irrational. This chaotic, imaginary space, full of innumerable incomprehensible people and activities, was both threatening and alluring. The danger was that, like entering the Malabar caves in Forster's *Passage To India*, a state of chronic temporal and spatial disorientation would result. These often contradictory representations were mapped onto the colonised realm in general and onto certain places in particular.

The following passage is culled from a particularly delirious representation of the Taj which highlights these themes:

> In chaste majesty it stands suddenly before you. . . . It is pure Arabian nights . . . it must be the fabric of a dream wafted through gates of silver and opal. . . . Oh Shah Jehan, Shah Jehan, you are bewitching a respectable newspaper-correspondent. The thought of you is strong wine. Shah Jehan, with your queens and concubines without number, their amber feet mirrored in marble, their ivory limbs mirrored in quicksilver; Shah Jehan who starved them in the black oubliettes, and hung them from the mouldy beam, and sluiced their beautiful bodies into the cold river. . . . And when I turn aside in your garden, shunning your fierce black and scarlet petals to bring back my senses with

English stocks and pansies, the sight of your Taj through the trees sends my brain areel again.

(Steevens, 1909, 140–3)

Although these themes are narrated in less intense ways than in the nineteenth-century heyday of the Orientalist imaginary, they continue to find an echo in the narratives of guidebooks, guides and visitors. In a contemporary 'coffee table' volume, *The Taj Mahal*, in a *Reader's Digest* series entitled *Wonders of Man* (*sic*), the short introduction includes the following passage:

> The Moghul court . . . was cruel and sensual as well as omnipotent on the vast subcontinent. As descendants of Tamerlane and Genghis Khan, the Moghuls delighted in bloody combat, savage sports, and hideous torture of their victims . . . Once crowned, the emperors sought unlimited pleasure in women, wine and opium.
>
> (Carroll, 1972, 11)

This overarching narrative framework that incorporates the Taj into colonial space is also frequently reflected in a lingering Orientalist exoticism amongst Western visitors:

> Erica *(23, student, from Cardiff, has been travelling for four months with no fixed end to her trip)*: It's like an Arabian dreamland, magical, mysterious and sumptuous. It's just a complete Oriental fantasy – your mind goes wandering off into mysterious thoughts.
>
> Ralph *(55, company director from Hertfordshire, UK, on a two-week package trip)*: It reminds you of the Arabian Nights, all the mystery and the romance. I keep imagining slaves and women from the harem padding across the marble, and the emperor sprawled out on the ground with his courtiers, smoking opium.

In this section, I have argued that narratives about the Taj Mahal transmitted and consumed by Western tourists are still, to a considerable extent, informed by the fantasies and codes that emerged out of the colonialist experience of India and the Taj. In fact, the very compulsion to visit the Taj, and gaze upon it at particular times, is part of the colonial construction of India and the world. Although rarely as delirious as the literature of the turn of the century, many contemporary accounts provide an echo of the reified images of ethereality, 'Oriental' femininity, cruelty, opulence, despotism and sensuality. The commodification of these narrative forms, typically in the shorthand soundbites of the package tour industry, fixes an understanding of the Taj that preserves a relationship founded in the colonial era which often remains deaf to other narratives. The Taj is typical of many destinations in serving as a site for the enaction of touristic narratives that continue the processes whereby the non-West is othered. The compulsion to classify and rank sites, and the articulation of desires and fantasies, is evident in historic and contemporary written accounts and in the present-day oral performances of guides and tourists at the Taj Mahal. The discursive production of the 'Orient', or the 'developing world', is reproduced in the commodified narratives of contemporary tourism. Yet while these rather reified discourses remain dominant at a global level – in the 'mediascapes' and 'ideoscapes' of tourist literature, Hollywood films and TV programmes for instance – other narratives challenge, and perhaps are breaking down their authority. And as I will demonstrate in the next chapter, while other performances of Western visitors to the Taj – walking, gazing, photographing and remembering – are inscribed by notions derived from these colonialist discourses, deviations and interruptions offer the chance to experience surprising sensations, to hear other stories, to engage in dialogue to produce discordant or hybrid accounts that decentre static colonial representations. In fact, just as other non-colonial representations of colonial space have always existed, so tourists are often unaware that they are also represented, usually in an unflattering manner, by the 'hosts' they visit (Crick, 1991, 12). This is aptly portrayed in figure 3.1 of early-nineteenth-century European tourists lounging at the Taj.

Nationalist narratives of the Taj Mahal

Combining mythical and official historical accounts, national narratives typically contain, 'a migration story, a founding myth, a golden age of cultural splendour, a period of inner decay and a promise of regeneration' (Hutchinson, 1994, 123) to establish national legitimacy and 'authenticity'. Bhabha (1994, 139–70) has explicated the 'double time' of the nation, wherein a retrospective notion that the nation has existed from time immemorial implies that national subjects must awaken to their destiny by projecting this past into the future. Although they are modern political forms, nations nevertheless lay claim to antiquity. However, a wide range of ideological and political movements assemble these components to enchant their own project to attain and contest power, each faction claiming to represent 'the people' and the 'national interest'.

Inevitably, national narratives are partial, articulating particular power bases by naturalising only specific subjects as great national actors. For instance, most myths tend to be constructed around exemplary (male) heroes. Metaphorically representing ideal national subjects in thought and deed, they 'perform legendary feats of strength', 'cross class boundaries with consummate ease' and 'effect miraculous escapes' (Samuel and Thompson, 1990, 3). These heroic narratives typically consign women to roles as 'camp followers, titillating distractions, rewards for male heroism or answers to male loneliness' (Kay, 1991, 442). Thus narratives interpellate only particular recipients, highlighting their national roles whilst relegating or obscuring those of others.

Figure 3.1 Taj Mahal with European sightseers, 1815
Source: Courtesy of British Library, London

Accordingly, dominant national histories often exclude the heritage of subaltern religious or ethnic groups, yet these groups evoke alternative histories as a means of identity transmission. There are always a profusion of competing narratives about identities within nations. Hegemonic narratives try to conceal these numerous micro-narratives since they appear to threaten the integrity of national space by identifying alternative sites of homage within the nation, or paying allegiance to a supra-national spatial entity.

Dominant national narratives are designed, however badly, as meta-narratives that speak for the whole nation. Yet however inclusive they may try to be, attempts to construct wholly inclusive accounts are well-nigh impossible. For example, the manufacture of 'official' histories that form a central part of the national school curricula requires a balancing act to incorporate retrospectively the various traditions and histories in the story of the nation. This must be an ongoing task since certain groups claim that they are not represented, and dominant groups complain about the admission of subaltern accounts. These inclusivist narratives are matched by exclusivist versions of the national story.

Exclusivist national narratives stir up fears of invasion and demonise 'enemies both within and without' (Samuel and Thompson, 1990, 5). Frequently, the appeal to a 'Golden Age' or a myth of origin conjures up fantasies of cultural (or racial) purity and the flowering of 'national genius'. Key events in national histories are often marked by the repulsion of invaders or the displacement of colonisers. Intervening events such as invasion, colonisation, immigration and the inflow of foreign influences are held to have tainted national character and space, which needs to be renewed and purged so that the nation may 'follow its own inner rhythms, heed its own inward voice and return to its own pure and uncontaminated pristine state' (Smith, 1991, 77). The implication of this rediscovery of the organic nation requires that domestic enemies and foreign influences be rooted out and the national space cleansed of non-indigenous elements. Subaltern groups may be described as 'enemies within', who ally themselves with a foreign power or propose 'unpatriotic' policies. This labelling them as people 'out of place' locates their identity according to historical and geographical references that are not situated within the national space.

As well as incorporating histories and myths about national heroes and defining events, national narratives also typically include stories that are set in symbolic landscapes and at significant sites which express aesthetic qualities and refer to historic qualities which epitomise and glorify the national character and culture. Moreover, narratives about the nation are performed at such sites. The Taj is widely understood to be a national monument and its significance to the nation is inscribed in school history textbooks and diversely narrated *in situ* by guides and tourists. As I will show, the interpretation of the Taj manifests the tension that exists between different Indian nationalisms, essentially between exclusivist and inclusivist notions of national subjectivity.

In India at present, historical arguments are vehemently expressed in the press, on the street and the academic disciplines of history and archaeology have become something of a battleground. For instance, the Annual Indian History Congress in December 1993 was notable for the numerous fulsome condemnations of the misuse of history by fundamentalist historians whilst the 'Hindu fundamentalist' group, the RSS, set up an alternative and parallel conference to give a 'correct picture' of Indian history (*Times of India*, 20/12/ 93).

The narratives I consider attempt to weave the Taj into the story of the Indian nation in contrasting ways. Employing widely differing constructions of national history and geography, 'secular' and Hindu 'fundamentalist' narratives diverge in the ways in which they tell the story of the Taj and represent its symbolic importance to the nation. These narratives are not as old as the colonial narrative discussed above and are transmitted through different forms of media, yet all are widely expressed by Indian visitors to the site. The 'secular' nationalist interpretation of the Taj is commonly related in history schoolbooks and in 'official' guidebooks to the site as well as by tourist guides at the site. The Hindu 'fundamentalist' accounts are generally to be found in propagandist literature and espoused by supporters at the site.

'Secular' nationalist narratives

As a strategy to unify the new nation of 1947, the new Indian elite manufactured a composite history designed to appeal to the greatest possible range of new national subjects. This syncretic history was part of the attempt to build up a national consciousness around 'secularism, non-alignment and socialism' (Desai, 1993).

Nationalist histories were weapons in the struggle against British rule when it became important to broadcast the achievements of historical eras and heroes to counter Eurocentric allegations of backwardness and claims about European superiority. In the early years, the achievements celebrated tended to be from the pre-Muslim Aryan eras and particularly the Hindu 'Golden Age of ancient India', the reign of the Guptas. This mythical example of social harmony, cultural excellence and spiritual enlightenment was portrayed as a goal to be recaptured. Similarly, the heroes eulogised were usually figures such as Shivajii, Rana Pratap and Guru Gobind Singh who had battled against Moghul rule. Reconstructed as exemplary figures worthy of emulation, they constructed a patriotic subject who was definitively non-Muslim (Chandra, 1993, 45–7, 56–9).

However, Independence in 1947 brought with it a sense that national unity should prevail, especially after the carnage following the division of Pakistan and India. The national imperative to incorporate the diverse peoples of India and gain their allegiance to the newly liberated, secular state required a national identity that recognised the contribution of various cultural and religious traditions. This secular nationalism, which is most commonly identified with the Congress parties, continues to dominate across India and particularly in the sensitive sphere of education. As a univocal 'retrospective illusion of nationalism', it produces a narrative which is hostile to alternative identities, 'be they religious, regional, linguistic or ethnic'. And these identities are 'rendered spurious, reactionary and vestigial' (Krishna, 1994, 507). Krishna points out that rather than take this production at face value as definitively 'modern' and 'civilised' as is often claimed, it is instead part of a 'larger package consisting of many standardised ideological products and social processes [including] development, mega-science and national security' (1994, 518).

To counter the distortions of colonial history which elevated European traditions and culture and vilified both Moghul and Hindu history and tradition, a national historical narrative has been concocted that largely disregards religious conflict. Thus, a reorientation which highlights positive aspects of Muslim Indian history characterises this version of the national story, wherein the Moghul age is designated the 'Second Golden Age of India'. The Moghuls are esteemed for their contribution to the unification of India (not then known as India in the modern sense, of course) as well as for their technical achievements and their endowments in the sphere of art and culture. Moreover, the Moghul emperor Akbar was added to the canon of great national heroes for his liberal regime; his patronage of Hindu holy men, artists, administrators and soldiers; and for his interest in all religions which culminated in his invention of a faith, *Din-i-Illahi*, blending different religious traditions.

The text of model answers for the CBSE examinations used by most secondary schools in Agra is based on the national syllabus for Indian history, and follows this liberal approach to history (Kundra and Bawa, 1991). The Moghul period is celebrated as the 'Second Classical Age' of India by virtue of its 'political unity', 'efficient administration', encouragement of national feeling, and especially its significant cultural and artistic progress (Kundra and Bawa, 1991, 134–43). The volume focuses on the religious advances of the liberal and syncretic Sufi and Bhakti cults and Akbar is stressed as one of the seminal figures in Indian history. In a key passage, he is described thus:

> Akbar completely identified himself with India and her culture. He did his best to advance the political, social, economic and cultural interests of this country like any such ruler who belonged to the Indian race and the Indian culture . . . he gave political unity to India which went a long way in forging the cultural integration of the country.
>
> (Kundra and Bawa, 1991, 61)

The builder of the Taj Mahal, Shahjahan is less eulogised, but again, his reign is praised fulsomely enough. Defects are admitted but overall:

> Keeping in view his personality as a whole, these weaknesses are insignificant. In history, he is known as the 'Prince of Builders'. He

deserves full praise for establishing complete peace and prosperity in the country.

(Kundra and Bawa, 1991, 71)

Foregrounded are the architectural achievements of his reign, most notably the completion of the building of the Taj in 1653, which is described as one of the 'Wonders of the World'. This harmonious version of national history continues to be the one received by most educated Indians.

This most prominent narrative of the Taj in India promotes the site as an Indian creation, not solely Islamic in style and inspiration, conceived and built during what is often referred to as the 'Second Golden Age of Indian Art' or the 'Second Classical Age', namely the Moghul era. This narrative emphasises the diverse influences and qualities of Indian heritage and the Taj has been constructed as a site which reflects this diversity.

This is the story which most domestic visitors to the Taj continue to narrate, and it is supported by secondary school textbooks and the majority of guides. The narrative recounted by a majority of Indian visitors and learnt by most Indian schoolchildren is that the Taj is a national monument which reflects Indian qualities as opposed to being merely representative of Muslim power. For instance, discussing architecture in the Moghul period, the 'model answer' in the local textbook for the question 'How can the Moghul period be called the "Second Classical Age" in Indian History?' states that 'under the Moghuls, the Hindu and the Muslim cultural fusion took place and there developed an Indian culture' (Kundra and Bawa, 1991, 135).

Another answer, to the question, 'Was Cultural Integration achieved during the Moghul Period?' epitomises the standard view projected of the Moghuls and their artistic achievements:

> The Moghuls . . . succeeded remarkably in establishing a cultural integration in India. They shed their religious bigotry and encouraged the sentiments of nationalism, which flourished under their patronage. In every sphere of culture . . . the people belonging to all religions and races worked together to produce masterpieces which are unrivalled. The specimens of art created under the Moghuls have become the common heritage of both the Hindus and the Muslims. It was undoubtedly the Moghuls to whom the credit goes for making possible the integration of the two sets of traditions.
>
> (Kundra and Bawa, 1991, 136)

Such answers foreground the Taj Mahal as a pinnacle of Indian cultural synthesis. In their 'model answer' to the question, 'Describe briefly the growth of architecture under Shahjahan', Kundra and Bawa state that Shahjahan's, 'architectural achievements, expressive of his genius and personality, have rendered him immortal'. The same answer also includes a statement refuting Hindu 'fundamentalist' claims that the Moghuls were foreigners:

> it is possible that the Moghul style (of architecture) might have been influenced by foreign styles but because its creators were Indian, it is absolutely wrong to say that their thinking was altogether foreign.
> (Kundra and Bawa, 1991, 140–1)

As with these school textbooks, most Indian academic historians stress the synthetic nature of the Taj and its national importance. Significantly, a history professor at Agra University with whom I spoke about competing versions of the origin of the Taj stressed the responsibility of historians to emphasise unifying strands:

> The Taj is an example of Indo-Islamic architecture, combining Hindu and Muslim art. There are so many Hindu architectural features, most of the ornamentation for instance. Maybe there was a Hindu temple there before Shahjahan built the Taj, but why bring these things up? We should not remember a past that creates controversy and division but instead, when we find the positive aspects of that history then we should emphasise them. There is no point in looking back if you can't look forward. No, you should create a history that can create unity.
> (Interview with Prof. P. Asthana, Agra University, 11/12/93)

Most in-depth architectural studies of the Taj have also emphasised the hybridity of its design as reflecting the much-trumpeted qualities of Indians to remain open to influences. The most authoritative and popular work avers that the Taj is:

> representative of the amazing capacity of the Indian artisan to adapt himself to changed conditions and to assimilate the inspirations to which he is introduced from time to time.
> (Nath, 1972, 5)

Besides these written accounts, most visitors stress that the Taj reflects Indian unity in diversity, as the following quotes exemplify:

> Rajesh *(33, civil servant, from Baroda, on pilgrimage to several sites with a family party of twelve)*: The Taj is an encyclopaedia of all religions, such is the diversity of architectural styles and the religions of the designers, labourers and craftsmen who worked on it. Of course, religious funda-

mentalists on both sides try to claim the Taj but, in fact, it is a gift to the world, a site for everyone to come to and see Indian culture.

Mohammed *(18, photographer from Jaipur, on a day trip with six friends)*: The Taj is a symbol of glory and national pride. It may be a symbol of Muslim power but it was built by Hindu artisans too. It is a national building and it reflects national characteristics, and every Indian has pride in the Taj.

Its world-wide fame tends to fuel a sense of pride about India, and the Taj serves as a place where Indian national identity can be reinscribed upon subjects through an act of homage to a symbolic national site, a place where they remember that they are Indian. The presence of thousands of foreign and domestic admirers intensifies this sense of national belonging.

A majority of domestic visitors place the Taj in the scope of this inclusive national narrative, expressing the sentiment that it is an important symbol of India. Its global importance conjures up feelings of national pride from both Hindu and Muslim visitors:

Shria *(35, civil servant, from Delhi, on a day trip with a family party of six)*: I wanted to show my children this national monument. It's such a thing of beauty and part of our history. . . . It is Indian. We Indians identify ourselves with the Taj. It is ingrained in our psyche from a very early age. We see it all the time, on biscuit tins and so on. When we see it we are made aware of our identity, our tradition. The fact that it is a Muslim monument is not important.

Raju *(40, businessman, from Lucknow, on pilgrimage to Mathura with family party of twelve)*: You see, the Taj was built by many labourers and artists; Hindus, Mohammedans, Christians, so it is not exactly a Mohammedan building. In any case, Akbar was a great *Indian*. He accepted Hinduism, and Shahjahan was his grandson. So here was the great example for Mohammedans and Hindus to live and work together peacefully. Now the elections are soon and Hindu politicians are stirring up trouble with all this stuff. They say the Taj is a Shiva temple. Maybe it was; but they have no proof. It is a great *Indian* monument – for *all* the people.

B.L. *(66, retired civil servant from Gujarat, on pilgrimage to Mathura)*: It is loved by both Hindus and Muslims, so it is a great thing. In fact, more Hindus visit than Muslims. We Hindus are great absorbers of all things.

But the Taj is a place where we can say '*Jai Jagat!*' (Hail World!). It represents not just a message to India but to the whole world.

Naseem *(52, hotelier from Lucknow, part of coach party on pilgrimage to Ajmer)*: It also expresses (Shahjahan's) love for his country and it should inspire all Indians also to feel this love for India. It is a beautiful place and it makes me proud to be Indian and appreciate the achievements of my ancestors. At this time when the country is divided by communalism, the Taj can be an example of peace and love to the people of our country. We all love the Taj and when we come we feel this national spirit.

Several Muslim visitors took the opportunity to emphasise their inscription within this national narrative, stressing their Indianness in response to accusations that they are not really Indians but the descendants of invaders. One man defiantly expressed his sense of belonging to India whilst visiting the Taj:

Mohammed *(58, shopkeeper and part-time priest from Bangalore, en route to Ajmer with a family party of seven)*: (The Taj) inspires godly love among *all* the communities of India; among Muslims, Jains, Hindus, Sikhs, Parsees, Christians. It is something for all religions. . . . It is a structure built for *all* Indians. It makes me feel like an Indian. I was born in India and have no desire to go anywhere else. I will live and die in this country.

The idea that the Taj can act as a symbol for India precisely because of the diverse cultural influences provides an inclusive sense of Indian identity. Whilst history is important in constructing a sense of Indianness, the narrative offered here does not attempt to identify some primordial and pure original national culture, but produces a syncretic identity, a host of different strands that are woven into a national story. The idea that India is a hybrid realm is mapped onto the Taj, a symbolic site which embodies and condenses diverse memories, myths, cultures and traditions which evoke a moral geography of inclusiveness. However, even an evidently syncretic cultural form like the Taj can be reinterpreted to symbolise a more exclusive sense of national identity as I will now show.

Hindu 'fundamentalist' nationalist narratives

The decline in support for the Congress parties in India seems partly to testify to the way in which the secular, liberal constitution and ideology erected after Independence is increasingly being questioned. Increasingly, the fragile secular consensus that has held together for the last fifty years is under threat from exclusivist forms of nationalism that accuse the politicians of minority appeasement, Westernisation and of disdaining Indian traditions in their pursuit of modernisation. As these secular politics are becoming increasingly questioned, so the Taj is also implicated in the reconstructed nationalist narratives which challenge them. The reinterpretation of national history is a central political strategy of the Bharatiya Janata Party (BJP) and its allies, the Vishwa Hindu Parishad (VHP) and the Rashtriya Swayamsevak Sangh (RSS):

> It would be no exaggeration to suggest that a communal historical approach has been, and is, the main ideology of communalism in India. Take that away and hardly anything is left of the communal ideology.
> (Chandra, 1993, 39)

The resurgent Hindutva movement emotively appeals for the reclamation of India to 'her' true self; a particular national destiny that is inspired by a specific mythical past. Its historical narratives, emphasising both colonialist and Islamic brutality in contrast to an idealised Hindu respect for cultural and religious diversity, holds considerable allure in the context of an upsurge of concerns over national identity and the future polity.

Contemporary communal historians have consolidated these nationalist narratives by highlighting the destruction of Hindu temples by Muslim 'invaders', practices which illuminate the contrasts between the 'barbarism' of the Moghul era with the 'idyllic enlightenment' of ancient Hindu epochs (Thapar, 1993, 4–6). The movement perpetuates the central myth of a 'continuous thousand-year old struggle of Hindus against Muslims as the structuring principle of Indian history' (Basu *et al.*, 1990, 2), a homogenising argument which proffers 'evidence' of 'the historical wrongs done by an undifferentiated and fixed body called "the Muslims" to another undifferentiated and fixed body called "the Hindus"' (Pandey, 1993, 11).

This retrospective projection enables often unfounded instances of violence to be labelled 'Muslim fundamentalist' and thus focuses on its alleged persistence. Many of the concerns about internal autonomy movements and the 'designs' of Pakistan are predicated upon these historical notions of Muslims as non-Indians and eternally hostile to the Indian nation. For instance, it is frequently pointed out that the Muslim's loyalty is to the wider space of the *umma*, and to Mecca, rather than India. However, as Basu points out, these retrospective constructions of a continuous strategic and systematic attempt by Muslims to take over India are ahistorical, for prior to the development of communications and economic integration, 'sharply defined identities and animosities across large expanses of space had relatively little chance of development' (Basu *et al.*, 1990, 3).

Hindu fundamentalists have criticised secular histories for their 'distortions', their move away from notions of 'intrinsic Indianness', and for 'lacking the vital core of an emotionally integrative principle' (Deshpande, 1994). It is contended that these narratives emanated out of a consciousness that was not shaped by

Indian concerns but by foreign ideologies. Yet it is claimed that the essential(ised) 'Hindu' Indian subject is untainted by 'foreign influence':

> in spite of all the tomtomming of the virtues of European modernity . . . the people of India have not really changed (or forgotten) their intrinsic Indianness, their essential rootedness in the Indian civilisation . . . centuries of efforts of alien rulers of various hues have failed to change the Indian consciousness in any meaningful way.
>
> (Bajaj, 1993, 12–13)

In response to these perceived deficiencies, in Madhya Pradesh, following the victory of the BJP in state elections, secular accounts in state school textbooks were replaced by texts that favoured a more Hindu-slanted history. Moreover, the RSS has set up a large network of schools across India which provide an alternative education which emphasises the values of the Hindu Right (Sarkar, 1994).

This competing nationalist project is attempting to reinscribe India as a wholly Hindu, non-secular space, and particularly wishes to reconstruct notable symbolic sites as Hindu to repair the damage wrought by Muslim and British colonisers. According to this conceptualisation:

> The *rashtra* (nation) is conceptually separated from the state and is defined as a cultural idea which embraces a community that resides upon a piece of land with which it shares an organic as well as an emotional relationship. . . . The Muslim remains forever the symbol of those who disrupted this sacred integrity and divided this holy land.
>
> (Basu *et al.*, 1990, 77)

It is argued that there is an intimate relationship between land and religion; that what defines the geographical boundaries of the Indian nation state is the historically continuous existence of a Hindu community within them. This posits the Hindu as the 'natural' Indian. Critics of the secular polity criticise the lack of political will to remove these 'symbols of defeat' from public spaces. For instance, Bajaj exclaims:

> It seems that we want to carry the whole burden of our historical defeats with us. We do not want to forget or erase any of it. We therefore have victory towers, triumphal arches, and statues of the victors occupying prominent public spaces in most cities. . . . And we have victor's mosques standing in the most sacred spots of Indian collective memory. The public spaces of India have thus become unbearable to the good sense of ordinary Indians.
>
> (1993, 8)

Recently, the political importance of history and geography has been re-emphasised in the protest against the secular policies of the Congress Party, who are routinely accused of appeasing the 'Muslim minority'. A programme of Hindu revivalism focused on the Babri Masjid at Ayodhya, in Uttar Pradesh. This campaign resulted in the immensely symbolic destruction of the mosque by the *kar sevaks* (foot-soldiers) on 6 December 1992. The mosque is alleged to have been built on the site of the Hindu deity Ram's birthplace by the Moghul king Babar, who destroyed a Hindu temple in the process. The evidence for the previous existence of the *mandir* is much disputed by politicians, historians and archaeologists.

The destruction of the Babri Masjid exemplifies the Hindu 'fundamentalist' project of righting the perceived wrongs of the past. There are particularly controversial mosques that were built by the Moghul Emperor Aurangzeb at Mathura, on top of the temple built on the site of Lord Krishna's birth, and in the most holy Hindu city of Kashi (Varanasi), which top the list of Islamic structures for which the revivalist Hindu movement demands demolition. However, there are many other structures and sites labelled as originally Hindu in origin.

There have been several provocative academic accounts which narrate the destruction wreaked by the Islamic 'invaders' upon Hindu temples, claiming that most well-known Islamic buildings were established on the site of Hindu religious structures. As Sita Ram Goel points out in his edited volume *Hindu Temples: What Happened To Them?*, the aim is to uncover 'a suppressed chapter of India's history: namely, the large scale destruction of Hindu temples by the Islamised invaders' (1990, I). The various writers in this edited volume homogenise Indian Muslims as 'invaders' – iconoclastic destroyers who are late-comers on the stage of Indian history. By contrast, 'we Hindus were not born yesterday . . . we are history personified, history with a capital H' (Dubashi, 1990, 49). Such beliefs are often articulated in certain symbolic public spaces.

The reinscription of all Indian space as Hindu has included the reinscribing of the Taj as Hindu in origin. The most notorious example of this relabelling is Professor Oak's *Taj Mahal. The True Story: The Tale of a Temple Vandalised* (1989) and the pamphlet, *The Taj Mahal is a Tejo Mahalaya* (1979). Many locals and visitors are familiar with this book and it was occasionally recommended to me as an exposition of the 'true story' of the Taj.

Professor Oak has built up a body of work which includes volumes refuting the Muslim origins of the Red Fort in Delhi, the abandoned city of Fatehpur Sikra and Agra Fort, which he attempts to prove were Hindu achievements taken over by Muslim rulers. This reinscribing of the Taj Mahal fits into his project to prove that:

> *all* historic structures in India currently ascribed to Muslim sultans and courtiers (including so-called tombs and mosques, castles, towers and bridges) are pre-Muslim Hindu constructions.
>
> (Oak, 1978, 29) [my italics]

His contention is that:

> The Taj Mahal is only a typical illustration of how all historic buildings and townships from Kashmir to Cape Comorin, though of hoary Hindu origin, have been ascribed to this or that Muslim ruler or courtier.
>
> (Oak, 1978, 25)

Oak holds that the people responsible for this state of affairs are 'court flatterers, fiction writers and senile poets who are responsible for hustling the world into believing in Shahjahan's mythical authorship of the Taj' (1978, 14). Apparently, these characters have misled Indians into believing that Shahjahan was responsible for the building, for Oak's thesis rests on the contention that the Taj is 'not an Islamic mausoleum but an ancient Shiva temple known as Tejo Mahalaya which...Shahjahan commandeered from the then Maharaja of Jaipur' (1978, 1).

In the pamphlet, he tries to substantiate his claim by providing 103 points of evidence. This includes philological testimony about the origins of the phrase 'Taj Mahal'; 'falsified' historical accounts designed to glorify the Moghul rulers; architectural features of the Taj which 'prove' its Hindu authorship; and botanical details of the species in the gardens which are held to be symbolic Hindu plants. Rubbishing the romantic element of the story, he offers some curious evidence. He contends that since Shahjahan had many affairs with other women he could not have felt much for Mumtaz. But conversely, if he had indeed felt anguish at her death, he could not have built the Taj since 'grief is a disabling, incapacitating emotion' (Oak, 1978, 19). Oddly, Oak also argues that his love for Mumtaz would also have prevented his building the Taj because:

> carnal, physical, sexual love is again an incapacitating emotion. A womaniser is ipso facto incapable of any constructive activity. When carnal love becomes uncontrollable a person either murders someone or commits suicide. He cannot make a Taj Mahal (which can only originate) in an ennobling emotion like devotion to god, to ones mother country.
>
> (1978, 19)

Much of the argument follows similar lines in discrediting and pathologising the Moghul rulers. He also bases much of his argument on hearsay about how features within the Taj have been concealed by officialdom, for instance, maintaining that there are hidden statues and a *linga* of Shiva in the Taj, and 'its walls and sealed chambers still hide the Hindu idols in it' (Oak, 1978, 17). He accuses the Archaeological Department of conspiratorially concealing the evidence.

A minority of Hindu visitors to the Taj follow the narrative that the Taj is really a Hindu site that was taken over by Muslims, and they often give obscure or apocryphal evidence to back up their statements.

Dwarka *(39, from Mumbai, hot drinks machine manufacturer, on a week holiday with eight family members)*: Well, it's an excellent building ... but people should remember that it's a Hindu temple dedicated to Shiva. If you read about it you will find this is the truth. It's something that was taken over by Shahjahan. The Moghuls were cruel tyrants who oppressed the Hindu masses. The Mohammedans converted all these temples into mosques. You will find that one of the rooms in the Taj is locked. Inside you will find a Shiva.

Sanjay *(21, student, from rural Bihar, on a one-week holiday with his friend)*: It is a building to Mumtaz Mahal they say, but it is built on the banks of the holy River Jamuna and in reality, it is a Hindu temple that Shahjahan took over.

Sunharilal *(34, harmonium player and teacher from Mathura, visiting Agra for the day)*: In fact if you read Professor Oak's book you will find that the Taj is really a Shiva temple. Look at the arch and you will see snakes – a Hindu image. And *Om*, the Hindu sign is written on the marble floor that the Taj sits on. There is the Hindu sign of three lines on top of the Taj and also, all Hindu places are built next to a river.

However, these 'Hindu' features – the snakes, the *om* and the three lines – are not clearly discernible at the Taj as far as I can see.

Besides those who refute the fact that the Taj is a Muslim monument, other Hindu visitors, whilst they accept that the Taj is architecturally and aesthetically impressive, dissent from the majority view outlined above that the Taj is an important symbol for India and represents a synthesis of Indian cultures. Although they recognise that it is a Muslim building, it is this very aspect that invalidates its importance:

Sujit *(29, civil servant, from Calcutta, on pilgrimage to Mathura with a party of nine)*: It is an asset to India only in terms of its architecture, not its historical significance. There are many more important times in Indian history than the Moghul period.

Patu *(30, civil servant, from Gujarat, on pilgrimage with a party of eight to various sacred sites)*: I have no impressions – no comment. I am a Hindu so it means nothing to me. . . . It is merely a good building. But it is a Muslim building and therefore nothing to me. . . . I have nothing to say as a Hindu. What can this mean to me?

Rakesh *(37, civil servant from Delhi, on a day trip with a family party of seven)*: It is a symbol of the architectural bent of mind of the Moghul kings. To me, like many of their monuments, these Muslims have built this only for their own glory and not out of any higher motive, not out of concern for the people, nor for their welfare, but only to show their own importance.

Although these narratives form a minority of domestic opinions regarding the significance of the Taj, they do reflect the contemporary political situation whereby the maintenance of secular consensus is under challenge from communalism. In this sense, the Taj represents an arena where the contesting ideas about Indian subjectivity, space and history can be articulated.

Muslim narratives of the Taj Mahal

In Chapter 1, I examined the ways in which semiotic inscriptions of sites communicate meaning and can be read as a text. It has been difficult for the Taj to retain its original significance as a funerary monument that communicates a particular Islamic meaning through its architectural symbolism. Instead, it is a site that has become 'encrusted with secondary images, values and associations' which have made it difficult to appreciate its original meaning (Rojek, 1997, 59). Nevertheless, many Muslim visitors continue to read the Taj as a sacred site.

Muslim narratives of the Taj have few written sources but form part of the understanding of local visitors who come to the site weekly to pray, and those who come from further afield as pilgrims. As the most famous Indian attraction globally, the Taj is a source of especial pride to many Muslim visitors who regard it as particularly symbolic of their history. At the same time, since the site is also considered sacred, it also implicates the wider Islamic geography of which it is part. This means that the significance of the site extends beyond India to the whole Islamic world. Those who worship at the mosque on the site orient themselves towards Mecca, the spiritual and geographical heart of Islam.

Although the Taj Mahal is undoubtedly the result of a synthesis of Indian architectural forms, it is stamped by Islam. Most obviously, one of the large buildings flanking the Taj is a mosque which is usually visited by Muslim visitors to the site. The Taj is at its busiest on Friday when the mosque is used as the main place of worship by Muslims from the adjacent area of Taj Ganj, a steady stream mingling with the tourists all day. Since the site is recognised as a place of worship, entrance is free to all on this day. Thus the Taj retains a sacred purpose that is not touristic and is narrated as such.

Rather than examining written narratives of the Taj, it is important to recognise that many of the features of the Taj Mahal and indeed its overall form and design are themselves textual in communicating Islamic cosmology and aesthetics to Muslims. This narrative is written on the site and can only be read by those who are familiar with the language. These inscriptions are closest to the original meaning intended by the designers. Rizvi describes the Taj thus:

> This is not the ordinary world; rather it reflects the heaven of the Islamic mystic, a perfection and security beyond space and time.
>
> (1987, 2,967)

The Taj then, was conceived and designed to articulate and appeal to Muslim sensibilities. For instance, according to Shearer:

> To a Muslim (the entrance) gateway has a specific spiritual purpose. It symbolises the transition from the realm of the senses to the realm of the spirit and is thus the entrance to paradise, the door to a womb of spiritual rebirth.
>
> (1989, 282)

Other Islamic meanings conveyed through the form and landscape of the Taj are the cosmological symbolism of the dome, and the reflection of the Taj in the river and central canal in the gardens, all of which reflect conceptions of heaven (Shearer, 1989, 285–7). The plan of the garden is full of cosmological allusions to heaven: the division of space into multiples of the sacred number four, the cypress trees symbolising death and fruit trees symbolising life (see Carroll, 1972, 91–6).

More obviously, besides metaphorical architectural allusions, the site is profusely inscribed with extracts from the Quran. There are 241 Quranic verses on the Taj and the surrounding buildings. As narratives, these address Muslims and they are understood only by those who can read Arabic. The Quranic text on the gateway establishes the nature of the relationship between the site and the visitor:

> O soul that art at rest, return to the Lord, at peace with Him and He at peace with you. So enter as one of His servants; and enter into His garden.

This textual inscription on the fabric of the site matches the narratives of many Muslim visitors to the Taj. For some, the Taj serves as symbolically important through what is considered to be the divine inspiration for the building, and as a place of pilgrimage where the sacred can be experienced:

> Kamal *(26, glass-bangle maker, from Firozabad, on a day trip with six friends)*: We've visited the Taj over one hundred times. It is the perfect place for a day out. Our Moghul king made a wonderful thing for us. We come again and again because it is the greatest building from our golden age, built by a Muslim king. Also, the Quranic inscriptions on the building fill us with happiness and inspire us. It is a representation of the beauty and glory of the Quran. Its inspiration is divine.

There are also many Muslims who visit the Taj as tourists. As I will discuss in more detail later, the peak season for Muslim visitors to the Taj is during the great December pilgrimage to the tomb of a Sufi saint at Ajmer when thousands en route wait in queues hundreds of yards long to gain entrance to the Taj. However, Muslims also visit the Taj throughout the year. Whilst many echo the secular nationalist sentiment that it is essentially an Indian building, built by and for Indians of all religions, the Taj is also frequently narrated as testimony to a 'Golden Age' of Muslim rule, to a past that possesses a strong affective meaning for Indian Muslims.

Such visitors usually spend longer than other domestic tourists at the Taj. They visit the mosque, read the Islamic inscriptions and visit the tombs, and they express an especially heightened sense of being at a symbolic site. They perceive the Moghul period as the era when India was under Muslim rule and, as such, this was its most enlightened historical period. Accordingly, these notions are incorporated into a narrative that emphasises achievement and expresses Muslim pride:

Sabir *(46, in 'the poultry business', from Mumbai, on pilgrimage to Ajmer with a family group of five)*: It was always my ambition for my children to see the Taj. This shows what the Moghuls gave to India. They were Indians, not foreigners as some people say, and the Taj was a gift by Indians to Indians – and the world – a gift of love. The Moghuls brought organisation to India, they were good administrators. They cared for the people and they brought culture and a love of art and buildings to India. Before them, these qualities were not there.

A visit to the Taj is also an occasion to reiterate a narrative of loss, which the building symbolises. For many, the brilliance of the Moghul era contrasts with the gloom of the contemporary Muslim predicament in India. Muslims' accounts suggest that they see themselves as heirs to a particular historical tradition which is remembered proudly, if wistfully:

Naseem *(18, student, from Delhi, on a day trip with family party of eleven)*: This is a memorial of our Muslim past. I like to come here to remember. As a Muslim in these difficult times, it gives me great heart to see the Taj and makes me feel for our past.

Ibrahim *(52, small courts magistrate, Mumbai, on a week-long holiday with a family party of thirteen)*: It (also) shows the Golden Age of Muslim rule, when there was peace and harmony in the country – not like today! Under Islamic rule, India prospered and was peaceful. For Indian Muslims of course, we feel a special pride for the Taj.

By way of concluding this section, I return to my brief discussion above about the salience of Indian history in contemporary India because I want to stress the way in which these Muslim, Hindu fundamentalist and secular nationalist notions affect the perception of particular sites and are activated at them. The existence of these enormously divergent stories, evoking inclusive and exclusive conceptions of national identity, highlight the difficulty of maintaining a sense of national cohesion in the wider national space that these accounts imply.

For the wider inferences of these narratives of the Taj articulate themes that are played out in many public spheres and do not merely circulate amongst those who are interpellated by them and relate them. For presently, Indian history and identity are in considerable ferment, and discussion about Indian identity and nationalist politics is quite ubiquitous, for instance enlivening many debates on the street. In Agra, the Taj serves as a focus for these considerations. To highlight this, I have reproduced an exchange between two local taxi-drivers, one Muslim, the other Hindu, who were debating the significance of the Taj with me over a cup of tea outside a successful marble emporium in Agra Cantonment:

RAVI: You see, the Taj is a Hindu temple in reality. These Moghuls, they destroyed many Hindu temples.

KAMAL: No, no. The site of the Taj was only a *garden* dedicated to Shiva. Shahjahan was friendly with the Hindu priest. He asked him if he could bury his wife there and the priest said 'Sure', and let him have the garden.

RAVI: This is not true. There was a *temple* there, a Shiva temple. The base of the Taj is the base of the temple. The priest and Shahjahan were not friends. He kicked the priest out. So really the Taj is a Hindu temple. If you read the old books you will find this.

KAMAL: There are no such old books. The only books are by these people who are stirring up trouble between Hindus and Muslims.

Anxieties about the identity of India are being articulated through two distinct historical narratives that are respectively exclusionary and inclusionary. Such dialogues are a feature of contemporary historical debate in India but here are played out locally on the street with reference to the symbolic space of the Taj Mahal. As a symbol which condenses ideas about India, the Taj is both a site where national narrations compete over the 'imagined geography' of the nation and local knowledges are contested. As I will now discuss, the tourist industry has produced a complex range of 'expert' accounts found amongst tourist guides, entrepreneurs and academics that constitute a valuable form of cultural capital as well as an economic resource.

Other narratives of the Taj Mahal

I have concentrated above on the narratives most frequently related about and performed at the Taj Mahal. There are, of course, other narratives. Shortly, I want to look at the counter-narratives that are told about the Taj, those interpretations which challenge the norms and assumptions of dominant accounts. Firstly, however, it is important to note that in Agra, in the universities, tourist institutions, and particularly in Taj Ganj, the area adjacent to the Taj, there are many local people who have researched and studied the history and architecture of the site in depth.

Because of its economic importance, there is a great wealth of expertise and knowledge amongst those dwelling and working in the nearby streets, many of whom have at one time or another worked as guides. Such knowledge has been crucial to their livelihood since intense competition between guides for custom means that it is a locally valuable resource. For instance, Dr Quamar, the owner of an STD telephone office close to the site, has written extensively on the marble inlay work and the architectural origins of the building, and Mr Mumtaz, the owner of a nearby marble craft shop, spoke to me about the dynastic quarrels of the Moghuls in the era of Shahjahan for forty-five seamless minutes. These 'experts' provide detailed narratives about aspects of the Taj. Eager to impart their stories, they are happy to spend time with Western tourists in conversation, and furnish a more interactive and less packaged form of information than the soundbites offered by guides. This might work as a strategy to keep tourists in their shops but there is also a sense in which pride in their knowledge constitutes a form of status which is enchanted by notions about expertise.

For many locals, their story of the Taj Mahal is based upon its economic significance. As a young local marble craft shop owner said:

> Abdul: Most Indians are poor but people come from all over the world and bring money to India because of the Taj. It gives us all a livelihood in Taj Ganj. It is like the goose that laid the golden egg. To me, the Taj is merely a local feature but for us locals, we have been presented with the wealth that having the Taj brings and we must preserve it.

This notion escapes the romantic idealised narratives of the Taj by stressing its pragmatic value. Other dissenting accounts of the site are constructed by some visitors. In the next chapter I will discuss the performances, dispositions and perspectives, and the spatio-temporal organisation of touring that stimulate these versions. Backpackers in particular reach unconventional interpretations of the Taj. The imperative for self-discovery and an awareness about being unduly influenced by normative Western constructions of the Taj can promote the desire to retain an independent disposition:

Mattheus (22, student, from Austria, travelling on his own in India for six months): I'd heard a lot of stories, good and bad, and I thought when I saw it I'd just throw away these stories and just make my own opinion.

This may be an unfeasible aim but it reflects the extent to which backpackers are extremely reluctant to be grouped with package tourists and is manifest in a critical approach to narrating the Taj. Accordingly, some tourists comment on how the Taj signified and commemorated power:

David (26, psychologist, from Christchurch, New Zealand, travelling on his own in India for two months): I think it represents a personal celebration rather than giving pleasure to others or showing your respect to a God. Ultimately it reflects a desire to go down in history more than anything else.

Nikki (26, junior doctor, from London, UK, travelling on her own in India for one month): I think really, it's the big difference between wealth and poverty. Power. Power in the first place, I would say. It's built to impress. It's an expression of one man's ego, a man's desire to be remembered forever.

Dominant notions about the romantic and aesthetic value of the Taj are reiterated by most Western tourists and yet they can clash with a more critical viewpoint which creates a degree of ambivalence:

Becky (30, social worker, from Bristol, UK, travelling with her friend for 'as long as the money lasts'): I think it's absolutely fantastic. It rendered me speechless – which is quite a surprise! And it sent butterflies through my stomach because it's so beautiful. This is the third day we've been to see it and it still looks brilliant. But I do think it's extremely extravagant and in some ways a complete waste of money.

Besides this critique of its opulence, there are also those who question the way in which the Taj is deemed to represent a pinnacle of aesthetic expression, and adopt a critical gaze to evaluate its aesthetic merit:

Pascale (28, radio journalist, from Liège, in Belgium, travelling in India on her own for one month): It's very pretty rather than beautiful. But there's no depth to it – it's rather superficial. There's not much to see really, especially inside the building. I wouldn't make that for my lover! It's OK but somehow it's not quite enough. It lacks something human.

Karl (59, semi-permanent traveller, from Enschede, Holland; has bought an Enfield motorcycle and is travelling around India for as long as he wants): It has its own sort of beauty but I don't like the symmetry of it much. It's too symmetrical. I would like to see some more magic in it, something less predictable.

In addition, there are tourists who question the suitability of the Taj as a symbol of India, and the relevance of the site as a central object of the tourist gaze.

> Kate *(27, nurse, from London, has been travelling around India for two years on her own, and is about to go back home)*: I've seen temples and monuments – and the Taj is very impressive, but I much prefer to sit and chat and have a chai. To me, that's much more part of it, to get to know the people and learn something from them. And something like the Taj Mahal, you've seen so many times before, so many pictures. I mean, anybody who's never been to India knows what it's like. I guess the Taj Mahal is to India what the Eiffel Tower is to France. But really, I don't think it represents India. It's not Hindu, and I mean, Hinduism is India.

Finally, there are narratives which appropriate the gendered construction of the Taj as a signifier of ideal love for a women and reinterpret it with regard to current social realities. Rather than a critical perspective, this highlights how symbols are flexible forms which can be freighted into political narratives to convey a powerful message:

> Sumathi *(22, P.E. teacher, from Madras, has come to Agra on an education course)*: It is an expression of love in such a way that no-one has expressed before or since. As a symbol of the total dedication of a man to his wife, it should inspire men to love their wives and care for them, but sadly this is so often not the case in India. There is a lot India's men can learn from the Taj.

Whilst symbolic places are the centres for a proliferation of written and orally transmitted narratives, in this chapter I have identified what appear to be the four most evident narratives that surround the Taj Mahal. Each has a distinct genealogy, located in particular cultural, historical and spatial contexts. This situatedness implies that narratives interpellate only particular subjects. Such tales, recited and consumed *in situ* at particularly symbolic places, can powerfully consolidate collective and individual identities. But by identifying the ways in which these narratives discursively construct imagined geographies into which the Taj is incorporated, it is possible to distinguish the processes whereby places can be conceived as the foci of multiple meaning systems. By recognising the simultaneous articulation of different spatialising projects at the same site, it becomes possible to disavow essentialising notions about the meaning of places, whilst discerning the traces of power and the relative political strengths of these discourses.

There are then, distinct audiences and performers for different narratives at the Taj. The continuous themes of colonial discourse are maintained, sometimes in startlingly unmodified forms but mostly as more polite versions of colonial fantasy. This raises a question about the extent to which these different narrators negotiate with those who relate other stories. It appears as if the Western narratives circulate amongst Western tourists and tourist industry personnel, and in texts such as travel guides, yet they rarely intrude upon the experiences of domestic tourists at the Taj. The spatio-temporal control exerted upon Western package tourists precludes much interaction with domestic tourists anyway, and so there is not much direct contestation between these narratives of place. But whilst there is little sign of intercultural dialogue, some of the themes originating in colonial narratives: that the Taj is a monument to love, a wonder of the world, an aesthetic pinnacle, are widely shared, although with subtle distinctions within each narrative tradition.

However, as far as the rival commentaries on the national significance of the Taj is concerned, these versions are part of a wider political debate in India, the efflorescence of which has affected many areas of Indian public life. This highlights how such political competition is activated and enacted at and around especially symbolic sites such as the Taj.

In the case of Muslim stories, which depend on a particular religious notion of the Taj, these narratives are not only transmitted orally but may be inscribed into the material form of a site and physically communicated by the language of symbolic, textual architectural forms. And as I will explore in the following chapter, the inscribing practices of walking along distinctive routes, notably by these religious visitors, is partly homologous to the inscription of writing.

Yet as I have shown, stories are told which escape the regular narratives about the Taj, usually where there is more time for reflection, a greater critical distance, and a disposition towards self-discovery. This different spatio-temporal experience of tourism is less supervised, predictable and subject to collective pressures, permitting experimentation, dialogue with other story-tellers, and unmonitored diversion from established and commodified scripts.

Of course, this account is an academic narrative, intended for a particular audience, using discursive tropes and conventions to frame my story about tourism, and this particular chapter is a story about stories. As an author, I have selected these voices out of the welter of interpretations I heard, hoping to convey the diverse tales that are articulated at and about the Taj. Yet as an attempt reflexively to map discourses in a symbolic space, this bricolage of narrative snippets, these multiple strands, hopefully give no authority to any one version, including my own. It is what Denzin has described as a 'messy text', multi-vocal, 'entangled in other texts' (1997, 234) which attempts to identify how identities and cultures are negiotiated and given meaning at a symbolic site. The story that I now tell about the Taj has effaced any previous narratives I might have consumed and reproduced; indeed I have listened to so many accounts that my own response to the site is mediated by thousands of voices, denying any confident attempt to represent it somehow objectively.

I have identified narration as one form of tourist performance, and in the following chapter, I investigate how differently embodied tourist performances organised around walking, gazing, photographing and remembering are enacted at the Taj. In most cases, given its fame, narratives about the Taj are already known before the site is visited and partly shape expectations and understandings. As I will show, the relations between representation and other tourist performances are strong. For instance, gazing and photography may be influenced by already identified features in texts; guided tours around the site are accompanied by a narration of well-rehearsed tales and conventionally recognised attributes; and remembering practices are often concerned with recording and then recounting the story of the Taj. Yet forms of representation cannot entirely condition experience. The performances that I will describe exist as distinctive tourist techniques which follow their own conventions and may obscure meaning produced by narratives or take precedence in particular instances. There may also be tensions between the desire to listen to or tell stories and carry out other enactments. Moreover, I will also go on to argue that a less mediated and improvisational forms of tourist performance and experience can act to decentre the consumption and the meanings of conventional narratives.

Notes

1 I carried out an extensive survey of contemporary guidebooks to Agra and the Taj available in the UK. The point made here, and those to follow on the themes by which the Taj has been and continues to be narrated, are echoed in virtually all these books but space precludes a more extensive selection. The guidebooks I reviewed are Alexander's *Delhi and Agra: A Traveller's Companion*; Shearer's *The Traveller's Guide to Northern India*; *The Collins Illustrated Guide to Delhi, Agra and Jaipur*; *The Cadogan Guide to India*; *Nelles Guide to Northern India*; *The Lonely Planet's India: A Travel Survival Kit*; *The Berlitz Pocket Guide to India*; T. Sendour's *Introduction to India*; *Insight Guide to India*; and *Fodor's India*.
2 Pal identifies and illustrates many of the ways in which Western artists, writers and photographers have depicted the Taj in the final chapter of his edited volume (1989).

4

WALKING, GAZING, PHOTOGRAPHING AND REMEMBERING AT THE TAJ

In this chapter, I will concentrate on the various embodied enactions played out in four main areas of performance – walking, gazing, photographing and remembering. Although this might suggest that these performative configurations are discrete, they are usually interlinked. Indeed, distinct sequences that combine these four activities are informed by particular conventions and understandings. These different conventions are conditioned by the degree of external constraint over tourists, peer-group pressure, notions of appropriate tourist etiquette, reflexive awareness, the relationship between site and visitor, and the nature of the stage, issues that were discussed in Chapter 2. As is the case with the performance of narratives, the culturally located nature of these more embodied performances is evident. Where appropriate, bearing in mind the comparisons between tourists and researchers, I have included aspects of my own performances at the Taj.

Walking

Tourism intimately concerns movement, that of a journey from an everyday situation to an extraordinary location. Tourism, as a set of embodied practices, is distinguishable from other social forms of practice. This passage through material space, as opposed to virtual movement, requires the activation of particular embodied techniques, dispositions and epistemologies which are enacted *in situ*. The aspect of tourist movement examined here is walking, a performance which 'entails movement through space in stylised ways' (Adler, 1989b, 1,366).

Walking is an activity central to tourism. Landscapes are criss-crossed and imprinted with the bodily presence of the visitor, and symbolic sites are negotiated via various paths. Walking and moving through space partly constitutes places, as 'the habitual routines of "place ballets" are concretised in the built environment and sedimented in the landscape' (Shields, 1991, 53). However, the amount of time tourists spend walking, the paths they take, and the extent to which they veer from the established trails varies. Thus, both the modalities of walking and the diverse constitutions of place are shaped by the different spatial and temporal designs of tours.

I use the metaphor of choreography to convey the ways in which tourists' bodies are tutored in 'appropriate' ways and form patterns of collective and individual movement through tourist space. I have discussed the political significance of walking in the city described by de Certeau, the way in which pedestrians negotiate routes that conditionally free them from the regulated nature of the space they traverse. Game also reveals how through walking,

> things extra and other, heterogeneous details and elements insert themselves ... practices ... that cannot be put into representation, cannot be seen, fragmentary pasts that cannot be read by others.
>
> (1991, 153)

However, whether through the regulation exerted by the scrutiny of tour personnel, fellow travellers, or self-surveillance, bodies following strict choreographies are less likely to experience the sensuality excited by less rigid choreographies. Where there are opportunities for visitors to construct their own improvisational trails, a potential escape from dominant narratives and practices is enabled. Casual wandering, lounging, and 'hanging around' may specify a disposition that implies a different relationship between pedestrian and place. As Game points out 'to wander is to err from the straight and narrow of linearity, of the order' (1991, 149), in this case, to deviate from organised passage through disciplined tourist space.

Places are also organised with modes of transit in mind. The kind of unilinear flows and obstacle-free streets of enclavic tourist space contrast with the numerous impediments and rough surfaces of heterogeneous tourist space. Tourist spaces, like certain cities, 'invite a writing of the stroll, others are closed, direct the walk, or make it impossible' (Game, 1991, 151). The variations of bodily contact and sensual encounter experienced by movement through these distinct stages structure the performances and choreographies of tourism. I will outline the diverse walking performances at the Taj, but within the context of the wider experience of tourist space.

For many tourists, especially those on package tours, their movements are shaped by a directedness that permits only a modicum of innovation. Since these tours are usually organised to fulfil the imperative to see 'as much as possible', to sample as many places as can be crammed in, the range of places to see and explore is paradoxically limited by a pre-determined, condensed itinerary. Moreover, the rigid dispensation of time necessitates the discouragement of lingering and so the opportunity to explore sites at a leisurely pace is often denied by tour personnel. Accordingly, most movement is encapsulated in buses, cars and planes and walking occurs only in brief bursts of collective sightseeing at attractions and by meandering through the regulated space of tourist enclaves; browsing in shops and restaurants, and wandering around gardens and golf-courses, stretching the legs over familiar territory.

In the structure of the holiday as a whole, for most package tourists the Taj is the most important sight/site on a visit to India. Of the several key attractions around which tours are organised, the Taj occupies centre stage. Tour organisers and guides whet expectations, emphatically predicting that the Taj will be the pinnacle of the trip. The site's centrality was conveyed to me by the tourists themselves who expressed how it was both anticipated and produced as the highlight:

> Wanda *(29, pharmacist, from London, on a two-week package tour)*: Most of our group have been completely and totally geared up to seeing it. This was the place we were all waiting to come to.

> Phil *(27, accountant, from London, on a two-week package tour with his partner)*: Everyone in our group kept saying it was going to be the highlight of the tour – and that's what all the tour guides were saying too.

After visiting the site, the assertion that the Taj was the highlight of the tour was retrospectively confirmed by 75 per cent of the package tourists I interviewed. It appeared to live up to the expectations of the majority of the package tourists and was favourably compared with other sights:

> Anne *(46, catering manager, from Leeds, on a two-week package tour with her friend)*: Well we liked the Red Fort, but the big thing has been the Taj. I mean, what a building. That was always going to be the highlight of the holiday.

Yet despite its central importance, most package tours only spend about one hour at the site. As I will discuss, this limited time is a matter of discontent for many tourists since visits to the Taj must be highly managed and organised so that what are considered to be the most important aspects can be crammed in.

At the Taj, obeying the instructions of guides and tour organisers, most package tourists follow prescribed paths, moving towards certain valorised spaces and features and not others. The performance of these disciplined collective choreographies constitutes a quite precise and predictable 'place-ballet' (see figure 4.1). Bodies are tutored and disciplined, kept together and directed by assumptions about what is deemed 'appropriate', by group norms, and principally by the orders of the guide. Upon entering at its side, groups congregate upon the platform by the central gateway for a few minutes while the guide dispenses information and tour members take photographs. Following this, the central walkway is negotiated, the platform at the crossroads of the water-course provides another gazing and photography point for a few minutes, the marble base upon which the Taj rests is ascended and the tombs are explored, and occasionally the back of the mausoleum platform is traversed. Besides these areas, few other areas are explored and only a fraction of the possible spaces, views, and

WALKING, GAZING, PHOTOGRAPHING, REMEMBERING

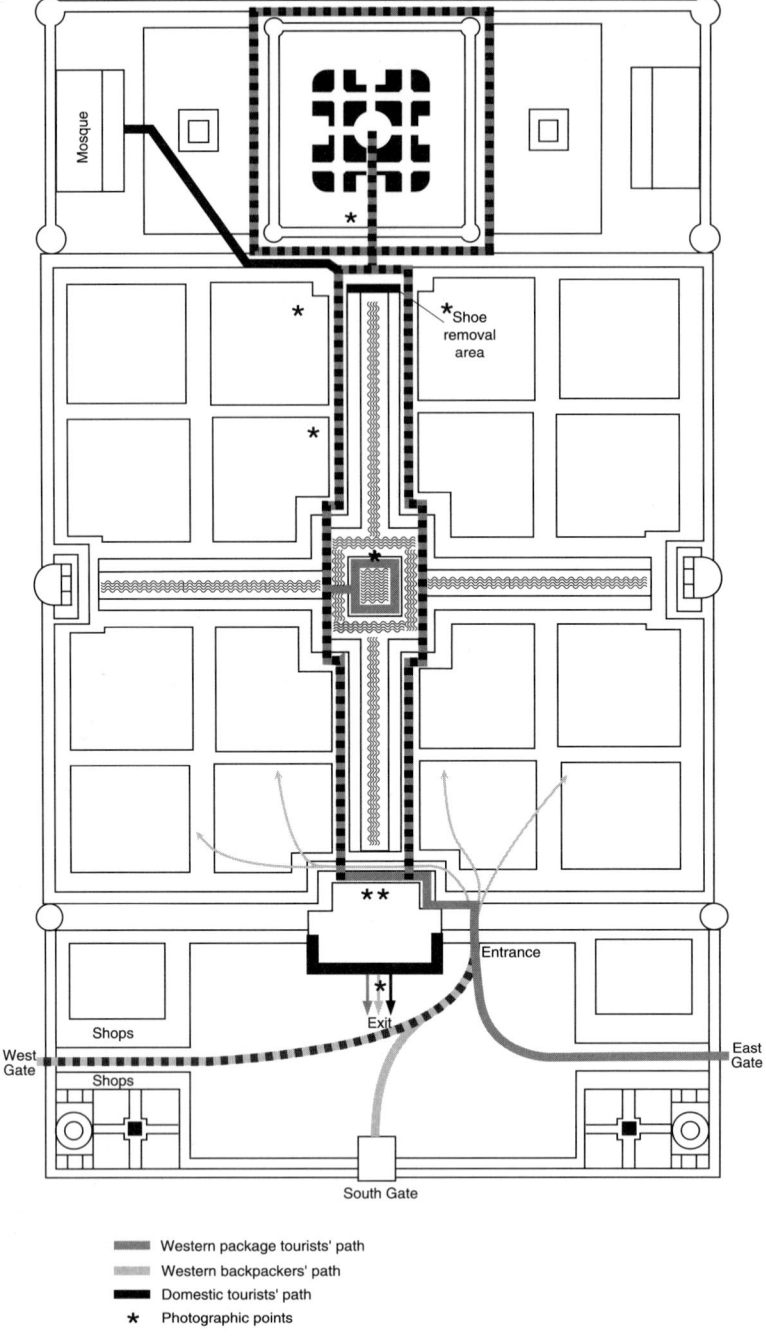

Figure 4.1 Tourist paths around the Taj Mahal

sensations in the grounds of the Taj can be experienced. These guided tours around the Taj are, with a few exceptions, highly regular. The tourist gaze is successively directed towards the following features as information about them is dispensed:[1]

> **Stage 1 (by the central gateway): The Taj as a whole: the famous global image looking down the water-course to the Taj**
>
> 1. a statement that the Taj is the most famous/greatest/largest building to love in the world; the romantic story of Shahjahan's love for his queen;
> 2. the extraordinary cost of the building; how long it took to complete; the numbers of workers; the myth that they had their hands cut off upon completion of the Taj to prevent any subsequent employment on other buildings;
> 3. architectural aspects: the special features synthesising Hindu and Muslim traditions, notably the dome, the minarets and the symmetry of the building.
>
> **Stage 2 (at the central platform)**
>
> much photographing – this is conventionally the point from which individual portraits of tourists are composed. Also, most guides indicate the seat upon which the lovelorn Princess Diana sat when she visited the Taj.
>
> **Stage 3 (at the tombs or by the mausoleum)**
>
> 1. description of the pietra dura inlaying with references to the types of stones used and always the application of a torch beam to the work to highlight its translucence;
> 2. the myth of the mooted construction of the 'Black Taj'; Shahjahan's imprisonment in the Red Fort by his son and his longing gaze towards his creation, the Taj.

These regular guide narratives, frequently mediated between the Orientalist themes of splendour, excess, cruelty and femininity, and the nationalist synthetic ideology discussed in Chapter 3, restrict the interpretation of visitors by the transmission of packaged information. Between the guides, the tour operators and the tourists themselves, there is a constant bandying about of clichés, superlatives and ways of looking at the Taj. Emphatically this ingrained 'place-ballet' epitomises the satisfaction of realising anticipated consumption, and then quickly moving the party on to another site of consumption – following a visit to the Taj, as for any attraction on their tour, the next stop is invariably a craft emporium. In the case of the Taj, the retail outlet concerned usually sells marble-inlay products, echoing the recently gazed upon marble and inlay work at the building and further commodifying the Taj experience. Consequently, tour guides are anxious to get to the emporia as quickly as possible to maximise the amount of time, and therefore, money spent there, so that they can increase the opportunities for collecting commission on the purchases completed by the tour group. Since the whole Agra tourist industry is typified by schemes for gaining commission for guides, drivers and other tourist personnel, there is a powerful incentive for tourist workers and organisations to utilise strategies that boost their potential rake-off.

Walking around the Taj fits into a wider pattern of spatial control over tour members, echoing the extremely directed choreographies of other sites. Passage is very specifically timed so that a maximum time may be spent at each stop on the march around the building. The organisational imperative to keep the tour party together means that discipline is imposed upon those who stray too far. In fact, the need to keep groups in tight formation is emphasised shortly before the party enters the site. Guides issue warnings such as, 'Don't get lost or we will have to leave you behind', and, 'Beware of dishonest people who will try to take advantage of you'. The construction of the site as one where great care must be taken is certainly exaggerated since there are numerous tourist police present to prevent transgressions.

However, the tightly constricted movement of packaged tourists can result in considerable frustration. For many tourists, the view from the back of the Taj – the meandering Jamuna River, the herds of buffaloes, the washing of clothes and bathing people, and occasionally, the passage of smouldering funeral pyres from the burning ghats further upstream – represents a timeless vision of the 'real' India. Movement towards and through this less regulated space is strongly desired. Tourists express the urge to go down to the river, to mingle with the buffaloes and cow-herds and yet rarely do so because of the aforementioned time-constraints and their own fear of the apparent 'otherness' they are looking at.

Tourists also express frustration with the onslaught of information:

> Guy *(48, lecturer, from Northampton, UK, on a ten-day package tour with his partner)*: The guide's been talking to us for about half an hour. He's taken us to various spots but he tends to bombard you with too much information. You try to have a look round but the guide says, 'Come on, we need to go' and he's only going to leave us on our own to do our own thing for a quarter of an hour.

But for many, given that a visit to the Taj is so eagerly anticipated and the main incentive for their trip to India, restrictions on time are the most keenly felt source of frustration, especially when they are whisked off to another craft emporium:

> Jeremy *(63, lawyer, from Oxford, UK, on a two-week package tour with his partner)*: We've been here one hour, which isn't nearly enough time, but

they say we've got limited time. We're going to see another marble shop now – thanks, but no thanks, we'd rather go for a beer.

Phil *(27, accountant, from London, on a two-week package tour with his partner)*: We went to the Taj and then straight after, to a marble inlay shop. They showed us how they made the things and then did the hard sell. I mean, that's happened everywhere, in Delhi and Jaipur as well, and honestly, it does get a bit much.

Dawn *(53, nurse, from New York, on a three-week tour with her partner which incorporates China, India and the UK)*: I've felt they've hustled us in some areas. I'd rather see the Taj than go shopping. You really get that everywhere you go on this tour. I mean, we've come all the way from New York to see the Taj, and then you've gotta go after a few minutes to some shop.

Yet despite this tension, many tourists seek distance from any external social interaction and a more physical engagement with the environment. Although the Taj is highly regulated and policed, unease at intrusions upon their progress around the site causes many package tourists to shrink from independent photographers and guides hustling for their custom. Upon reaching the platform on which the mausoleum stands, visitors are required to remove their footwear in recognition of its Islamic significance and as a mark of respect to the dead, and store them in an area by the stairs, leaving a small tip for the custodians. Domestic tourists go barefoot onto the platform but many package tourists prefer to pay an extra charge to keep their shoes on and tie a cloth bag around their feet. This provides an apt metaphor for the way in which package tourists insulate themselves from the physical sensations and imagined potential diseases in the Indian environment, forever retaining a certain distance from the crowds.

In heterogeneous tourist spaces where there is not the same form of surveillance, tourists traverse spaces where routes are not laid out, and activities are not tightly regulated. This is not to deny that there are particular touristic practices which adhere to a style of travelling, but there is the possibility of mobile exploration and escape from these norms. Where tourists have greater time at their disposal, they have the opportunity to explore a wider range of spaces on foot, to consider sights and attractions from different angles, to wander off the 'beaten track' and find a preferred spot. The average time spent in India by Western backpackers is 3.48 months (see table 5.1, Chapter 5). This time is generally unstructured and schedules tend to be improvised. Individual travellers, or those in small groups, therefore, tend to be more improvisational in their movement, contingent decisions to stay here or go there being made at short notice.

Many backpackers are aware of this distinction between themselves and package tourists, a demarcation they are keen to point out by way of emphasising what they consider to be their superior, more individualistic mode of travel and their deeper level of perception. While many backpackers do visit the Taj Mahal, most assert that it is not central to their itinerary.

The following quote exemplifies the way in which this attitude influences their decision to visit the Taj:

> David *(26, writer, from Glasgow, UK, travelling on his own in India for six months)*: I feel very reluctant to pander to, to go to specific tourist type areas, particularly buildings and monuments. But there's normally a couple of times when I throw caution to the wind and go. I thought this would be a monument that I'd want to see, especially because of the energy of the place. I think that's what these kind of places are – high energy places – and that's what draws people to them. You can accumulate a lot of knowledge about a particular place but ultimately it's down to the actual vibrations and the emotional aspect.

It is notable that David stressed that he wanted to 'throw caution to the wind' in visiting the Taj. Presumably he felt that his status as an independent traveller might be compromised in some way and there is a clear notion that a traveller such as he should not 'pander' to these attractions. Also, he values emotional and spiritual responses in opposition to the collection and consumption of information about the Taj, and these are typical backpacker imperatives as we shall see. This indicates some of the motivations that impel such travel to India.

Although it is not a central focus of their travels, backpackers who do visit the Taj Mahal spend far more time there than any other tourists. Most stay longer than two days in Agra and thus make use of the opportunity to visit the nearby Taj (the area of backpackers' hotels is adjacent to the Taj) on more than one occasion. Many spend most of the day at the Taj and the average time spent there at any one visit is five hours. Since there is rarely any pressing need for them to keep to a schedule, many visit the Taj two or three times to 'hang out', socialise, watch people or read. Thus, time is not only spent gazing at the Taj but entails a diverse range of activities.

Having a greater control over their own use of time, backpackers cover a wider spatial range. The 'place-ballets' of backpackers tend to be less confined (see figure 4.1). At the Taj, they wander over the whole area of the site, sit amongst the trees, sprawl out upon the lawn and stroll down lateral paths. This choreography incorporates a number of different movements as backpackers move from one spot to another, taking in the views or watching the passers-by. There are no regular locations at which backpackers position themselves and there are no external constraints over where they may roam. The Taj often serves as a site for social intercourse, backpackers often sit in groups and chat, or talk to domestic tourists or locals. Indeed, the space of the Taj represents something of a meeting place where they can sit and share experiences and recommendations about their travels.

These individual, improvisational movements indicate a desire to remain unrestricted. Indeed, backpackers do not usually employ guides to tour the Taj since this is believed to restrict their freedom in looking and moving. Likewise, most are not concerned with consuming a large quantity of information about the monument by reading about its history and architecture. It is generally considered better to gain more immediate impressions from the site than in consuming information, for it is through reflexivity and supposedly unmediated impressions that one can get a 'feeling' for the Taj:

> Michael *(39, strategic consultant, from Melbourne, Australia, travelling in India with his friend for one month)*: You can read about it but it doesn't help at all in experiencing it. It's the same with a guided tour. Having someone who explains the individual features is not of great interest. It's what stays in the mind; the essence.

> Fiona *(31, EFL teacher, London, travelling in India on her own for an unfixed period)*: I love the space here, it's beautiful, but I don't like to think about it in these ways: Why read about it? Why go on the guided tour? You have to meditate on it as a spiritual symbol.

The stress on this mode of consuming the Taj also connotes the aforementioned backpacker desire to be identified as different from the package tourist by virtue of their greater individualism:

> Karl *(59, semi-permanent traveller, from Enschede, Holland; has bought an Enfield motorcycle and is travelling around India for as long as he wants)*: I'm an individual. I don't like to follow a leader. And I don't like so many people round me. I like company, certainly, but not this way. When I have got my own impressions and worked them out, then I like to read about it.

Besides, the opportunities that they have for dialogue with both Indians and other diverse travellers at the site means that meaning can be negotiated and shared. In a sense, this also accords with the desire for self-realisation and the notion that India forms a space in which such enlightenment can be achieved. This individualistic pursuit engenders a certain reflexivity amongst backpackers, which is manifest in the ways in which much of the time spent at the Taj involves meditation, sketching and journal-writing. The experiences confronted are reincorporated into located ways of containment and comprehension as part of a larger project of self-education, and the enaction of certain choreographies in tourist space is instrumental to this goal: the wandering through space absorbing stimuli and drifting off into fantasy and memory; the repose in yogic meditation; and the movement towards 'otherness'. This less-organised movement can lead to chance occurrences that destabilise culturally located epistemologies and common-sense impressions.

Another form of touristic choreographed movement, the most specific and formalised, is performed by those tourists who partake in ceremonial procedures to commemorate and signify their link with particularly symbolic sites. This form of walking is discussed below in the section on remembering. The rituals may be formalised calendrical occasions or individual actions that inscribes the relationship between site and visitor.

Although there are certainly elements of such ritual performances in the disciplined tourist choreographies discussed above, I am referring here to the many Muslim visitors to the Taj, who stay for a much longer time than other domestic tourists, on average about three hours. They tend to approach the Taj with veneration and linger for a long time in the grounds. Collectively or singly, Muslims slowly walk around the mausoleum, reading the Quranic messages embedded in the structure, stand inside gazing upon the tombs, and sit on the marble terrace in silent contemplation.

A visit to the tombs of the emperor and his wife is a sacred activity in itself. Prayers are recited and visitors may stay in the chamber for several minutes as if paying homage to the departed. In fact, the Muslim guardians of the tombs, who keep a twenty-four-hour vigil inside the mausoleum in shifts, are known as *Khadims*, and are selected on a hereditary basis, some claiming descendance from the time of Shahjahan. Paid by the local government, these men also carry out specifically religious functions in regularly praying for the departed and defending the tombs. Muslim visitors also cross the square to visit the mosque to the East of the mausoleum, a space where few non-Muslim visitors go. Thus the movement of Muslim visitors follows a purposive and predictable spatial pattern. The very meaning of the space, saturated with notions of the sacred, informs a practice which is concerned with rapid movement to spiritually significant features.

Besides the constraining demands imposed by most package tours, most forms of group travel involve a certain amount of peer-group pressure. There are often demands to stay within the orbit of the group and engage in collective activities which limit individual trajectories. Group-oriented activity depends on the confining of individual desires. Thus, tourist groups that are not organised by a travel company nevertheless are disposed to 'stick together' and follow collective paths.

There are few solitary domestic tourists since a trip to the Taj is primarily an experience to be shared, usually with the family. This collective mode of travel highlights normative social life and identity, in which the family, caste group and community is integral to a sense of security. Social occasions such as religious rituals, pilgrimages, parties and holidays typically bring the members of extended Indian families together. About 75 per cent of domestic tourists are part of family groups, comprising from three to fifty persons, with the average group numbering approximately ten. As I have remarked, during pilgrimage season large coach parties of villagers visit the site en route to sacred centres. This communal approach to visiting places structures choreography.

These groups tend to stay extremely close to one another whilst walking around the Taj. Different points are stopped at collectively and tourists tend to move off en masse. This collective movement is not a matter of seeking safety in potentially dangerous space or a response to any perceived threat of epistemological chaos. Whereas package tours are regulated by agents such as guides, this place-ballet signifies a powerful sense of group identity and particular norms of collective spatial practice, such as a lack of self-consciousness about keeping one's distance. Most forms of leisure in India are similarly communally oriented.

The choreography of these groups is also shaped by the manner in which the Taj is consumed visually. The non-enaction of a romantic gaze means that domestic groups rarely linger at the entrance gazing upon the Taj. The usual procedure is for them to walk quickly down the central walkway, rapidly enter and exit the tombs, sometimes walk around the building, and then turn back, usually exiting without a backward glance. It is as if the building has been witnessed, admired, and is part of the day out but of no special affective importance, producing a series of movements which are not slowed down by reflexive contemplation.

The rapid coverage of space is reflected in the relatively short time that most domestic tourists spend at the Taj. Over half stay at the site for less than an hour and 25 per cent spend less than two hours there although occasionally groups will sit on the grass, chatting.[2] However, this is rendered less appealing by the fact that in comparison to most other public spaces in India, regulation of the Taj prohibits eating in the grounds. Tourists complain that picnicking is very much part of the Indian day out and should not be forbidden. Due to this restriction, many visitors eat their lunches outside the site. One guide, Vinod, reported:

> Indians are great picnickers, they have a picnicking mentality. The average Indian has no great knowledge about the Taj. It is just a famous thing to see. Any outing is an excuse for a feast. If food was allowed in here, it would be a vast scene of families eating, litter everywhere.

Of course, if the rules restricting eating in the premises were relaxed, the choreographies of these visitors would take a very different form.

The social function of a visit to the Taj is reinforced by the belief that it is a good place at which to meet other Indian and Western tourists. Accordingly, groups frequently make contact with each other and step off the central paths to converse, and Western tourists are approached, chatted to and often photographed with the group. The national symbolic significance of the site and the co-presence of members of the 'imagined community' of India mean that national pride and solidarity – unity in diversity – can be celebrated:

> Kusuma *(22, housewife, from Bangalore, on a four-week honeymoon)*: The Taj makes us feel great about India, feel great love for our country. It reveals

our culture to foreigners, and it's wonderful for all kinds of Indians to visit the Taj and meet people from all over the country.

Passage around the site then, is co-ordinated by the group. Like Western backpackers, domestic tourists have little interest in partaking in a guided tour, requiring neither information nor guidance:

> Jaysing *(31, sergeant in Indian Air Force, on pilgrimage to Mathura with a party of twenty-three)*: We have no interest in guides. What's the point? We can see it! A guide is not necessary for the enjoyment of the building. They only want money and to waste our time. We prefer to form our own impressions.

> Ratilal *(47, jeweller, from Ahmedebad, on pilgrimage to various sacred sites with a party of ten)*: We would have no freedom. A guide would restrict our movements and tell us where to go and what to look at, and so we would not use our own minds but concentrate on boring details.

Besides tourist use, the Taj is widely used by locals as a place to meet, stroll around, watch domestic and foreign tourists, worship, and hang out. As they are let in free at all times, local boys tease the tourists or plague them with requests for money when the tourist police are not around and, for them, the Taj serves as a large playground. Amongst the bushes and trees at the sides of the gardens, on the banks of the Jamuna, and all over the site, local boys play, weaving paths of childhood adventure (see figure 4.2).

Access for local adults is restricted to Fridays, when entry is free. On this, the busiest day, the influx of local Muslim worshippers visiting the mosque transforms the atmosphere of the site. For the local Muslims in Taj Ganj, the mosque is the most popular in the area. A second mosque also forms part of the Moghul complex, just outside the West gate. Because it is a religious building, local Muslims feel they should be granted access at any time and deeply resent what they regard as the unconstitutional entrance charge which effectively debars many of them from going as often as they would like:

> Mehmood *(30, shopkeeper)*: The Taj is a holy building therefore there should be no tickets for anybody. Why should there be obstacles put in the way of people to visit the Taj, a building they love, for religious reasons?

On Fridays, young local men approach foreigners and attempt to strike up conversations, practising their English and engaging in political, religious or other issues about which they are curious. This is a regular pastime for some of these youths. A fifteen-year-old schoolboy told me:

Figure 4.2 Local boys exercising on the banks of the River Jamuna

> Sanjeev: We like to look at the tourists, try and guess where they come from and then ask them. We come here every Friday after school and we like to talk to the tourists so that we can learn about different countries and also give information about our lives, and practise our English.

Meeting and conversing with strangers is a common leisure practice amongst Agran youth and the Taj is the pre-eminent site for this pursuit, and has been for many years. Besides being the site where local youths meet foreigners, several elderly men hang around on Fridays, reading, and frequently approach English visitors, with whom they feel they have an historical connection through colonialism and an affinity of interest in literature, in order to strike up discussions.

The temporal and spatial control which determines local use of the Taj, highlights how the site, like most major historical tourist attractions, is subject to surveillance. Tourist police prohibit 'undesirables' from entry, bags are searched, and certain types of behaviour are proscribed, such as touching artworks, eating and drinking, or failing to remove shoes in particular areas. Thus, spatial control has intensified, impacting particularly on locals. Local men told me that when they were younger and fewer visitors came to the Taj, they had much more freedom to do as they wished. There used to be no admission charge so they could go at any time, and the site was not policed to the extent that it is today. Consequently, the range of activities engaged in at the Taj was greater. One man summarised this change, highlighting how such activities were increasingly passive and visual:

WALKING, GAZING, PHOTOGRAPHING, REMEMBERING

Jawarhal (45, perfume seller): In the old days it used to be fun. We would come here any time we wanted to, and we would play cards and drink beer all afternoon. This has now been stopped and we are not allowed to do anything except just sit here and look.

This intensified control over the space of the Taj reflects the increased spatial regulation over tourist spaces in Agra as I will discuss in Chapter 5. The control of access and movement in the Taj is apparently partly a response to the perceived threat of terrorist activity with the upsurge in communal tension in the past decade and lingering mistrust of Pakistan. The queues waiting to enter the Taj are subject to surveillance and kept moving by officious police. Bags and over-garments are checked and no electronic equipment other than cameras (though not video cameras) are allowed in. Once inside the grounds, tourist police stop visitors from picnicking and throwing litter and generally keep watch over the crowds. Control is maintained over touting and only officially sanctioned workers are permitted to ply their trade. Previously, the Taj was open for twenty-four hours and visitors were able to satisfy their desire to gaze at the Taj under moonlight, but this is now not possible since it closes at 7 p.m.

This surveillance and control extends to a rather different performance at the Taj which affects both tourists and locals, namely the commandeering of the Taj for the visit of foreign dignitaries. On these occasions, the site becomes even more policed than usual; tourists awaiting admission often have to wait until the VIPs have completed the visit and those who have already entered are ushered to the sidelines by baton- and rifle-wielding soldiers so that eminent visitors have an unimpeded passage down the central walkway. If an especially important foreign personage is arriving or one for whom stringent security is thought necessary then the Taj can be closed for a large part of the day, an enormous inconvenience for those tourists who have a limited stay in Agra. The space of the Taj then becomes totally subject to official control, all visitors or nearby strollers are subject to concentrated surveillance. Here then, the ultimate spatial control of the Taj is exercised by the Indian government who at this official level, further inscribe the Taj as the pre-eminent attraction for visitors to India.

My own spatial performances at the Taj were varied. In order to identify the regularities of performance and the diverse spatio-temporal patterns by which tourists organised their tours of the Taj, it was necessary to spend as much time as possible at the site. Unlike tourists then, and more akin to the many workers at the site, I spent long periods of most days over a six-month spell carrying out work *in situ*. Much of the time I spent sitting at the most obvious vantage points – upon the three platforms – so that I could identify the routes taken by tourists. At other times I would follow guided tours, listening to guide's commentaries and the remarks of tourists, and also cover all marginal areas of the site so that I could identify ways in which particular tourists might be drawn to them. Interviews with domestic tourists were usually recorded on the platform of the mausoleum, so that the tourist police were less likely to see my small secreted cassette recorder, and interviews with backpackers were generally carried out on the lawns. It proved difficult to interview package tourists at the Taj given their limited time and the extent to which they were required to adhere to their party. This meant that I had to carry out research in the evening at the hotels in which they stayed, when there was more time and no pressure from tour personnel. To maximise opportunities for ethnographic research and to ensure I interviewed a wide range of tourists, I had to follow the choreographies of a large diversity of visitors. My walking performances of necessity followed many and various routes. Whilst this sort of research meant that I had to be disciplined and instrumental in my strategies for information retrieval and hence in my movements, this was frequently foiled. Because I became something of a familiar fixture at the Taj, I was apt to be engaged in conversation at any point with local visitors and guides, often important key informants, who might interrupt any ethnographic strategy I was pursuing. Thus, out of politeness and a desire to converse, research had to be combined with pleasure. In this sense, then, besides being a site of work, the Taj was for me, as it is for other workers at the site, a stage upon which sociable encounters were played out.

The distinctive walking performances that I have described impinge upon the ways in which the tourists gaze upon the Taj Mahal. For instance, the coverage of particular routes dictates the angles and views that can be consumed, the length of time spent at the site determines the degree of scrutiny the monument can be subject to, and the norms of collective behaviour condition the importance of gazing to experience the Taj, as I will now discuss.

Gazing

The visual dominates the sensory consumption of tourist attractions much as it prevails in the image-saturated societies of contemporary capitalism. In the ocularcentric West it has been considered 'the noblest of the senses' (Crawshaw and Urry, 1997, 177) and yet according to Howes, this sensual preoccupation means that other senses such as smell and hearing are underdeveloped (1991, 170). In tourism, gazes are socially organised around a set of techniques which lay the basis for visual performances. The ascendancy of the ocular has arisen out of historical tendencies to construct tourist sites in particular ways, and construct a normative set of gazing practices. As Urry contends, 'to gaze as a tourist is to insert oneself within a historical process and to consume signs or markers of particular histories' (1992, 182). Thus the organisation of tours emerges from situated aesthetics and ways of seeing which reflect particular ideologies and norms.

For Western tourists, Adler avers that 'sight itself has been differently conceived in the course of tourism history'. For instance, she describes how sixteenth-century travellers were more concerned with discursive performance and learning than ocular absorption. Thus the word was considered more important than the image, and the ear and tongue predominated over the eye (Adler, 1989a, 8). Gradually, however, experiences gained through sight came to be perceived as mirroring reality. At first, the duty of the traveller was to classify and quantify things seen through an 'emotionally detached, objectively accurate vision' (ibid., 14). However, by the end of the eighteenth century this was replaced by a more romantic gaze as

> the well trained 'eye' . . . made authoritative judgements of aesthetic merit, as travel itself became an occasion for the cultivation and display of taste. . . . Experiences of beauty and sublimity, sought through the sense of sight, were valued for their spiritual significance to the individual who cultivated them.
>
> (Adler, 1989a, 22)

These romantic performances were encouraged by, and stimulated, the development of the picturesque tour which normalised the contemporary notion that visual contemplation of the extraordinary is appropriate, and that such a practice develops the sensibilities of the onlooker. The obligation to gaze in this affective way continues to inform much contemporary tourism and yet there is now a proliferation of things, people and sites to gaze upon, transforming them into touristic spectacles. There are various techniques to regulate and direct the tourist gaze. The products of the media and the images disseminated by magazines, adverts, tour brochures, films and TV drama and travel programmes confirm and introduce objects worthy of gazing upon. These common-sense notions as to what sorts of features ought to be gazed at are frequently ordained by guides, guidebooks, information boards and signposts which direct tourists to 'outstanding' features. MacCannell (1976) terms this secondary inscription of significant attractions 'sight sacralisation'. The kind of landscape constructed here is a curious one where the unquantified and ill-defined terrain of non-tourist space is punctuated by tourist spectacles against which it is the backdrop. Following this selection of objects to be gazed upon, particular techniques of visual representation frame tourist performances and experiences. The collection of souvenirs, postcards and photographs help to order the 'range of often disparate and relatively unconnected sights' (Urry, 1992, 181) and structure the tourist gaze.

But whilst there are predominant tour technologies that are reinforced by normative tourist performances, tourist gazes are performed in different ways and are directed to a range of objects, as Urry has described, distinguishing between types of tourist gaze (1992, 184). I will show how different visual performances may be enacted at the same place.

Tourism involves both the collection of archetypal quotidian cultural signs of otherness (Culler, 1981), and the journey to gaze upon extraordinary places. There are 'common sense' hierarchies of those attractions most deserving of such attention, as the popularity of various seven wonders of the world in the nineteenth century indicates. Whether remarkable or quotidian, sights have come to capture metaphorically the essence of a place. However, rather than gaze upon places and objects in any pure or natural form, tourists confront a series of cultural discourses that distinguish places in terms of particular values. We see a 'canyon-as-a-geological-wonder', 'a field-as-historical-battleground' or 'a painting-as-a-work-of-genius' (Neumann, 1988, 22), and the theming processes discussed increasingly frame and mark out these distinctions.

For most Western tourists, the Taj continues to be the principal site for gazing at, and consuming India. As an example of the sights and signs collected by contemporary tourist-semioticians, the Taj, as a constructed symbol of the 'Other', is a synedoche for India. Although globally the most famous and reproduced sight of India, and therefore, in a sense, 'already seen', it nevertheless remains the focus of the tourist gaze, notwithstanding the existence of landscapes in India that offer manifold juxtapositions of images, visual diversity and unpredictable sights.

In the colonial era, a British travel writer asserted that, 'Once one has seen the Taj, one has no further interest in the town of Agra. The descent from the topmost pinnacles of sublimity to the ordinary fatuousness of everyday is ridiculous' (Steevens, 1909, 40). Likewise, some Western package tourists declare that seeing the Taj was their only motivation in choosing India for their holiday destination:

> Bess *(62, retired head teacher, from Staffordshire, UK, on a two-week package tour, with her friend)*: I had no great desire to come to India at all, except to see the Taj and see another Wonder of the World.

> Grace *(over 70, retired ward sister from Nottingham, on a two-week package tour with her friend)*: I was not particularly interested in coming to India – it held no great attraction for me – but I did want to see the Taj Mahal. I have always wanted to see the Taj Mahal before I die.

To travel to India solely for the pleasure of gazing upon one building testifies to the production of the Taj as an important global site and a symbol of India. The intensity of tourist expectations and the significance of the site further generates the compulsion to gaze romantically at the Taj.

Tourist personnel work to produce normative gazes, 'coaching tourists into the right sort of gazing through both tuition and exemplification' (Crang, 1997, 150). On highly structured tours, tour personnel screen out sights that are considered unimportant or unpleasant and direct the tourist gaze to key sites. At such sites, the gaze is further directed towards only specific features as I have indicated above in my description of tours around the Taj and the specific bites of information and objects highlighted by guides. En route, other scenes can only be witnessed at speed, and as a series of fragmented images, it may be difficult for tourists to incorporate these sights into an epistemological framework, and consequently they are discounted, not fitting into the visual highlights which the tour promises and is designed to accommodate. Such tours and condensed schedules require the inculcation of a 'spectatorial' gaze to facilitate the rapid collection of images as groups serially move from site to site, seemingly epitomising a 'postmodern' consumption of 'depthless signs'. Yet the opportunities for enacting a sustained 'romantic' gaze are apparently limited by these condensed schedules.

For although the desire of package tourists is to gaze romantically at this 'picturesque' or 'sublime' object in solitary immersion, this is thwarted by the numbers of tourists at the Taj. Echoing the colonial convention that scenes were best depicted without 'natives' cluttering up the picture, many package tourists expressed surprise and disappointment, bemoaning the hordes that spoil the serenity of the scene and clutter the romantic vista:

> Maureen *(45, housewife, from Manchester, UK, on a two-week package tour with her friend)*: The Taj has beauty, balance, equilibrium — it's just beautiful, serene actually. I mean, you could just sit and look at it all day — apart from the milling crowds. But if you could just block them out, you could just sit and look at it.

> Irene *(42, receptionist from Sheffield, on a ten-day package tour with her partner and another couple)*: What's surprised me, and it affects the atmosphere, is all the people — because it ought to be a peaceful place to rest and look but all those people — it's just too crowded, which is a shame.

The longing to experience this Western visual convention, which stresses the value of looking at scenes in blissful solitude, epitomises a tourism which conceives the world as a place to be looked at; a visual consumption of cultures on display which edits out perceived unsavoury aspects.

However, since the structure of the tour and the commission requirements of tourist workers usually keep visits short, some tourists return, chaperoned by tour guides and drivers. This compulsion to view the Taj at sunrise or sunset partly satisfies their desire to gaze in solitude and spend more time at the site:

> Dorothy *(66, retired head teacher, Staffordshire, UK, on a two-week package tour with her friend)*: Well, we didn't get that much time there this morning so I went back this evening as well, to see it in the sunset, so I've spent virtually the whole afternoon there, and it was still perfection.

Again, a major complaint made by package tourists at the Taj is that the tight structure of the tour does not allow sufficient time for solitary detachment and contemplation of the building:

WALKING, GAZING, PHOTOGRAPHING, REMEMBERING

Michael *(47, soft-furnishing retailer, from Buxton, Derbyshire, UK, on a two-week package tour with his partner and co-manager)*: I think that's the thing, with this schedule it really is tight for time and the guide's got to get everything in. At the Taj today, we just had no time to look at the thing, and we want to look – I mean that's what we came for.

Many tours are organised so that they visit the Taj at sunset and/or sunrise. This timing of the gaze continues the influence of a particular nineteenth-century discourse which is rooted in colonial methodology of how to consume 'romantic' sights. Nearly all accounts from this time discuss the time of day which provides the most favourable conditions in which to gaze upon the Taj. As the debate on the most fruitful time to gaze intensified, the proponents of particular times were labelled 'morningites', 'eveningites', 'moonlighters' and 'mid-dayers'. For instance, in Hamilton's guide, *The Taj Mahal Of Agra*, there is a chapter titled, 'When should the Taj be visited?' (1937, 23–9).

This is now echoed in all contemporary guidebooks, which elucidate the benefits of timing one's gaze during particular periods of the day. This discourse exerts a powerful influence on contemporary tourist itineraries and practice. A majority of package tourists are concerned with gazing at the Taj at particular times of day, notably at sunrise and sunset (security measures restricting entry after dark have curtailed tourists gazing during the most celebrated time for gazing, at full moon).

The Agra Development Corporation has capitalised on this desire to be captivated by the Taj at special times by introducing a new pricing policy whereby admission to the Taj between 7 a.m. and 10 a.m., and 4 p.m. and 7 p.m. is one hundred rupees. At all other times it remains 20 rupees. This has generated much opposition amongst Indians since it effectively prevents most of them from visiting during the periods when admission is more expensive. Recently, there were even proposals to install powerful lights to simulate the effect of moonlight upon the Taj, in order to satisfy tourist desire.

Whilst Western package tourists are often frustrated in their desire to gaze romantically at the Taj, the backpackers who visit the site have plenty of time in which to indulge such a visual performance. Although backpackers can view the Taj from a wider range of angles than package tourists, and despite their claims to individuality, many backpackers do enact a romantic gaze towards the Taj, and are more located in a Western tradition of tourism than they think. Indeed, such apparently footloose travellers often rely upon the selective criteria of the *Lonely Planet Travel Survival Kit* to inform them about what should be gazed upon. The greater time at their disposal means that any desire to engage in solitary visual immersion may be realised.

I have mentioned the way in which colonial India frequently served as a realm of the 'other' where, it was believed, 'authenticity' and the 'mystical' could be discovered. The contemporary mutation of this trope is in the search for alternative psychic and spiritual experiences, the quest for enlightenment or self-discovery that continues to impel young Westerners to visit India, and influences backpackers' practices and interpretations at the Taj. Practices associated with the transcendental and mystic properties of Eastern religions, such as yoga and meditation, are performed on the lawns of the Taj. And this tendency to imagine India as the dominion of the metaphysical, the opposite of Western rationalism, is reflected in certain dispositions towards gazing upon the Taj. A romantic gaze is enacted but one informed by a valorised mystical 'otherness':

> Mattheus *(24, student, from Frankfurt, Germany, travelling on his own in India for four months)*: It's a very proud building. And it has an aura, you know – you can feel it. And when I saw it the first time I heard a sound like 'Om'.

Accordingly, this way of looking at the Taj highlights how the space of the 'other' becomes enchanted, especially at selective symbolic sites which have become the focus of Western 'New Age' spiritual sentiments.

Likewise, the persistent pursuit of cheap drugs by many Western travellers means that the space of the Taj can be explored by pharmacologically inspired imaginations resulting from *bang lassi*, a yoghurt drink containing hashish, widely sold to backpackers in the local cafés in Taj Ganj. At 15 rupees, this is a very cheap way to get 'high' and many travellers spend a day at the Taj stoned, watching the surroundings for hours. Other drugs such as 'grass' or LSD are also popular ways of enhancing the experience:

> Robert *(23, traveller, has been travelling around India and South Asia for two years and has no plans to stop)*: It's fucking brilliant! I came here this morning. It was great; really lovely. Well, man, I took a tab of acid before coming down here. Fucking brilliant, man – a trip at the Taj! That's why I came down here. It's like, so intricate, and things were moving all over the place, I can tell you!

Nevertheless, although backpacker visions of the Taj are informed by romantic conventions which may mutate in drug-induced hallucinations, the availability of time, the space for reflexivity, and the improvisational nature of much backpacker movement means that the unorthodox, sometimes critical views of the Taj that I discussed in Chapter 3 emerge from intense gazing:

> Clive *(30, 'jack of all trades', from Wellington, New Zealand, has been travelling for four months and does not know how long he will stay in India)*: The Taj is the thing you're supposed to see, isn't it? I was impressed when I first set eyes upon it. But you know, to be honest, it seems rather overrated. Is it really so beautiful? And when you think of what it represents – the ego of a ruler – it makes you squirm to think of what else could have been done with the money.

In addition, surprising sights and changing conditions are witnessed by the sheer amount of time spent at the Taj by many backpackers:

Gordon *(47, Buddhist monk, originally from Sydney, Australia, he stays in various monasteries throughout Asia, intends to stay in India for three months)*: This is my eighth time here. The first time, I slept in the gardens here. In the space of twelve hours, I saw this place with sunset, full moon, rain and sunrise. I played a flute in the gardens and then watched a corpse float down the river with a vulture perched on it.

Although backpackers generally enact a romantic, intense gaze at the Taj, as I will subsequently examine, in the heterogeneous tourist spaces which they inhabit, the performance of such a gaze is not possible. Unlike at the Taj, there are no markers or attractions delineated by the tourist industry, few normative codes of behaviour and frames of reference. Indeed, there is little possibility of sustained gazing because of hazards, the movement of people and vehicles and continual distractions. Rather, incomprehensible and untranslatable sights present a visual cavalcade that mobilises the enaction of a distracted gaze. However, it is clear that although certain spaces present a highly managed appearance and are designed to channel gazes, this can break down under critical scrutiny, where the enaction of unorthodox performances and oblique ways of looking reveals unexpected aspects, cracks in the carefully regulated edifice of disciplinary and commodified spaces.

Urry considers that what he terms the 'collective' gaze involves a less reflective mode of looking (1990). Contrasting with the intense self-absorption of the solitary romantic gaze, this gaze is conditioned by affiliation to the group. In this case, the solidarity of the group is paramount and a trip to a symbolic site might, for instance, be a relaxing day out for a family to a local tourist attraction, or a group visit where collective witness may be deemed appropriate.

The notion that the Taj is a symbol of India is also articulated by many domestic tourists as I have described in Chapter 3, yet the gaze that they perform is of a different kind to Western visitors. Of the domestic tourists I interviewed 35 per cent cited their desire to visit a 'wonder of the world', and 80 per cent stated that they want to see the Taj because of its fame. Questions as to why they wanted to visit the Taj were often reproached as being too obvious; the reasons were straightforward and commonplace, the responses below being typical of those given by a majority of domestic interviewees:

Rakesh *(31, civil servant, from Delhi, on a day trip with a family party of seven)*: As a tourist I want to visit especially beautiful and famous places. We came here as a sightseeing excursion so that our children can see this national monument.

> Jadhav *(51, civil servant from Delhi, on a day trip with a family party of nine)*: We came quite simply to see a famous historical place, of course.

> Naaz *(20, history teacher, from Mumbai, on pilgrimage to Ajmer with a family party of five)*: Because its a wonder of the world. We have heard about the fame of this monument from early childhood and we have wanted to see it for a long time.

Thus it is the fame of the Taj that attracts people, its renowned beauty and history. Although first identified as a world wonder in the colonial era, the notion has been appropriated by Indians to enchant their sense of national identity and prestige. However, the desire to see the symbolic site is not accompanied by a desire to gaze at or experience the Taj intensely. Instead, a visit to the Taj is typified by a communal *witnessing* of a national monument with family, friends or fellow-villagers, as well as millions of other Indians. More than anything else, this shared gaze celebrates the collective identity of the group, and reinforces national identity. In this case, although there is no directing of the gaze, peer-group norms constrain the visual range of what can be gazed upon by their insistence on collective witness.

This collective gaze is not intense. The Taj is looked at briefly, along with the tacit recognition that it is a remarkable building of national significance. However, an aesthetic appreciation is not the result of being awe-struck, but reflects a common-sense understanding that the Taj is an achievement of excellence. Most domestic visitors use single adjectives to describe the building, such as 'unique', 'beautiful', 'marvellous', 'magnificent', 'world-class', 'artistically excellent'. There is little sign of the defeated struggle for adjectives to capture the object of the intense gaze, the conjuring up of exotic, mystical and ethereal imagery to describe the Taj common amongst Western visitors. The unreflexive, non-analytical gaze is criticised by some Western tourists on the grounds that a hurried, unserious and distracted passage around the Taj whilst conversing and laughing fails to mobilise the appropriate form of looking. In the opinion of these critics, this reflects an incompetent tourist performance:

> Linda *(33, financial consultant, London, on a three-week package tour with her friend)*: I think Indians are really crap tourists. They just don't know how to be tourists, rushing around, talking all the time and never stopping to look at anything – even here at the Taj Mahal!

This response highlights the extent to which tourist performance is typified by an entrenched set of codes which circumscribe which enactments and dispositions are appropriate. Where two forms of tourist performance coincide on the same stage, the potential for one group to participate or appreciate as an audience the performance of the other group may be curtailed by these conventions.

The failure to enact an intense, contemplative gaze does not mean that such practices are absent in Indian social life, but that a tourist visit to a famous building is not an occasion to perform them. However, any response that emerges out of a more reflective engagement with the Taj tends to be diverted towards other than aesthetic aspects, again producing critical interpretations, such as those depicted in Chapter 3. These more phlegmatic impressions include:

> Chaturvhaj *(60, trader, from Saurashtra, Gujarat, on pilgrimage to Mathura with a party of fifty villagers)*: At first, I was impressed, but upon closer inspection it gives me little pleasure. The white marble is beautiful but not the red sandstone which is not a pleasant material and spoils the artistic effect. The Taj is not a particularly important place although the place has been immortalised.

> Ilias *(53, foreman in construction, from Bangalore, on holiday with a family party of ten for three weeks)*: A wealthy king has shown his pride by squandering an enormous amount of wealth which he could have used for the welfare of the poor. But it is no better as a building than many modern architectural structures, and what use does it have?

Other ways of looking at the Taj could be called mediatised, since as the pre-eminent romantic site in India, it is often used as a stage in a more conventional sense, as a setting for a 'masala' movie. The influence of these films is considerable and people, especially children, re-enact scenes and dances from movies and perform songs, testifying to their power to colonise the popular imagination. Many visitors recall movie scenes when they visit the Taj (particularly the 1961 epic *Leader*, starring Dilip Kumar and Vijayantimala), in a sense superimposing a filmic image on the scene before them. Recently, a Tamil film called *Nagma* was filmed at the Taj (see cover). For many, these films are the most familiar source of information about the site:

> Pandit Maharaj *(40, religious singer, from Vrindaban, on a day trip with a party of fifteen friends)*: I haven't read much but there is a movie about the Taj Mahal which we've watched many times. And coming here, we remember the song where Mumtaz sings *What you've promised you must carry out*, about Shahjahan's promise to build the Taj for her.

However, not all domestic tourists perform a collective or mediatised gaze at the Taj. Whilst the romantic gaze described above primarily involves the contemplation of an aesthetic(ised) object, what I term the 'reverential' gaze focuses on the divine, the sacred or the commemorative. Indeed, a reverential gaze may not even have the object itself at the forefront of its focus but rather view it as a symbol, a metaphor or metonym for a religion or community. This visual performance may be collectively enacted as when a sacred or highly symbolic site is visited during a ritual or pilgrimage, or it may be performed by solitary devotees. Muslim visitors to the Taj enact a reverential look as they consume the sacred site, particularly intensifying their gaze towards the mosque, the tombs and the Quranic script inscribed on the buildings. This gaze is not particularly concerned with consuming romantic scenes or even collecting mental images but is a means to an end; a route towards significant spiritual feelings which are not exhausted by the visual. It is formed through adherence to religious duty and ritual rather than being motivated by a desire to consume beauty or the sublime.

The gaze is as central to ethnography as it is to tourism. Urry has described the 'anthropological' gaze which is solitary but less concerned with romantic gazing and more with scanning sights and actively interpreting their meaning (1992, 184). This approximates my own gazing performances, and indeed that of any ethnographer. Rather than the Taj itself, the objects of my gaze were tourists and their guides, the routes they took and performances they enacted. When I first arrived at the Taj, although I had been there before, I was inevitably drawn to the spectacle of the mausoleum, but gradually this no longer provided the central focal point as my gaze became more diffuse, and extended to the rest of the site – to the trees swaying in the breeze, to the brilliant green flashes of parrots on the wing, to the bullock carts used by gardeners, and the host of workers maintaining and restoring the site. My initial romantic gaze also became dislocated as I listened to the critical accounts of some tourists and began to doubt whether the Taj was as magnificent as was claimed, and finally, this romantic aura vanished with the site's familiarity to me. Moreover, as I became conscious of the other sensual elements of the site – the different sounds of footfalls on marble and grass, the shrieking interruptions of parrots, the stench of the river and the sweet aroma of *bidis* (cigarettes), the sound and touch of the humid breeze – the visual stimuli were complemented by other sensual nourishments.

Photographing

The gazing practices I have identified above influence tourist performances organised around photography. Photography has become synonymous with tourism. Banal and familiar images of travellers carrying mighty cameras to capture sights and large crowds of tourists clicking away en masse indicate the ubiquity of photography amongst tourists. In a sense, touristic photography attempts to capture and materialise the tourist gaze. The apparently objective evidence offered by the photograph further entrenches the notion that what is gazed upon can be comprehended by the discerning onlooker, without revealing its codes or ideology, and as such, reaffirms colonial notions about capturing the reality of the other.

Yet the dramatic representation of symbolically important places and occasions is largely informed by the conventions of framing photographic images in brochures, magazines and travel programmes. Albers and James maintain that the ways in which 'pictures are selected, combined and symbolised' (1988, 137) organises meaning and institutionalises how tourist attractions should be gazed upon and photographed by tourists. Such images are framed by the 'theatrical conventions' required by entry into specific tourist 'dramaturgical landscapes' (Chaney, 1993, 86). Accordingly, tourist snapshots:

> complete a hermeneutic circle, which begins with the photographic appearances that advertise a trip, moves onto a search for these pictures . . . and ends with travellers certifying and sealing the very same images in their own photographic productions.
> (Albers and James, 1988, 136)

As I have mentioned in Chapter 1, the commodification of places, cultures and heritage involves the selection of images to sell to tourists, and marketing strategies advertise only certain aspects and angles, imposing a dominant form of spatial representation. The global consumption and reproduction of these images ensures their continual circulation and reinforces hegemonic understandings in the economy of signs. And whilst the repetitive incorporation of familiar objects of tourist interest through photographic technologies testifies to the serial reproduction of images, where unfamiliar sights are gazed upon photography also provides a means to incorporate difference and circumvent ontological disorientation. By following 'a repertoire of actions when confronted by the "other"' (Crawshaw and Urry, 1997, 183), photography is a strategy to recode and enframe experience outside themed, enclavic environments.

The reproduction of dominant ways in which places, cultures and people are seen and understood is assisted by the propensity of tourists to communicate their relationships with each other, with places, and with other cultures, by using photography as a popular 'ceremonial form' to capture meaning (Chaney, 1993, 82). This inscription of the self in time and space by creating a material record of presence at a site sustains subjective notions about belonging to collective identity, a history and a geography, and consolidates particular metaphoric or metonymic values attributed to sites, thereby enhancing styles of symbolic association.

However, although conventions of framing, posing, selecting, excluding and including dominate the photographic practices of most tourists, Chaney argues that tourist photography is best conceived as an intermeshing of 'professional and amateur generated images' (1993, 109). This suggests that tourists bring particular preoccupations and skills to photography which can never be entirely captured by convention. Accordingly, there are different conventions by which tourist photography is organised, and less customary ways of incorporating tourist sights.

At certain sites, the imperative to photograph is almost a duty. Package tour companies which visit such sites as part of itineraries are organised to enable

WALKING, GAZING, PHOTOGRAPHING, REMEMBERING

photographs to be taken and, as I have shown, co-ordinate passage around the site to arrange photogenic views. Such encouragement makes a visit synonymous with photography. For instance, one guide, prior to his group's morning visit announced:

> Well, today you are visiting the Taj. This is the part of our trip you have all been waiting for and I can assure you won't be disappointed. So remember to bring your cameras and plenty of film!

A large proportion of the package tourists' limited time at the Taj is spent in photographing the building. The desire to collect visual mnemonic aids to recall the scene, and the importance of consuming the Taj through the romantic gaze, are consolidated by the practice of photography. Western package tourists are most preoccupied with collecting photographs of the Taj and their array of hardware signifies the centrality of this concern. The compulsion to carry out this work is evident in the rapid shutter action and frenetic manoeuvring for angles.

> Tony *(48, clerical officer, from Birmingham, UK, on a two-week package tour with his partner to celebrate their wedding anniversary)*: Today, at the Taj, I've taken more photos than I've ever taken in my life. We've had two cameras going so we're going to have piles of photos.

> Ernest *(43, manager of a haulage firm, Bristol, UK, on a two-week package tour)*: My camera's overheating but I can't help it. You can never say you've took enough photos 'cause if you miss one scene you'll regret it for ever.

One man, although he had taken many photographs himself reflexively admitted that there was a limit to how many photographs could be taken and that such activity might curtail gazing as another mode of visual consumption:

> Jeremy *(63, lawyer, from Oxford, UK, on a two-week package tour with his partner)*: I haven't taken many photos by other peoples' standards actually, I've just taken two rolls. But some people in our group have taken twenty rolls so far. One wonders if they've seen anything properly.

The consumption of depthless images is part of a dystopic, postmodern scenario and it does seem that much package tourism consists of the serial capturing of scenes. As Urry remarks, frequently 'travel is a strategy for the accumulation of photographs' (1990, 139). Yet the notion of the mechanical collection of photographs, whilst certainly prevalent at the Taj, does not capture the zeal with which such acquisition proceeds.

As I have said, the restrictive 'place-ballet' enacted by these tourists confines the gaze and the range of photographs that can be taken and this is further controlled by the suggestions of the guides about where suitable views present themselves. Most tour guides offer advice on suitable photographic angles and subjects, and provide interludes where passengers can 'capture' a vista. The most clichéd and best-known view of the Taj is taken en masse by package tourists inside the main gate almost immediately following entry. The tourists' photographic strategies commence with this view and then continue as they snap all the way down the walk to the Taj, stopping at the platform at the crossroads of the water-course, from where they are usually encouraged to photograph the Taj.

For many British tourists, their photographic ambitions also include a photo of themselves in front of the Taj on the seat that Princess Diana sat upon; highlighting the way that packaged and repetitively networked global soundbites and images of famous faces and places shape the way those places are experienced:

> Doug *(51, sales manager, from Sheffield, UK, on a three-week package tour with his partner and two other couples)*: I always wanted to see the Taj. And I wanted to sit on the same seat as Princess Diana, which we did, and had our photographs taken.

Perhaps this conjunction of two romantic icons, one a symbolic British figure, confirms British identity in the space of the 'other'. I surmise that given the recent death of the Princess, and the ways in which this image was served up once more to capture notions of the loneliness of Diana and her detachment from the royal family, the iconographic significance of the Taj as a romantic site will gain extra poignancy for many tourists.

Whilst these time-consuming visual practices are compulsively carried out by package tourists at the Taj, ironically their centrality frequently leads to feelings of dissatisfaction. This shortage of time creates a tension between the pursuit of fulfilling two desires; to consume the Taj through photography and to gaze at the Taj romantically, for both visual practices cannot be pursued with any degree of satisfaction:

> Keith *(48, production manager, from Brighton, on a two-week package tour with his partner)*: I haven't had a good chance to look at it yet. I've been taking photos and even though you're staring through that lens you can't really appreciate it 'cos I'm thinking, 'Oh, I hope this comes out all right'. I want to just sit and look at it for a bit, you know, absorb the place, but it seems like we're running out of time.

Diverse photographic practices are differently conditioned by the spatio-temporal organisation of tourism. The solitary tourist wandering through heterogeneous tourist space may stop and photograph the unexpected. At the Taj, photography is carried out by about two-thirds of backpackers but is a far less central activity than for the time-pressed package tourists. Those who bring a camera can capture the Taj at their leisure without pressure to 'cram in' the requisite number of shots, but they are generally less concerned with taking a great number of photos. Moreover, because of their greater spatial and temporal freedom, they have the opportunity to roam around the area of the site, gazing at, and photographing the Taj from multiple angles. This greater visual exploration of the site potentially allows the production of less clichéed views which may include unexpected elements spied askance from the sides and corners of the grounds, rather than the views photographed during the typical linear tour.

To avoid the imperatives of photographic performance and the normative codes which organise visual consumption, some backpackers deliberately leave their camera at home, believing that they will see 'more clearly'. Whilst this is often partly an attempt at gaining cultural capital by distinguishing themselves from mere 'tourists', it is also believed that the imperative to photograph would constrict their gazes and cauterise their imaginations:

> Fiona *(31, EFL teacher, London, travelling in India on her own for an unfixed period)*: Photos stop you looking at things and they're a status symbol to show the folks back home. The only reason people come here is to take photos, but you never really see anything through a lens. You imagine them going home and looking at photos and saying, 'Did we really go there?'

> Trevor *(41, plasterer, from Bristol, UK, spends half of his time working and saving so that he can travel the rest of the time, has been travelling around India since the sixties)*: I never bring a camera with me. I can always remember the places I've seen. I mean, what's the point of taking a shot of the Taj from the gateway, or from the seat Lady Di sat on? There are so many photos already. I suppose they *(the tourists)* just want to show they were there.

The poses and positions of those inside the frame follow photographic conventions which facilitate and naturalise story-telling and modes of collecting and labelling. Thus the performance embodied in photographs often enunciates institutionalised roles. At the Taj, of course, the most regular conventions are those in which groups or individuals stand in front of the mausoleum.

The adoption of ritualised stances are ways of relating to a site but more generally capture moments of personal display. They provide an opportunity for expression within a format. As such, this moment captures dramaturgical performances whose fashions vary between tourists. These interludes of acting typify much tourist behaviour and they can vary from the highly formal posing with gravitas to a collective form of play and 'acting daft'. As enframing spaces, tourist sites provide the stage upon which the practice of photography permits certain forms of performance: 'The seeing is framed by implicit theatrical conventions in which we are, as an audience, located within a particular dramaturgical landscape' (Chaney, 1993, 86).

The conventions of Western tourist photography typically foreground solitary tourists in front of the Taj. Stances testify to the seriousness of the occasion and the desire to use photographs as a means of 'proving' that one was there. However, many photographs do not include members of the party at all but focus on the building, attempting to enframe as few tourists as possible so that the building may retain its aura as a romantic site uncluttered by the mundane. These strong enframing conventions are occasionally broken by 'post-tourist' acts which undermine the norms of photographic practice through mockery and a self-conscious awareness of the role playing such performances requires. For instance, a group of American tourists enacted the following ironic performance as they stood upon the platform inside the grounds, posing before the Taj for a member of their party wielding a video camera:

Tourist 1: OK guys, line up and look astonished
Tourist 2: Yeah, but . . . it's great – but what does it do?
Tourist 3: Bob had the best line – 'The Taj is amazing, but boring'
Tourist 1: Come on, let's do the photo so we can get outta here.

However, although a minority engage in ironic role-playing such as this in front of the camera, performing mock looks of astonishment or perform acts of horseplay, the presumed seriousness of the Taj minimises such dramas.

The common photographic practice of domestic tourists is to snap the group together on the path going down to the Taj and rarely are shots solely of the building taken. This conforms to the ways in which the Taj is visited first and foremost to witness a famous site and as part of a collective excursion and the photograph is testimony to the visit. The posing of the group photograph is typically hierarchical and the dispositions are dutiful as if an obligation is being met. Only a few of these group photographs are taken and photography does not take up the bulk of the time.

They are usually taken by one of the group but sometimes a photographer is employed so that all party members may be included. There are also some forty working registered photographers at the Taj who mainly serve the demands of domestic tourists. Besides the group shots, 'novelty' photographs are taken such as the tourist leaping in the air or saluting. The photographer acts as director to the tourist and suggests ways in which amusing images can be constructed. This calls for an unserious and playful performance in front of the group which is at variance to the serious posing of Western package tourists, who regard such irreverence as inappropriate, or gauche, in this context. The most popular novelty photograph is one creating the illusion that the tourist is holding up the Taj between thumb and forefinger (see figure 4.3).

Photographs also mark occasions. The production of a set of selective visual cues to reconstruct a life-story or travel narrative is illuminated by the

Figure 4.3 Boy holding up the Taj

compulsion of tourists to visit the Taj to enchant personal and symbolic events. The photographs subsequently taken, in which participants usually perform a romantic pose, associate the site with personal and shared milestones:

> John *(49, office manager from Southampton, UK, with his partner on a three-week package tour)*: Well, this is our silver wedding anniversary, and really, the Taj is the reason we're here. We've always wanted to come and see the Taj and take photographs of ourselves here, and the twenty-fifth anniversary is the best possible reason.
>
> Sandra *(38, housewife, from London, on a two-week package tour with her partner)*: Well, this is gonna sound really corny, but the reason we wanted to visit the Taj is that we've got a really happy marriage and we're really in love. And this is the place for romantics.

The Taj is also a popular spot for Indian honeymooners. The motivation to reaffirm and testify to the strength of a relationship, ritually to marry the potency of special times with special places for remembrance, signifies the power of the image and concept of the Taj for many Western visitors. And thus the symbolic moment is performed at the Taj, and commemorated in the resulting photograph.

Besides these performances, the gaze of domestic tourists is directed towards the foreign tourists at the Taj, who are unfamiliar to those who dwell outside metropolitan areas. Many domestic visitors ask to be photographed with the tourists from abroad, and whole groups can be seen crowding round foreign individuals to cram themselves in the frame. These photographs involve a performance whereby the foreigner is the centre of the frame and gestures of friendship such as the placing of arms around shoulders are enacted. As a regular visitor to the Taj, I was frequently asked to pose with family groups and individuals, and so although I took no photographs at the Taj (although I did elsewhere in Agra) there are numerous photographs of the Taj in which I feature!

Of course, all tourist photography is concerned with commemorating trips and visits to symbolic sites, and it is to the diverse performances of remembering that I now turn.

Remembering

The tourist practice of remembering cuts across the performances of narrating, walking, gazing and photographing that I have discussed above. Different tourist gazes and movements, forms of narration and conventions of photography involve the particular organisation and reproduction of collective and individual memories (Urry, 1992, 182).

Remembering is not simply a psychological function of a particular part of the brain, but is socially constructed, communicated and institutionalised. In a contingent and continuous process 'the past is endlessly constructed in and through the present' (Urry, 1995, 4). As Samuel argues, memory is not 'merely a passive receptacle or storage system, an image bank of the past', but is:

> historically conditioned, changing colour and shape according to the emergencies of the moment, that so far from being handed down in the timeless form of 'tradition' it is progressively altered from generation to generation.
>
> (1994, ix–x)

As locations where the social organisation of remembering and forgetting are often played out, tourist sites feature multifarious ways in which remembrance and reminiscence are differently practised *in situ* by groups and individuals. Memory can be activated, transmitted and concretised through the performance of specific actions.

Lowenthal has commented on the way in which collective remembering is mobilised towards particular places. Historical sites:

> remain essential bridges between then and now. They confirm or deny what we think of it, symbolise or memorialise communal links over

time, and provide archaeological metaphors that illumine the process of history and memory.

(1985, xxiii)

Such places are 'condensation sites', replete with polysemic interpretations, which 'precis much more complicated stories and messages into a mnemonic or shorthand form' (Cohen, 1985, 102). These diverse readings are expressed through particular practices and depend upon distinct modes of transmission, for example, through the narration of myths or the construction of 'expert' accounts, the erecting of memorials, the bodily organisation of groups during ceremonies of remembrance, political oration, and the collection of photographs and videos.

Specific features and incidents tend to become forgotten as particular memories predominate, and discursive and performative formations evolve which silence competing memories and ways of remembering. At symbolic tourist sites, narratives and performances of remembrance are increasingly organised and commodified by commercial and institutional forces. However, at international sites, the proliferation of performances of remembering highlights how the stability of traditional and parochial memories are undermined by globalising forces:

> with the realisation of the increasing flows of images, ideas, information and people across borders, so the process of social remembering becomes even more disjointed, speeded up, hybridised and fractured.
>
> (Urry, 1995, 18)

Whilst confusing global processes can force a turning back to the comfort of old memories and styles of remembering, they may encourage the formation and expression of subaltern memories and mnemonic performance by groups who pay allegiance to competing traditions. Whichever may be the case, the performative aspects of remembering at symbolic sites inscribe tourists into a particular remembered tradition or history and suggest wider spaces such as the nation, the wider tour itinerary (or the space of an individual's tourist history), a wider sacred space. This construction of these subjective histories highlights the ways in which tourist sites are important places for the construction of identities that resonate across time and space.

I have discussed how travel narratives and photography are used as mnemonic devices to recall holidays. This emphasises the ways in which tourism can serve as a Western, romantic ploy whereby memories of holidays, of the 'other', of escaping, are used to ease the stress of the everyday. This praxis emerged out of an eighteenth-century European romanticism which reacted against the first signs of industrialisation and chose as its object that which was, by contrast, conceived as natural, traditional and authentic. This anti-modern sentiment was inspired by the classical and renaissance sights of the Grand Tour, the sublime and pantheistic realm of 'nature', and the figure of the 'noble savage'. Wordsworth sums up the ways in which a romantic aesthete survived the clamour and chaos of the modern world through the succour of sweet memories of 'nature' in his 1798 poem *Lines Written a Few Miles Above Tintern Abbey*:

> Though absent long,
> These forms of beauty have not been to me,
> As a landscape to a blind man's eye:
> But oft, in lonely rooms, and mid the din
> Of towns and cities, I have owed to them,
> In hours of weariness, sensations sweet,
> Felt in the blood, and felt along the heart,
> And passing even into my purer mind
> With tranquil restoration . . .

He continues, as he gazes upon a 'romantic scene':

> While here I stand, not only with the sense
> Of present pleasure, but with pleasing thoughts
> That in this moment there is life and food
> For future years . . .

This strategy for collecting memories is part of the common-sense understanding of what holidays are for. The need to take an annual holiday has become part of the normative temporal organisation of lives, a special time when ordinary constraints are lifted and the self can undergo temporary transformation. As such, holidays are marked out as extraordinary periods, stocked with valuable experiences, the gaining of knowledge, and the acquisition of sights and commodities. Selected sights and moments from holidays are recorded so that they can fit into personal life-stories, and provide stimulating and satisfying memories in times of boredom or stress. Memories can be incorporated into personal narratives; such collected fragments point to the 'self-conscious attempts by people to struggle to have a biography, to own experience' (Neumann, 1988, 26) and sustain continuity in personal life. However, such practices constitute the 'work' of tourism and are an investment in future enjoyment. They are acts of recording, concerned with the compilation of memories that will be used at a future date.

Although improvisation is circumscribed by the limited repertoire of emplotted stories, story-telling is the most contingent process of remembering. I have pointed out how dominant histories and myths are written and performed to inscribe the ideologies and identities of the powerful at the Taj. Attempts to fix 'official' versions of history pervade popular forms of story-telling in the media and school textbooks. Yet the 'rhetorical organisation of remembering and forgetting', what stories are told and how they are shaped, highlight how such narratives contingently juggle with historical 'facts' and myths (Middleton and Edwards, 1990, 9). As we have seen in the narratives of the Taj, myths are flexible discursive forms, enabling wide scope for interpretation and are ideologically 'chameleon' (Samuel and Thompson, 1990, 3). They may be appropriated to provide antecedence and continuity to widely varying political objectives (Tilly, 1994, 247).

Of course, tourist photography is the most central mnemonic tool through which experience can be converted into an image (Sontag, 1979, 7) in order to materialise and order 'significant moments in a biographical record' (Chaney, 1993, 103). The act of photography marks out and dramatises those sites and events considered to be important and provides a temporally ordered set of images which lend themselves to a recounting of the story of the holiday. This collection of visual memory prompts is often supplemented by the journals which tourists keep of the places they visit and the adventures they experience, which are written, like diaries, for the purpose of future recollection. Part of the evening, or moments of rest, are spent in recollecting and ordering the day's events. However, like other cultural texts, travel experience can provide enduring references for thought whose interpretation remains open to change (Adler, 1989b, 1,369).

The identity of places is bound up with the dominant histories which are told about them (Massey, 1995, 186). The production of remembrance around certain artefacts is inscribed by power in two senses. Firstly, dominant performative formations evolve either through assumptions about what is appropriate to remember and how, or the establishment of particular rituals of remembrance. Secondly, the powerful are able to memorialise their key figures and commemorate incidents through their inscription onto the landscape in the form of monuments.

Such memoryscapes materialise memory by assembling iconographic forms which provide stages for organising a relationship with the past. Memorials follow different semiotic conventions and articulate particular meanings which reflect the iconographic conventions of the era in which they were built. Yet public familiarity with the rhetoric of such material statements can decline and they are interpreted according to contemporary visual understandings (for instance, see Warner, 1993).

The Taj Mahal is a memorial which Shahjahan built for essentially private purposes of remembrance since access to the site was not usually available. Until he was imprisoned in the Red Fort by Aurangzeb, his son and successor, the Moghul emperor and his immediate family visited the site but it was not a public space. Whilst, no doubt it was also a project that aimed to transmit a sense of power and glory, to imprint the importance of Shahjahan for posterity, it was never intended for wider consumption and was thus never meant to represent 'love' in a general sense, a metaphoric allusion that all may tap into. The religious cosmological allusions materialised at the site are not accessible to most contemporary visitors. This is not, of course, the case with many Muslim visitors who enact particular narratives, gazes and movements as I have indicated. These performances are intimately connected with remembering the Moghul tradition, a vanished Muslim power, and the emperor and Mumtaz.

The notion that the Taj is a site of remembrance is specifically Muslim. Bhardwaj draws a distinction between the ways in which different religious traditions perceive and use sites of death or 'necral landscapes'. Islamic practice 'localises the dead through entombment, giving rise to some of the most imposing tombs in the world' (Bhardwaj, 1987b, 332) whereas in Hindu practice, the body is cremated and is not considered to exist after death. Rather than serving as places of remembrance, cremation places are regarded as impure, 'places for the departure of souls, not the residence of bodies' (ibid., 326). Since there is 'no room for place-person specificity after death' (ibid., 325), there is little purpose for Hindus to build memorials for the dead. Bodies are cremated, placed in sacred rivers and are considered to become detached from earthly matters. Accordingly, Hindus do not usually consider the Taj to be a necral landscape, but when they do, they are not likely to linger at the tomb since the soul has departed and the dead body is believed to be unclean. Indeed, for some Hindu visitors, the Taj is tainted by its association with death. As I will shortly discuss, many domestic tourists purchase small alabaster and marble model souvenirs, yet some refrain from doing so because of the building's association with death:

> Kusuma *(22, housewife, from Bangalore, on a four-week honeymoon)*: Well, we would never buy a model of the Taj and keep it in the house. We are superstitious about it, I know, but the Taj is also a symbol of death, of impurity, and who knows what bad luck such a model would bring us.

Interestingly, two necral landscapes coincide at the Taj, the mausoleum itself and the Jamuna River along which the burning pyres float after their immolation at the funerary grounds to the north.

I have described how the Taj Mahal acts as a symbolic Indian national site for both domestic tourists and foreign visitors. Attempts to map national memory and identity onto territory depend upon particularly symbolic landscapes and sites around which performances are organised. At the Taj, the nation's history is remembered by most Indians in the ways in which the architectural features of the building are interpreted to stand for Indian syncretism rather than Islamic power.

To return to rituals of remembrance, Connerton has developed the idea that memory can be either inscriptive or incorporating. The inscriptive discursive and representational processes of remembering are, according to Connerton, less powerful than incorporating rituals which are impressed upon the body so as to form part of 'social habit memory'. He argues that groups transmit and sustain their memories by mapping them onto symbolic and familiar spaces through ritual performance (1989, 37). Unlike the interpretative scope for innovation in myths and written histories, rituals lack scope for improvisation. Participants are obliged to observe stylised and repetitive actions, which are regulated by calendrical, verbal and gestural codes. This regular ritualistic practice inscribes habit-memory upon the participants' bodies, a process which Connerton asserts provides 'insurance against the process of cumulative questioning entailed in all discursive practices' (1989, 102). Manifesting and expressing ideological norms, rituals constitute powerful programmes for the enaction of collective remembering and systematic forgetting. Accordingly, such rituals specify the relationship between performers, and between the performers and the symbolic site (and the wider symbolic space into which it is incorporated).

As the centre of such rituals, symbolic sites attract tourists who may participate in these rituals or witness them. Ceremonies may be organised by national elites, military sections, religious or ethnic groups, local power-holders and businesses, and a host of special interest groups such as battle re-enactment societies and 'New Age' groups. Indeed, symbolic sites may be a focus of contesting rituals such as at Stonehenge where Druids, New Age travellers and English Heritage vie to carry out their ceremonies (Bender, 1993).

Again, disciplined, commemorative performances are most typically enacted by Muslims, in their homage to Shahjahan and Mumtaz in the mausoleum, the reading of the Quranic text, and the rituals performed at the mosque. In their regularity, these incorporating ceremonies inscribe a particular sacrality on the bodies of the Muslim performers, specifying their relationship to the site in particular and to Islam in general. The same can be said of the more routine rituals which locals enact at the mosque each Friday. The cosmological symbolism of the Taj and the holy text written upon it mesh with incorporating performance to provoke an intense emotion and sense of belonging:

> Abdul *(62, motor mechanic from Pune, on pilgrimage to Ajmer with a party of 17)*: Our hearts compel us to visit the Taj for its beauty and for its importance for our Muslim people. It is Allah's creation, and the tomb of a great ruler and we often come, whenever we are near, to remember him. This is our duty as Muslims.

Each year on the anniversary of the death of Shahjahan, on 26 and 27 *Rajab* of the Muslim calendar there is an *Urs,* an occasion of remembrance for the queen and Shahjahan. The *Urs* was initially introduced in the reign of Shahjahan when nobles and courtiers were invited to commemorate Mumtaz and alms were distributed to the poor (Kapoor, 1962, 26). The contemporary ritual now attracts thousands of Muslims to the Taj to perform prayer-rituals en masse in the gardens. They ritually walk around the Taj and pay homage to the tombs of the two royal personages, reinscribing the monument with Islamic significance. There are musicians playing outside the main gate in celebration of the occasion and banners are hoisted which recall the glory of Moghul reign. Moreover, expectant mothers come to the tomb to ask for the blessings of Mumtaz, offering gifts such as wicker baby rattles, to ease the pains of childbirth (Kapoor, 1962, 22). Again the explicit link with Islam is reinforced by these ceremonies but the celebratory nature of the occasion, and its sensuality, co-exist with the disciplinary incorporating rituals described by Connerton. It may be that the combination of sober ritual enaction and more carnivalesque festivities actually provides a stronger basis for reproducing the commemorative significance of the Taj than the disciplinary performance alone.

Connerton's notion of remembrance also seems to capture the procedure of guided tours around the Taj discussed above, which are organised around the collection of information and images that can be easily consumed and remembered. However, his insistence on the ordered discipline necessary for the truly effective transmission of memories neglects the contingent individual and group processes by which people perform memory at symbolic sites. In concentrating on a particular order of remembering that is usually official and authoritative he ignores looser and more improvisational rituals of remembrance.

The commodification of memory, evident in the intensified mediatisation of popular symbols, myths and icons, is part of the process whereby the social production of memory becomes externalised, situated and staged outside the local community. Increasingly, elements of popular remembrance are commodified by the film and television industries which exploit the popularity of mythic heroes, sites and events. Augé argues that such commodification 'makes the old (history) into a specific spectacle, as it does with all exoticism and local particularity' (1995, 110).

As key nodes in travel itineraries, symbolic sites are foci around which the mnemonic devices of travel narratives and photography are structured. The construction of these narratives is served by the provision of commodified memories. As part of the recent massive repackaging of the past and the 'exotic'; the widespread commodification and mediatisation of images, clothes, artefacts, styles and food, the tourist industry capitalises on the burgeoning nexus between consumption and leisure. Furthermore, the saturation of tourist information, guided tours, booklets, interpretative cassettes, information boards, audio-visual presentations, and themed simulacra, attempts to capture the 'feel' of a historical period, evoking events and capturing characters.

At tourist sites, memory is increasingly organised according to a commodified 'heritage' which 'fixes history' and thereby limits the interpretative and performative scope of tourists (Crang, 1994, 341–2). The package tours at the Taj are structured around the production and consumption of commodified memories, as routes follow well-rehearsed patterns. Regular narratives are enacted by the guides; not too detailed so they may not be absorbed but with a few key themes and tales that facilitate remembering. As I have described, suggestions about what sights and angles are worthy of remembrance shape visual consumption. The compilation of memorable sights and objects persists before and after a visit to the Taj (see figure 4.4).

Figure 4.4 Postcards from Taj Ganj

Typically, the common-sense ubiquity of souvenir collection is encouraged by visits to marble shops where articles designed to suggest the marble inlay work on the Taj are sold. Alternatively, souvenirs may be purchased in the tapestry, carpet and jewellery stores. Emptied of any social meaning and the conditions of their production under these conditions of rapid exchange (no bartering or haggling) such mementoes are bought in environmentally regulated, quality-controlled outlets. Accordingly, they are highly fetishised objects, standing for the Taj, and their purchase sustains the tourist industry's promise that the tour will be 'an experience you will never forget' (see Pal, 1989, 234–5 for a discussion of souvenirs of the Taj and nineteenth-century examples).

As mentioned above, many domestic tourists also purchase cheap alabaster models of the Taj as mementoes to commemorate their visit. Indeed, enormous numbers of these small craft items are sold at numerous outlets. For instance, at the domestic bus terminal (see Chapter 6), several stalls are solely devoted to the sale of these items. Western tourists, with their different aesthetic preferences and means of distinguishing status, tend to joke about the 'tastelessness' of these model Taj Mahals, preferring to purchase commodities of 'better' quality and taste. However, the aesthetic qualities of these models do not appear to be important; indeed several domestic tourists cited to me their cheapness and function as material mnemonics as reasons for their purchase (see figure 4.5).

While commodified and official memories do usurp popular memory, they rarely obliterate the personal contingencies of remembrance. For instance, souvenirs and photographs can conjure up the remembrance of personal incidents and odd experiences, and they can also be bought in a 'post-tourist' sense in which a knowing mockery of their commodified nature and supposed taste is enacted. For instance, backpackers in Agra buy all sorts of souvenirs, from fake marble artefacts to everyday objects from local markets.

In heterogeneous tourist space, the admixture of disparate and contradictory elements, visual unpredictability, sensual overcrowding, disrupted progress, the degree of social and physical contact, and the difficulty of self-insulation, mean that potted memories are not available. Whilst much commercial activity takes place, the space itself is not commodified, packaged and interpreted for tourists.

As a result, the sensual qualities of memory, 'involuntary', unpredictable memories rekindled by sounds, smells and 'atmospheres', are apt to be elicited in heterogeneous space. The visual inscriptive practices of organising memory are less important here. Whereas voluntary memory represents and is conscious, these involuntary memories are 'characterised by the operations of the unconscious' and are 'affective, relating to senses of touch, taste and smell' (Game, 1991, 108). Barthes captures the distracted state typically induced by passage through heterogeneous space, averring that what the pedestrian perceives is multiple and diverse, coming from a:

> variety of substances and perspectives: lights, colours, vegetation, heat, air, slender explosions of noises . . . passages, gestures . . . All these incidents are half-identifiable: they come from codes which are known but their combination is unique . . .
>
> (1977, 159)

Walking through heterogeneous tourist space permits the invocation of involuntary memory through sensual immersion. Indeed, this is the compelling attraction of such space for the Western tourist. The sensual and often undefinable recollections of childhood, and the furtive memories of stories and fantasies can be involuntarily resurrected in the welter of movement, sights, sounds and smells.

Whilst quite regulated, the Taj is also a sensual space, constituting neither an obvious enclavic or heterogeneous space. Moreover, the opportunities for spending a long time there permit exposure to, and awareness of, sensual

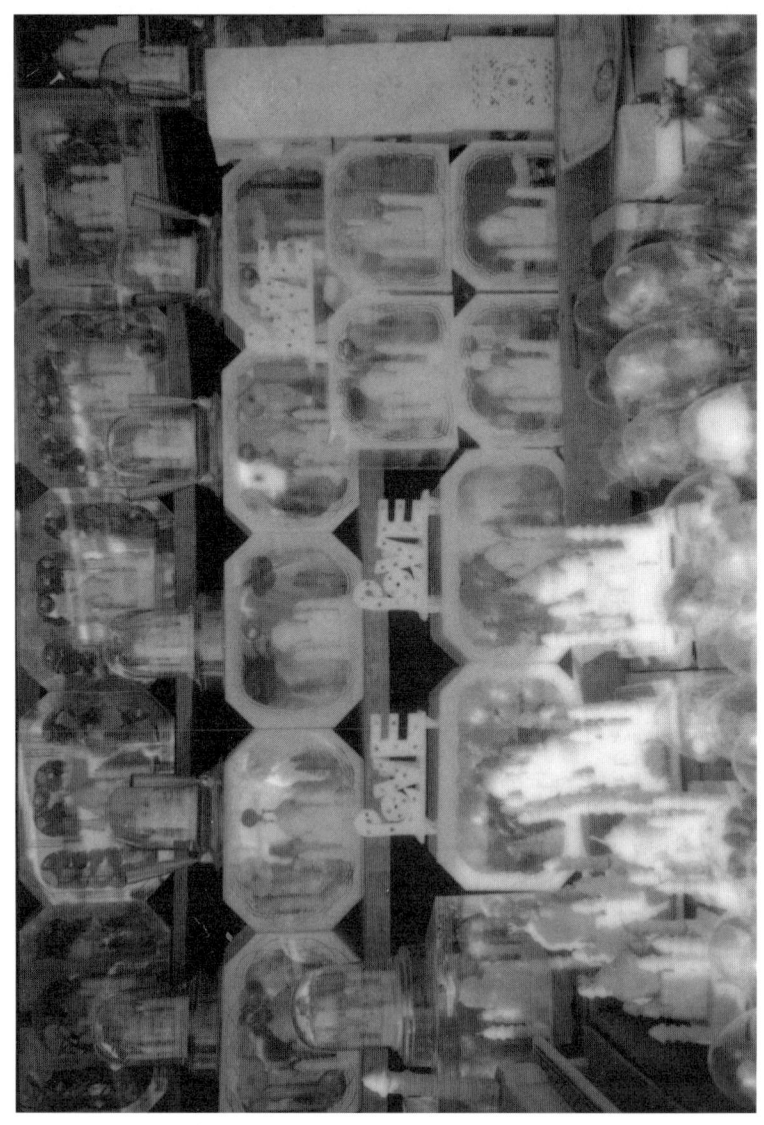

Figure 4.5 Model Taj Mahals on a stall in Agra

experiences that have nothing to do with the commodification of the site: the noises, the scent of the earth and grass and bullocks, the wind in the tall trees and the subtle changes in temperature, light and humidity. Their predilection for reflexivity encourages backpackers to write letters and journals, and sketch the scene. Whilst these activities smack of the Western urge to collect travel memories, they potentially stimulate involuntary memories and permit the gathering of unorthodox, personal, sensual memories.

Symbolic sites also provide a theatre, a backdrop or a nodal point in the quotidian activities and routes of local inhabitants. The local memories provoked by visiting, glimpsing and passing through these sites cannot be subsumed by the kinds of externalisation and commodification described above. Mainly rooted in childhood, these memories often provide a reassuring sense of security and continuity (Lynch, 1973, 40). I want to use some of Bachelard's writings to explore how such local forms of remembrance are enacted at the Taj.

Bachelard considers the areas within a house that constitute 'felicitous' and 'eulogised' space, namely those protective, inhabited domestic spaces, that embody self and value: 'By remembering "houses" and "rooms", we learn to abide within ourselves' (Bachelard, 1969, xxxiii). These 'corners of our world' are the fundamental basis of 'home' and foster a sense of locality. Within the house there are also particular places that have especial symbolic import. Bedrooms, attics and parlours contain smaller spaces where the sensual experience of texture and micro-atmosphere are absorbed in the dens of childhood imagination. Bachelard says of the house that 'each one of its nooks and corners was a resting-place for daydreams' (ibid., 15). The power of these reveries is revealed as 'our memories of former dwelling-places are relived as daydreams' and persist during our lifetime (ibid., 5–6).

We can use Bachelard's conception of the house as 'one of the greatest powers of integration for the thoughts, memories and dreams of mankind', to apply to the wider locality. Like pieces of organic furniture in one's (home)town, familiar sites, routes and features can provide a rich source of memory. The nooks and crannies of derelict buildings, the backstreets, the forbidden zones, the routes of childish adventure, the fields and woods, and the symbolic spaces of the town square, the park and famous historical sites are the sensual theatres of childhood performance. The adventurous child concocts a map of familiar routes and sites of play which constitutes an imagined geography that precedes the more pragmatic adult spatial networks. These more practical frameworks are, however, continually invaded by dreams and reveries stimulated by the earlier map. Passing or sighting the sites of childhood sport can disrupt the business-like progression towards a destination with the sensual memory of an indefinable childish experience.

In Agra, many local adults reminisce about how they used the Taj as a playground when they were children and often lamented the fact that the pressure of work prevented them from continuing to visit regularly. The Taj can be conceived as forming part of the imaginative geographies based on the well-worn routes of childhood. Passage by or through the grounds of the Taj sets off a host of memories and affective sensations amongst locals that apparently evoke a more carefree era in which space and time were experienced as less constrained:

> Purshottam *(25, watchmender)*: I went innumerable times as a boy. I used to play there all the time. Now I have no time, I only go on Fridays sometimes. Sometimes I sit on my roof and look at the Taj and remember when I played there as a boy.

> Tarachand *(43, fabric dyer and cleaner)*: Most of my childhood was spent there playing, up to the twelfth grade at school. Now I have little time since I work so much, but I wish I could go more often than once a month to remember those childhood times.

Clearly, the remembering practices connected with local use of the Taj are more organised around personal memories which reinforce a sense of continuity in place, and it is likely that ways of gazing upon the site are not shaped by the imperative to focus upon the most striking features but are more directed to the sites of childhood play.

This examination of the diverse tourist performances that centre upon the Taj Mahal has exemplified the sheer diversity of activities that centre upon one symbolic site. Like the narratives discussed in Chapter 3, these practices articulate their particular situatedness and reveal tourists' historical and geographical relationship with the site. The symbolic and emotional importance of the Taj is different for domestic and foreign tourists, religious and secular visitors, and directed groups and backpackers.

I have identified a range of walking practices around the site. The diversity of these movements, expressing dispositions to roam or stay close to established paths and in close contact with groups, and their contrasting purposive and distracted modes of covering ground testify to different levels of spatio-temporal control. These varied choreographies are also distinguished by the degree to which performances follow established rituals. The sensual abandon of the body in liminal space associated with tourism is rarely stimulated by the more directed forms of tourist performance.

Modes of gazing and photographing are powerfully shaped by customs of travel and informed by particular narratives about the site. Thus such performances are often shaped by and reproduce representations manufactured by the tourist industry, but they also may create new forms and generate unpredictable experiences. There are a range of gazes enacted at the Taj. I have identified the romantic gaze practised by most Western visitors, the collective witness performed by many domestic groups of tourists, the reverential gaze activated by Muslim visitors, and the psychedelic, drug-influenced gaze of some Western backpackers. These gazing practices affect the disposition to engage in particular photographic practices and the centrality of photography to a visit to the Taj. The study of these photographic pursuits has highlighted distinct theatrical approaches and recording imperatives.

Remembering is a particularly important practice for tourists. The purposive attempts to compile memories is avidly followed by many tourists at the Taj through souvenir and photographic accumulation and the keeping of travel diaries. Indeed, tours are organised around the collection of commodified memories. However, the Taj is also itself a monumental inscription in space. In this necral landscape, adherents of particular belief systems approach such memorialisation in distinct ways. Muslims follow incorporating mnemonic rituals whereas other forms of remembering are inscriptive. I have suggested though that, as a sensual space, passage around the Taj can stimulate involuntary memories that escape the ritualised and commodified performances of remembrance. And tourist performances of remembering, like those of walking and gazing, contrast with the ways in which locals walk round, gaze at and remember the Taj.

I have portrayed the varied performances carried out by domestic tourists to the Taj, partly to decentre ethnocentric generalisations about tourist meaning and practice, but, more importantly, to identify the diversity of interpretations and performances at the Taj. These various enactions highlight the ways in which tourists can combine spiritual and secular practices and meanings in visiting symbolic sites, and also how forms of collective travel can be shaped by a different set of communal understandings and techniques than those articulated by groups of Western tourists. Norms of gazing, photographing, walking and remembering tend to be less shaped by the romantic desire to visually consume sights and the compulsion to collect experiences. Rather than being directed by tour personnel, these collective performances are informed by shared notions of collective pleasure and witness.

I have stressed throughout this account that tourist performances are strongly influenced by the spatio-temporal organisation of their tour around the Taj and the different social pressures exerted by group norms, or the lack of such collective constraints. The propensity for reflexivity, enquiry into difference and improvisation are conditioned by the level of regulation and the nature of the space moved through, and the time available to the tourist. At the Taj, there is a measure of regulation; it is a tourist space which is stage managed and bounded. But it is also a sensual space, with the Jamuna River, the scene of local activities flowing behind the mausoleum, and bright green parakeets screeching through the trees, as well as the more obvious visual, auditory and other bodily pleasures it offers. Moreover, because a rich diversity of visitors assemble there, there is a potential, sometimes realised, for unlikely meetings to occur.

For package tourists who have limited time here, and whose movements are constrained by the structure of the tour and the stage directions they must follow, the performances they enact are usually restricted to gazing and photography, and yet these controls are frequently the source of frustration and tourists face the dilemma of having to choose between enactions: to photograph? to gaze? to wander? For those who are less temporally and spatially restricted, a different set of performances are followed, not always any less predictable, but offering the potential for a more reflexive, improvisational and surprising experience.

In the next chapter, I will extend my examination of spatial regulation and design by exploring the wider spatial contexts within which Western tourists organise their travels. In Agra, there is a rather evident division between what I have termed enclavic and heterogeneous tourist spaces as I will describe. The different groups of Western tourists who temporarily reside in these distinct spaces rarely move through the same areas of Agra, except when they visit the Taj Mahal. In the wider schemes by which their tours through India are organised, there is a pattern whereby these distinct groups tend to move between enclavic or heterogeneous tourist spaces respectively. And the Taj is incorporated into these different travel itineraries as one of the tourist spaces which are linked together. The above account of tourist performances then cannot be abstracted from the wider spatial and temporal conditions in which these travellers move. In the final chapter, I will discuss a range of proposed tourist developments which may impact upon the distinct spaces discussed in the next chapter, and alter the circumstances within which tourist performances are enacted.

Notes

1   These features of the guided tour were those most commonly cited by the guides. I followed fifteen separate guided tours around the Taj and they proved to be highly predictable in their presentations. In all the cases guides were locally based; either official, trained guides who were licensed by the Archaeological Survey Department and based at the Taj, or they worked for travel companies and were employed to accompany tourists around Agra on day tours. The narratives I have highlighted are those related by at least twelve of the guides.
2   Over the course of three days in January 1994, I monitored the time spent by domestic visitors. This information complemented that compiled from the interviews I carried out.

5

ENCLAVIC AND HETEROGENOUS TOURIST SPACES IN AGRA

In Chapter 2, I introduced the notions of enclavic and heterogeneous tourist spaces. The Taj does not fit obviously into either of these forms, constituting a hybrid. Tourist performances at this particular tourist stage are partially affected by its regulation and boundedness, but a greater influence is that extended by tourist personnel and fellow tourists. At a more general, global level, the proliferation of tourist space tends to produce both large-scale, capital-intensive projects such as holiday villages and complexes, and more informal, less-planned areas to serve independent tourists, which can be equated with my categories of enclavic and heterogeneous forms. Spatial forms are rarely as separate as my idealised division suggests, for ambivalences and contradictions which disrupt spatial processes of ordering cannot be extinguished. But while ordering processes are inevitably uneven, and enclavic and heterogeneous spaces usually have a relationship with each other, they are sufficiently demarcated in order for the distinction to be sustained. In Agra, the Cantonment area and Taj Ganj particularly correspond to these spatial formations.

I am interested in the design codes, kinds of social interaction, range of activities and forms of regulation that (re)produce these spaces. The material and social forms of organisation characteristically found in Agra Cantonment and Taj Ganj are part of a wider context whereby tourists serially reside in, and visit, similar tourist spaces during their travels though India. These themes, the common experiences they engender, and the ways in which they are reinforced through tourist processes are the subject of this chapter.

To introduce the discussion I identify the itineraries which are followed by those tourists who stay in these distinct spaces. This situates the Taj within a spatial sequence of destinations, but more importantly as far as this chapter is concerned, it shows how different tourists move between similar forms of space during their trip to India. I am concerned here only with the ways in which foreign tourists use and experience space in the 'City of the Taj' since the majority of domestic tourists rarely linger in the city after their visit to the Taj.

Following this brief analysis of the structure of tours which incorporate these discrete spaces, I will describe the main features of the package tourist enclave in Agra Cantonment and the backpacker area of Taj Ganj. Between these spaces lies an intermediate zone which accommodates those tourists (commonly called 'foreign independent travellers') who are desirous of greater comfort and organisation than backpackers but are unwilling to travel according to the tight schedules and enclavic structure of the package tour. Accordingly, they frequently move between the Cantonment and Taj Ganj, mixing a desire for comfort with ventures into the bazaars. They generally approach travel with an independent outlook but are willing to pay for the organisation and facilities that ensure comfort, and tend to use flexible travel companies with whom they negotiate an itinerary. Here, middle-range hotels and small emporia predominate. Either side of this zone lie the bazaar and the enclave.

Most package tourists are attracted to Agra to see the Taj Mahal, the most famous and popular attraction of package tours to India. Accordingly, Western package tourists in Agra far outnumber backpackers but although they numerically predominate at the Taj, in other areas of Agra backpackers have a marked presence on the streets. To give an idea of the difference in numbers, during the height of the season from November 1992 to March 1993, 1,011 Western guests stayed at three budget hotels in Taj Ganj, for a total of 1,851 bed-nights. During the same period, 31,804 Westerners stayed at the five-star Moghul Sheraton Hotel for a total of 50,230 bed-nights.[1] Yet these vast numbers passing through experience only minimal interaction with Agra and its denizens.

In order to bring out the distinctions between these different tourist spaces, I compare the ways in which tourists and locals are regulated, the organisation and experience of shopping, and the forms of spatial and social exploration that are constrained and enabled. Particular tourist experiences produce distinct ways of understanding India that often confirm preconceptions but, as I will suggest, those moving through heterogeneous tourist space have opportunities to critically reflect on these assumptions.

Package tourists in Agra Cantonment

A majority of package tourists visiting India spend between one and three weeks in the country. This limited amount of time means that tours organised by large travel firms usually offer predictable itineraries which are scheduled to visit particular sites. The shorter the time available, the greater the need to cram in the requisite number of sights. The experiences of tourists are considerably affected by this tight time-budgeting.

Weightman examined thirteen package tours to India and discovered that 'selective spatial and temporal biases' were 'directed towards the North, the city and the past' (1987, 232). This tourist experience was 'mainly that of Moghul influenced India', and 50 per cent of sites visited were of historic architecture (ibid., 234). Selected sites on these itineraries are commonly constructed as representative of India and the structure of the tour reifies these notions. As Weightman observes:

A tour to India minus Agra and the Taj Mahal or Jaipur and the Hawa Mahal is unthinkable. Repeated presentation of these and similar landscape elements has made them objects, symbols of the essence of the nation.

(1987, 234)

Many tourists perceive advantages in this mode of touring. The most common justification for selecting a package tour was that it removed the difficult process of organising routes and choosing which places to visit:

> Charles *(40, 'in property', from Bristol, UK, on a ten-day package trip)*: I like doing tours like this because they select the things you want to look at. It's all organised for you. You get to the hotel at ten and then it's off at eight the next morning. I certainly wouldn't like to tour India differently. I don't think I could cope with the bureaucracy. I wouldn't even think about it. It's not even on the edge of possibility.

Here, there is a common assumption that there are sights that should be seen – 'the things you want to look at' – and this is reaffirmed by their inclusion in itineraries. This hermeneutic process follows a sequence whereby the sites are rated, anticipated, experienced and consumed, and retrospectively highlighted in recounted narratives.

Tours such as this should be conceived as modes of travel and not presumed to cater for specific kinds of people, for package tours to India are believed to circumvent the difficulties which self-organised travel would entail. Some tourists report that they do not usually go on organised tours but think that India provides too many practical and epistemological impediments.

> Will *(36, teacher, Shropshire, UK, on a ten-day package tour)*: If you did it yourself you'd spend so much time trying to get things done. And, well, the culture and the life are totally different. We're not used to it. This way, at least you get some degree of protection and normality.

This reproduces the widespread colonial notion that India is utterly 'other', a space to be negotiated carefully to minimise disorientation. In this sense, the package tour contextualises and tames the difference, emplacing it in a predictable epistemological setting of tourist itineraries, narratives and activities, and providing environments and experiences which only suggest the exotic. Yet despite these carefully monitored provisions, some tourists still find that they are unable to find any purchase on the difference they confront.

> Penny *(40, soft-furnishing retailer, from Buxton, Derbyshire, UK, on a two-week package tour with her partner and co-manager)*: It's totally different. So

difficult to find your feet here. Even after a week it's still a bit of a mystery to us, everything seems confused and chaotic.

Indeed, some of those who had ventured outside the enclave were often shaken by their experiences:

> Anne *(46, catering manager, from Leeds, on a two-week package tour with her friend)*: We went to a bazaar and not only did you have people touching you, dragging you from stall to stall, you also had beggars following you round. It was all too much.

I have discussed the ways in which package tourists visiting the Taj are carefully managed through a combination of tour structure and scare tactics to remain within the orbit of the tour operators. This pattern is serial in that the package tourist moves from one enclave to another in transport capsules, stopping en route at shops, restaurants and attractions where the presence of disturbing differences in the form of people, sights, smells and sounds are minimised. In Agra, enclavic tourist space is produced and consumed in the Cantonment area of the city where the British colonial offices and dwellings were located. Ironically, almost fifty years after British colonial dominion ended, the Cantonment is again occupied by large numbers of Westerners.

The Agra Tourist Guild, a body representing most large tourist-related enterprises in the city, has striven to preserve the spacious, orderly and green characteristics of this space. The wide roads of the Cantonment area are well maintained. The roundabouts and verges are manicured and no temporary buildings are permitted to clutter the spacious environment, contrasting with areas abutting this tightly controlled space where tea houses, dwellings and businesses sprawl onto the street. The old colonial bungalows provide accommodation for municipal and tourist offices, and homes for wealthy Agrans, and the British sports facilities of football pitches, tennis courts and golf course remain. Typically, package tour groups staying in Agra centre upon three spaces: hotels, emporia and historical attractions (the Taj, Agra Fort, Fatehpur Sikra).

Along the main arteries of the Cantonment are situated the four five-star hotels, the *Agra Ashok*, the *Clarks-Shiraz*, the *Taj View* and the *Moghul Sheraton*, as are most of the large emporia and up-market restaurants. There are many other hotels in this area, and some in the process of construction.

The hotels combine 'international' standards and design features with aspects of Indian 'exotica'. The most expensive hotels are air-conditioned at all times, producing an atmosphere at variance with the climatic conditions outside. Large lobbies, expensively furnished with plush furniture, serve as the meeting places for groups and relaxation. Adjacent to the lobbies are in-house shopping arcades, replete with small retail outlets selling local crafts, Indian clothes and jewellery. The hotels have a selection of cafés and restaurants, and a flexible menu which permits guests to choose Western or indigenous dishes. In the lobby, music is usually played as piped muzak, or performed by local pianists and occasionally, Indian classical musicians.

Other facilities on offer at the upmarket hotels are satellite TV, mini-golf, croquet and swimming pools, several bars and musical entertainment. The chairman of the Agra Tourist Guild admitted that there was a distinct lack of night-time entertainment in Agra; no special tourist night-clubs, concert venues, cinemas or discos. Moreover, guests are warned not to venture outside. Thus most have little choice but to spend the evening in the hotel where they eat and drink, peruse the shops, or attend special functions arranged for them.

Despite their globally homogeneous characteristics, these hotels try to remind guests that they are in India by including particular design features such as friezes and posters, sculptures, pieces of furniture and carpets, and the odd architectural trait. Within the context of the overall architectural design, these characteristics are emplaced within an aesthetic orderliness that *showcases* the exotic, an arrangement which contrasts with the different spatial patterns outside the enclave. In a sense, this decor strategy is a metaphor for the contemporary construction of tourist space: the exhibition of features in a decontextualised enclave. These highlighted items, torn from their usual setting like artefacts in a museum, are a small taste of the world beyond the hotel compound. As an instrumental version of *Don't Cry For Me Argentina* was piped into the lobby of one hotel, the resident astrologer commented on these minor simulations:

> Madhukar: In this hotel we give them a taste of India – the Indian things like astrology, magic shows, *ghazals* and theme parties. There, you see, they are playing your music, there are all the conveniences of the West. This is not the real India. This is an international hotel – they're the same all over the world. What do they learn?

Colonial fantasies about the 'mystery' and 'romance' of India are further evoked by several other features. Several hotels employ very tall, immaculately attired doormen, resplendent in tunic and turban, conjuring up the obedient bearers and servants of the Raj. At the entrance to one hotel is a snake charmer, and all the large hotels employ astrologers, an integral part of Indian life, which proves popular with guests.

This rather mild construction of 'otherness' is required to compensate for the restrictions on the movement of guests, yet some visitors are aware of this 'staged authenticity':

> Peter *(60, food manufacturer, Bedford, UK, on a three-week package tour with his partner)*: To be honest, we're staying in a five-star hotel, and you could be anywhere in the world. I know they try and stick to the

Indian theme but it's so artificial. It doesn't feel like India at all and I find that rather off-putting.

A major production of simulated 'otherness' are the themed garden parties for which guests pay an additional 20–40,000 rupees. The parties offered usually follow the 'Moghul' theme, the 'Village' theme or the 'Lane' (*Chowk*) theme.

On the 'Moghul' theme night guests are encouraged to attire themselves in the appropriate period costume, with fancy dress provided by the hotel, consisting of flowing, sparkling, embroidered robes and turbans. The event is held in an outside tent, supposedly arranged in the style of a Moghul banqueting hall, where the numerous attendants serve 'authentic Moghul cuisine'. Musical entertainment and dances are performed in this setting to 'recreate the ambience of Moghul India', according to the programme. A variation on this theme is the introduction of a 'hunting' theme where barbecued meat is eaten off 'rough split log tables' and guarded by 'Moghul sentinels'.

At another hotel, the entertainment manager reported 'we aim to create the ambience of a village in our grounds'. To this effect, potters and marble craftsmen, bangle sellers, palmists and snake charmers dress up as the 'traditional' retailers in the village. Suitably attired visitors are encouraged to assume the roles of villagers by sitting on *bhudas* (wicker stools) and relaxing on *charpoys* (rope beds), taking rides on bullock carts, participating in village dances and having *mendhi* designs imprinted upon their hands. Other features include dancing bears and monkeys, a selection of farm animals and traditional musical entertainment. Unsurprisingly, this 'staged authenticity' omits awkward details such as the caste composition of most Indian villages.

One of the features of the 'village' night is that two of the guests are proposed as participants in a 'typical Hindu marriage ceremony'. Wearing the proper ceremonial garments and tutored in the basic rituals, the couple act out the marriage in front of the other 'villagers' who participate in and take photographs of the scene.

The irony of these productions is that most of these hotel guests are almost entirely excluded from the life of the street or village by the structure of their tour. To make up for this absent experience, the re-creation of what they do not witness at first hand includes an element of performing as stereotypical Indians. This postmodern, theatrical playing with identity in an ordered, yet ludic space, could be enacted in any similarly regulated space anywhere. The occasion and place – away from home and in the realm of the (nearby) 'other' – provides a collective dramaturgical game in which guests fantasise and act out situations that they imagine but will never confront, with the legitimising factor that this ersatz experience did occur in India. At the same time, this immersion in a bogus 'village' India, is often accompanied by a knowing, post-touristic attitude that acknowledges and enjoys the inauthenticity of the occasion. Additionally, the adoption of Indian roles constitutes something of an inversion and reproduces carnivalesque moments. For instance, at one theme party, a man dressed up as a

Moghul princess, causing much merriment amongst his group. Such parties thereby provide one of the few 'liminoid' occasions on the package tour. However, these stagings of a highly stereotyped 'otherness' require the construction of a particular kind of tourist space – ordered yet close to the space of the 'other', incorporated into an enclavic itinerary and linked to other enclavic spaces.

Shopping is central to the package tour experience. Besides the shops in the hotels, most trips to the famous sites are combined with visits to large craft emporia. Most of the package tourists I interviewed had bought or intended to buy local craft products, some having spent hundreds of pounds. The most important retail industries in the Agran tourist sector are those selling marble inlay products, embroidered goods, and semi-precious stones and jewellery. Many small outlets sell these products in Agra, but the large concerns are concentrated in Agra Cantonment and it is these emporia that package tours visit.

The largest concerns are the huge *Oswal* marble emporium and the profitable *Cottage Industries* which serve many coach parties. The approach road to the latter sweeps off the appropriately named Mall through a landscaped garden, and the whole building is enclosed by a high perimeter fence. Inside the air-conditioned shop, the decor is as pristine as the immaculately garbed staff. At *Oswal,* which apparently secures the custom of tourists by paying the highest commission rates in Agra, there is a giant model of the Taj Mahal to reinforce the link between the marble inlay industry and the building which ensures its popularity. The business buys the products of over 1,000 craftsmen and the goods range from small inlaid boxes to marble tables retailing at 35,000 pounds sterling.

To return to the theme of the production of simulacra of India in enclavic space, at one of the marble emporia popular with coach parties, the management have employed and positioned several marble craftsmen in a low building adjacent to the entrance of the showroom. Here, upon disembarking, the tourists take photographs of the men at work while a salesman provides attendant commentary. Most Western tourists appear intrigued by this exhibition of 'backstage' working. Ironically, however, such working practices are far from backstage in Agra. If the tourists were to walk a few hundred yards down the road they would witness many such marble craftsmen working in a similar fashion on the edge of the street outside their small shops. The Western distinctions between backstage and frontstage are not always delineated by work and retail activities in India. In the bazaar areas of Agra one can observe the work of bookbinders, pharmacists, blacksmiths, tailors and a host of other workers at the edge of the street. In enclavic tourist space by contrast, a stage-managed Indian space is provided.

The principle foci of package tours are symbolic tourist sites. In Agra, besides the Taj, most package tours also visit Agra Fort, whilst a smaller proportion venture further to the abandoned Moghul city of Fatehpur Sikra, forty-nine kilometres west of the city. Other minor attractions are Itmad-ud-daulah, often called the 'Baby Taj', and other Moghul tombs and gardens. Accordingly, the city is experienced by visiting several historical monuments and making a sequence of purchases. At other attractions, tourists follow the prescribed route and narrative of a guided tour as they do at the Taj Mahal. The smells and sounds of the city, its people – the beggars, touts and traders, the school-children and the elderly – and the diverse shops and services, are all missed by the exclusive movement of the package tour through these regulated spaces.

Spaces other than the famous attractions and enclavic tourist space are avoided by most package tourists. Since their limited time and movement is so rigorously controlled and adhered to, they have little opportunity to explore the bazaars of Agra. Even when they leave the hotel or emporia, and the encapsulated environment of the tour bus, touts are kept at bay by tour personnel and, as at the Taj, the group moves as a tightly bounded collectivity. The static enclavic space of Agra Cantonment is replaced by a mobile enclave, usually the tourist bus, which moves through time and space, equally shielded from the perceived chaos of the 'other'.

However, less regulated local spaces cannot be wholly avoided by package tourists as they travel en route to attractions. The shock at witnessing degrees of poverty and perceived disorder in the form of uncollected rubbish and wandering animals can produce emotional and cognitive discomfort, even though such space is not physically entered but merely bypassed. The following response was given by a middle-aged man in the midst of a world tour as he arrived at the Taj.

> Courtney *(55, factory inspector, from New York, on a three-week tour with his partner which incorporates China, India and the UK)*: It's a beautiful building but it's surrounded by poverty. You step outside the gate and see what's there – Jesus! They always put pictures in the book about the good things but they don't show what's outside the gate. You wouldn't want to go out there, all that mess and garbage.

Very few package tourists visit these other areas of Agra and when they do the experience can be uncomfortable. A member of a party visiting the city's largest bazaar said:

> Honour *(46, civil servant, from Leeds, UK, on a two-week package tour with her friend)*: Until you've been amongst it you don't realise how bad it is. You get fed up of haggling, people come up and touch you, and it was really crowded, very busy. And not only did you have people wanting to sell you stuff, you also had beggars following you. I couldn't handle it at all, it totally upset me. I had to get away as quick as I could. Very traumatic.

As I suggested in Chapter 1, the lack of engagement with other spaces seems to reproduce negative Western representations of India and the 'Third World' which have their roots in colonial discourses. The quick glimpses of local spectacles perhaps suggest the depthless media images of 'poverty', 'begging', 'disorder' and 'dirt' whereas a more prolonged engagement with such scenes might provide a less superficial understanding which could not be easily recapitulated into these regimes of representation. While package tourists know full well how to negotiate enclavic environments and are guided around tourist sites, most never learn the techniques of negotiating spaces of difference, and never develop interactive repertoires in non-enclavic settings.

Although I have so far described the tight organisation of enclavic tourist space and the restrictions imposed upon tourists, a large minority of the tourists who occupy and move through the enclaves are frustrated and dissatisfied precisely because of these constraints. For whilst there is a concern to avoid extreme difference, there is also a countervailing feeling that the partiality of the tour means that they miss out on experiencing the 'Other'. The following sentiment captures the tension that arises from this ambivalence:

> John *(31, dentist, from Lincolnshire, UK, on a twelve-day package tour with his partner)*: I would like to have more time to ourselves on the tour. We think they've got guards who are paid to look after us while we're wandering round sites. I find that quite hard because I want to meet the people. But then again, if we'd gone in feet first we would have been destroyed in two days.

Similarly, many package tourists are apt to express dissatisfaction with the concentration of the tour upon historical buildings when they reflect upon the signs of apparent 'difference' they have merely glimpsed:

> Barry *(50, estate manager, from Wakefield, UK, on a two-week package tour with his friend)*: To be honest, we're a bit sick of monuments by now. We've seen the villages from the coach and we want to go amongst the cow-dung houses and the people, to look at the agricultural system and the way they work but we've been kept away from all that. It's a case of you go from one big tourist attraction to another.

> Paul *(55, painter and decorator, from Wakefield, UK, Barry's friend)*: We went to Fatehpur Sikra, the hotel, the Taj, the Fort and then to a marble-inlay shop. They did the hard sell and, I mean, that's happened everywhere. I find that quite hard because I want to meet the people. The only Indians we've met have been those connected with tourism. We're being kept away from the ordinary life really. It's being sanitised for us. We've been shielded in every way. But we're grown men, we know how life is.

Since the controlled experience of space and time limits the possibility of unique adventures, the tourist quest for the authentic and the surprising are thwarted by the predictability and haste of the tour:

> Bob *(28, computer programmer, from London, on a two-week package tour)*: It's been so fast, the speed with which we've visited places. And also, you're visiting places that have been visited by thousands and thousands of tourists before, so you don't see them fresh.

Reflections upon the partiality of sites visited also demonstrate an awareness of the limited places visited and themes experienced, along with the attendant repetitive tourist performances that are called for:

> Brenda *(25, patent agent, from London, on a two-week package tour with her partner)*: I would have liked a bit more time on my own, or at least seen some different things. We're whisked about from place to place. It's ten minutes here – look at that – take a photo – buy a souvenir – then go somewhere else and do the same. Is that all there is?

> Belinda *(29, student nurse, from Lincolnshire, UK, on a twelve-day package tour with her partner, John)*: Well the Taj is very big, very white, but very much like an awful lot of buildings we've seen in India. It's ridiculous! We seem to have taken no end of photographs of long straight roads with a bloody great building at the end of it. All the time!

The constraints over the space and time of tourists means that a lot has to be pack(ag)ed in. Such tours are emphatically not always a leisurely experience as was pointed out by several interviewees:

> Wanda *(29, pharmacist, from London, on a two-week package tour)*: Rather than a holiday it's rather working hard at getting an experience. I mean it's been quite gruelling. You haven't time to be ill or tired, you just have to keep going, keep moving.

For most package tourists, enclavic space nurtures the strong urge to remain insulated from the disturbing and different, and yet there is also a contradictory desire for the 'other', fuelled by fantasies of exploration, the exotic and the novel. Exemplifying this alternative yearning for excitement, certain tourists regarded the highlights of their tour as those rare occasions when they escaped from tight schedules and regulated spaces and ventured into non-enclavic space. These adventures often encountered only mundane aspects of Indian urban life yet the frisson of excitement that they provided had a considerable impact:

> John *(49, office manager from Southampton, UK, with his partner on a three-week package tour)*: The best bit of the holiday so far was the drive from

Delhi to Agra, seeing the countryside. And the bloody taxi in Delhi – Christ! Down the wrong side of the street, lorries coming straight at you! Mind, it wasn't half exciting.

Wanda: The best thing was wandering around these little streets in Delhi. We went to places where they'd never seen a white person before. The best value for money was probably the motor-rickshaw ride around Jaipur – fantastic. That was more enthralling than anything.

Rob *(36, accountant, from Leeds, UK, on a two-week package tour)*: I think the highlights have been not the monuments but what we've seen on the bus travelling along: people going about their business, waving, smiling at us. And the kids coming up to the bus shouting 'one pen', 'one rupee'.

This tension is typical of tourist ambivalence in searching for ordered experience and physical and epistemological safety, and at the same time, desiring the 'other' and the transgressive. In fact, the rigid monitoring of movement towards non-enclavic space curtails any realisation of the latter tendencies. In Agra, tourist industry personnel are motivated by strategies which aim to keep the tourist involved in consumption for the maximum period and co-ordinate the organisation of large groups.

The Cantonment area serves as a self-contained space where most of the needs of the tourist can be met, and managers aim to confine tourist consumption to these services. The tours in and around Agra always visit the large emporia which are chosen according to where tourist personnel have established deals over rates of commission.

In the same way that guides instil fear into tourists who would like to explore space and spend more time at the Taj, hotel personnel and tour managers purvey horror stories about the likely result of any venture into non-enclavic space in Agra. They shake their heads, disclaiming responsibility if the tourist does not follow their advice and relate stories about how tourists get ripped off by disreputable traders who sell them fake items (ironic considering the high rates of commission charged at plush emporia), how they will be subject to unending harassment, how tourists have been given drugs and raped or robbed of their possessions, and of the potential violence outside. Most package tourists already perceive India as strange and 'other' and these stories are generally sufficient to curtail their wanderlust. However, a minority are sceptical:

Barry : We'd have liked to have had a look round the centre of Agra but we've been advised by the tour representatives not to go out for fear of robbery and thieves. He was emphasising that the people would be hostile if we were walking round on the streets. But to us they seem fairly gentle. OK, you get the beggars and they'll hassle you, and the kids, but so what? We feel we're missing out a bit.

These tall tales of danger reproduce a jaundiced view about India amongst many package tourists. The rumour that the city is dangerous is a source of anger to many Agrans. Small traders are denied custom by the strategy of large businesses to keep tourists in enclavic space, whilst other locals would like to meet foreigners and feel they are being unjustly maligned:

> Aran *(53, manager of medium-sized jewellery emporium)*: The tourists are told that they must be careful – pickpockets, thieves, *goondahs*. But India is not like that. You walk down the street, it is safe. People like to talk to foreigners. The visitor is treated like a god, as a duty. Money is not everything: a man will leave his work to spend time with you. The guides should tell of these things but instead they talk about the beggars and the thieves.

The staff in the large luxury hotels are trained to adopt the 'appropriate' demeanour towards visitors. Unfailingly polite and deferential, their conversations with guests are informational and brief. The scope for meeting other locals is limited since guests rarely venture outside the enclave and even rickshaw drivers are not allowed into the hotel grounds. Another point of contact with locals is in the emporia where the formal ritual of the display of wares and haggling over prices involves tourists in social interaction. However, many tourists are unwilling to enter into the process of bartering and either pay the first price cited, or withdraw from the transaction:

> Carol *(38, accountant, from Reading, UK, on a two-week package tour)*: Personally, I object to the visits to craft shops. The people there latch on to you, pester you – the pressure of the selling. They say they're just showing you things and you don't need to buy. But I feel intimidated by it and I haven't bought anything.

Tourists' main encounter is with the tour guides, who tailor their delivery and persona to the party concerned. However, it is from these tourist personnel that package tourists gain an extra insight about matters such as religion, politics and the family. Given the rigorous adherence to the daily timetable, the opportunity for extended conversation is limited, yet if tourists ask about matters unconnected with the potted tour narrative, they are usually rewarded with an attentive response.

The most intimate encounter for many visitors is with the hotel astrologer to whom they may divulge personal information and be open to his suggestions. Tellingly, his antipathy towards their emotional and material preoccupations revealed the circumstantial power relationship between one astrologer and his Western customers:

> Madhukar: They have only three concerns; sex, marriage and money. They're sixty and they ask me about marriage! This is unthinkable for an Indian! At this age they should be turning their thoughts to the soul, towards religion. They are very materialistic, obsessed with their investments. While here they buy big marble tables. I want to say, 'Don't think about money all the time.' But they are the elite. If they complain I could lose my work.

One form of local connection which some tourists make is through prostitution. Several of the rickshaw drivers who wait outside the gates of the hotels are the contacts, and in the event of a stray male tourist venturing out on his own, they will approach the man and suggest that he meets a girl. The usual offer is either for the rickshaw wallah to take the tourist to the house of the 'nice Indian girl', or to bring her to the hotel. The fee quoted is between 600 to 1,000 rupees for a night in the hotel, a small amount for the tourist but a large sum for most Indians. The story goes that many of the women prepared to do this sex work are students who are unable to pay their fees although there are 'red light' areas in Agra, and the prostitute population is relatively high compared to other Indian cities, partly because of the large garrison.

According to local legend, a three-star hotel in Agra Cantonment procured nearly a hundred young women to provide sexual services for Western residents and wealthy locals. Enticing the women by promising a substantial sum for a one-off service, the manager of the hotel subsequently blackmailed the women with disclosure to relatives about their 'immorality' if they did not continue to prostitute themselves.

Although sex tourism in India is not overt, it goes on discreetly in the major tourist centres. The Western desire for the sexualised 'other' no doubt fuels the demand for prostitution in Agra and the pimps and contacts stress the attraction of the exotic and erotic to the tourists, mentioning the Eastern sexual techniques in the *Kamasutra*, the beauty of Indian 'girls' and their youth. The complicity of these local pimps in broadcasting these 'Orientalist' sexualities reproduces colonialist discourses and since most of the sex workers speak no English, these assumptions are less likely to be challenged by any verbal dialogue.

In concluding this section, I want to emphasise the extent to which the experience of Agra for most package tourists is extremely partial, with a bias towards the historical, asocial and commodified. The production of controlled environments, rigid itineraries, potted narratives about attractions, and simulacra of local features; the superficial encounters between tourists and locals; and the centrality of shopping produce an experience that screens out the smells, sounds, sights and people of Agra. The commodified and highly enclavic production of memories, images and photographs, souvenirs, narratives and information is partly subverted by glimpses, chance meetings and hidden desires, yet such occasions are contained within the spatial and temporal organisational imperatives of the tour.

Whilst I have focused on Agra here, the similarities of the interlinked, themed surroundings which these tourists move through and stay in construct a pale simulacra of India within a familiar environment. Such an itinerary produces a space which is defined by particular design codes and themes and fulfils the consumption–production cycle of representation. This imagined geography reproduces India as a historic space of exotic palaces, glamour and romance, cruelty and opulence, which contrasts which contemporary chaos and squalor, but it is also experienced as a landscape of consumption, convenience and luxury. However, whilst global mediascapes and Western-based corporate tourist advertisements reproduce these 'Orientalist' notions, they also constitute a valuable economic resource for entrepreneurs and workers in the Indian tourist sector who capitalise on the fantasies of Western tourists.

Backpackers in Taj Ganj

Other forms of tourism are far less regulated by spatio-temporal constraints. For instance, backpackers form an increasingly large percentage of international tourists. Although they travel for diverse reasons and have emerged through a combination of distinct tourist processes (Loker-Murphy and Pearce, 1995, 820–6), their spatio-temporal practices follow distinct patterns.

By virtue of their small budgets, most backpackers are unable to stay in 'international' standard accommodation. Their travel networks may be quite extensive as they usually opt to construct their own improvisational itineraries over a longer period of time. Although they may visit many of the same symbolic sites as package tourists, they generally stay in non-enclavic tourist space, and have the opportunity, through the lack of an enforced schedule, to explore tourist attractions such as the Taj in greater detail and investigate a wider diversity of spaces. Such itineraries are contingent on chance meetings, instant decisions and recommendations received en route, although many travel choices are directed by consultation with budget guidebooks. The pursuit of these less rigid itineraries means that places that are of marginal tourist significance may be included in the journey. In fact, the less-travelled path 'has a high degree of mystique and status conferral' (Riley, 1988, 321) amongst such travellers.

This greater flexibility over time and space is the principal factor in influencing where these tourists stay, who they meet and what they see (ibid., 327), which potentially facilitates a greater degree of reflexivity about the sights, cultures and people that they confront. This also extends to a self-reflexivity which is often inspired by the desire for self-realisation, which impels many backpackers to commence their journey and is practised in the journals in which they record their adventure (Riley, 1988, 322). This reflexivity is also facilitated by random and unexpected sights and occurrences in heterogeneous space. As Adler states:

> Paradoxically, disorientation and lack of knowledge pertinent to a travel site only further free encounters to be seized as the stuff of private dream and enacted myth.
>
> (1989a, 1383)

In many cases, the amount of time that backpackers intend to spend in India has not been determined or is dependent on the contingencies determined by their travel funds. The varying lengths of backpacker sojourns outside their country of origin is suggested by the figures in table 5.1 which details the time spent in India by 1,000 tourists staying in three hotels in Taj Ganj. This suggests that 40 per cent of backpackers remain in India for longer than three months, which reflects the one-off nature of many of these trips and the preferred form of travelling over a longer period of time.

Backpackers are usually keen to emphasise the rationale behind the improvisational nature of their tour and to distinguish their mode of travel from that of package tourists:

> David *(26, writer, from Glasgow, UK, intends to travel on his own in India for six months)*: I didn't plan anything, I just came. It's a lesson because there's so many inconceivable things that just arise, it's not worth trying to organise something. It's the best way to see it or you just see what everybody else has seen. On a guided tour you miss so much of the atmosphere, only looking at the finer aspects. Certain things may not be pleasant to see but it's better to have a thorough picture than a selective one.

In fact, this 'improvisation' is usually negotiated through contact with other backpackers. Evenings in the hotels and restaurants of heterogeneous tourist space are spent comparing experiences and recommending sites as worthy of a visit. This backpacker lore surrounds such matters as what bargains are to be

Table 5.1 Duration of stay in India

Duration of stay	Percentage
1 month or less	18.5
2 months	18.5
3 months	23.0
4–5 months	11.5
6 months and longer	28.5

Source: Fieldwork 1993[2]

had, what good backpacker 'scenes' are to be found, where drugs, good *ashrams* and 'authentic' atmospheres are to be discovered, and where remarkable and unheralded sites exist:

> Nicola *(23, student, from Vancouver, Canada, intends to travel on her own for three months)*: I arrived here with no plan at all but I've met people and travelled with them for a while before going my own way. You hear stories and advice on where to go and what to see and I've travelled according to those suggestions, from place to place.

Backpackers are often extremely competitive concerning the 'authenticity' of their experiences, the extent to which they experience the 'real' India and meet the 'real' Indians, the bargains they procure, and other forms of cultural capital they acquire through charity work, drug taking or spiritual experience. In regard to constructing itineraries in India, almost all backpackers carry their own 'travel bible', *The Lonely Planet Travel Survival Kit* (Finlay et al., 1993), a volume of over 1,000 pages, furnishing details of what to see, where to stay, how to survive and where to go. The text recommends which places are most worthy of a visit, concentrating particularly upon the historical, natural and ethnic attractions, and manifesting an ambivalence that celebrates and reviles what are seen as anti-modern aspects. In this it is another heir to an Orientalist tradition in travel literature about India, albeit one with a greater sensitivity to, and sympathy with, Indian cultures.

Most backpacker itineraries are constructed in consultation with *The Lonely Planet* which, although it contains a vast amount of information covering a plethora of sights, is nevertheless a pre-selected menu from which to organise one's route. Although serving the flexible, DIY requirements of the backpacker approach to tourism, for some 'old hands' of backpacker tourism in India, *The Lonely Planet* is unacceptably constraining, and is spoken of with contempt:

> Trevor *(41, plasterer, from Bristol, spends half of his time working and saving so that he can travel the rest of the time, has been travelling around India since the sixties)*: You see them with their *Lonely Planet* and their toilet roll. I think they miss out by using the *Lonely Planet*. Everything in that book they follow. I prefer to go to out of the way places and just come across things and you always do come across things in India. When I do look at the *Lonely Planet*, I find that I have been to many of the places it mentions but only by stumbling across them.

Backpackers construct itineraries which usually incorporate some of the most famous tourist attractions but are rarely structured around such places. In emphasising the improvisational nature of their itineraries and distinguishing themselves from package tourists, many backpackers present a visit to the Taj as an afterthought. While not a central focus, there is often a desire to gaze at it because 'it is so famous', 'it's the number one sight in India' or 'you can't go to India without seeing the Taj', although it is rarely regarded as a highlight. Moreover, the greater amount of time available to backpackers means that their itineraries do not need to be organised around 'highlights', and a more contingent mode of travel can be facilitated. Accordingly, the range of places visited can expand to include those not normally identified as tourist spaces.

Despite their presentation as improvised and contingent, there are certain themes according to which backpackers structure itineraries that follow colonial, Orientalist assumptions. The search for mystical and religious experiences, strangeness and cheap drugs reconstructs India as an idealised space in which one can rediscover something of one's true self. These desires are articulated in accounts which identify the best narcotic high or the profoundest spiritual experience as the highlights of the trip:

> Eric *(24, casual labourer, from Edinburgh, UK, has been travelling around India for eight months with no immediate plans to return home)*: The Parvati Valley, that'd be my highlight. The best hash in the world, man, very nice stuff. I've been travelling for two years now and I don't need to carry anything extra around. All you need to get is some good hash. With all these hassles all the time, my supply from the Parvati Valley has kept me cool.
>
> Greg *(25, casual worker, from Christchurch, New Zealand, intends to travel for four months)*: Rishikesh was the spiritual highlight – very enlightening teachers. There were enough Westerners to make it normal, but not too many – whereas at Manali where everyone's trying to get more cheap drugs, it's like an English scene transplanted to India.

Greg also highlights the conditional encounter with 'otherness' which typifies many such adventures; normality is defined as Western and denoted by the comfortable presence of fellow white tourists. Yet as I have mentioned, the motivation for much backpacker travel is the quest for self-discovery, which relies upon this discursive construction of India as a space that will challenge received wisdom and shake up preconceptions:

> Gunther *(23, film technician, from Munich, Germany, intends to travel on his own for six weeks)*: I wanted to challenge myself before coming, this was my intention. It's my first journey alone and I wanted to see how I'd manage. I'm always looking for change.
>
> Stephanie *(21, student, from Adelaide, Australia, intends to travel with her friend for five weeks)*: The main reason for coming to India was to change myself in general, and change my perceptions and its certainly doing that.

The particular stage in the life-course of backpackers is crucial to this desire for self-transformation. Many are students travelling before starting work and travel in India represents a last chance to wander at leisure before the discipline necessitated by entering the world of work, often seen as synonymous with entry into full adulthood:

> Jem *(21, recently graduated from university, from Newcastle-upon-Tyne, UK, intends to travel with his partner for six months)*: I'm taking a year off after uni and I'm probably going to work with my Dad's firm when I get back. I guess this is the last chance to travel like this before I get tied down with responsibilities.

Besides students, there are other visitors at different stages of their lives who feel impelled to embark on their travels. These backpackers are often conscious of the temporary character of their 'freedom':

> Becky *(30, social worker, from Bristol, UK, travelling with her friend for 'as long as the money lasts')*: I've always wanted to visit India and I'm getting on and still have no mortgage, no husband, no kids, so now seemed a good time to do it.

This break from the predictable life of home and work may be inspired by a more momentous decision to leave what they were doing and travel to escape their routines:

> Jolene *(31, from San Francisco, has been travelling for five months across Asia and has no plans to stop)*: When I think about what I was doing before as a computer operator, it's too stifling. I worked for eight years – thank goodness I jacked it in. Growing up in a US city you have a limited perspective and coming here gives you a new perspective on life, opens up horizons. In America it's so isolated and ignorant. We don't get much world news. Here you meet a lot of Asian and European people and you realise there's a world out there.

Another group of backpackers are those who have been visiting India for many years. These backpackers usually manage to alternate periods of hard work with budget travel. Putting their 'career' as travellers into perspective, these older 'India hands' contextualise their early experiments with drugs and the quest for spiritual enlightenment by conceiving them as part of an initial stage in their relationship with the country:

> Trevor: You still get hordes of Westerners looking for the truth, for their spiritual master. I've been coming to India for twenty years now. Actually, at first I was into the drugs and the religion. But I never did

find my guru, my holy man. Being here was wild and strange and the drugs contributed to that. But I soon grew out of the drugs.

Other regular visitors have a long-standing mystical or spiritual relationship with the country:

Gordon *(Buddhist monk, see Chapter 4)*: I think I must have a streak of masochism because I keep coming back, something draws me back. I was called to India from childhood, I don't know why, but it called me. And it was here in 1970 that I stumbled across Buddhism and I had the strange feeling that I was coming home after a long time. So India's my spiritual homeland. But it's not the modern India, it's the ancient India.

These accounts also highlight the aforementioned traditions of the search for spiritual enlightenment and drug-related experiences. However, the most common reason for selecting India are to experience difference:

Mattheus *(22, student, from Austria, travelling on his own in India for six months)*: India for me, is a country with a lot of different extremes of culture and kinds of life. I think the attraction is mainly the fascination of the unfathomable. I came here to develop as a person, to learn, to see these differences.

This search for alterity is conjoined with the search for self-realisation:

Greg: I was feeling in need of a culture shock and India seems to be the place where there are so few parallels to the place I come from. It's like a total immersion in something different. I love how multifarious it is. It assaults your senses all the time. Coming from New Zealand, it's quite difficult to pinpoint what exactly is my culture and it's helped clarify for me what aspects of my own life I value.

The priorities of backpacker travel, the requirement for cheap basic accommodation and moderate tourist infrastructure, and the centrality of particular symbolic places on the typical itinerary have led to the development of specific forms of tourist space. *The Lonely Planet* provides a comprehensive listing of cheap accommodation in most areas tourists visit and backpackers tend to follow the recommendations. The evolution of a circuit of backpacker destinations has helped to produced the heterogeneous tourist space that I have described in Chapter 2.

The vast majority of backpackers visiting Agra stay in an old market area in the city, Taj Ganj, the quarter surrounding the Taj Mahal. Taj Ganj is an excellent example of heterogeneous tourist space, in which tourists can experience everyday local life and interact with locals. Taj Ganj provides a contrast to the order of the Agra Cantonment. The area is a mixture of domestic dwellings, public offices and commercial establishments, and shops, hotels and restaurants serving the tourist trade. The small shops and stalls typical of urban India are here: sweet shops, bookbinders, pharmacies, tailors, cassette vendors. The area is inhabited by a large proportion of both Hindu and Muslim residents and although particular streets or quarters tend to be occupied by one or the other, they live together in close proximity. Hindu–Muslim riots following the demolition of the Babri Masjid in Ayodhya resulted in several fatalities and there is still some tension in the quarter. There are both mosques and mandirs here. As well as the site for religious expression, political campaigns are mobilised. During the state elections of December 1993, there were loud marches, street rallies and sloganeering loudspeakers throughout the area. As everyday public space for locals, as well as tourist space, Taj Ganj contains schools, administrative buildings and the offices of political parties. Thus there are many children to be found in the area, who frequently pester tourists for money or small gifts.

In 1993, there were fourteen hotels in Taj Ganj, situated alongside other tourist enterprises, local shops and dwellings. These backpacker hotels provide 'budget accommodation', having cheap rates and 'basic', functional amenities, although there are degrees of comfort and cost. At the bottom end of the market there are dormitory rooms and at the top end there are a few en suite rooms. Decor is rudimentary and exacting standards of cleanliness and comfort are not observed. Most hotels also contain cafés which supplement the other eating houses in Taj Ganj. Service in both cafés and hotels is informal and typified by friendly exchanges between proprietors and waiters, and tourists. *The Lonely Planet* supplies information about these hotels, indeed serves as their major publicist. Some duly advertise this with signs which claim that they are 'Recommended by Lonely Planet' (see figure 5.1).

The hotels and restaurants provide the focal point of backpackers' recreational activities in the area. They are places where these tourists 'hang out', write their journals and postcards, read, chat and gaze at the street; meet each other, swap stories of their trip, share travel lore, and form new, often temporary alliances. Although there is a high degree of contact with locals, for most backpackers, association is predominantly with each other. The cafés of Taj Ganj are alive with these tourists, whose public presence in the area co-exists with groups of locals in other locations, principally on the street (see figure 5.2). Thus there are different but undemarcated spaces in which locals and backpackers socialise.

The food in the cafés provides food to satisfy local tastes but also makes concessions to Western preferences. The 'no-frills' service, crowded tables and basic menu suit budget requirements. One item served by most of these budget cafés is *bang lassi*, and cafés and hotels are also sites where backpackers may get drunk and stoned.

A curious feature of these backpacker haunts, and indeed many others in heterogeneous tourist space in India, is that the 'golden age' of hippie travel to

ENCLAVIC AND HETEROGENOUS TOURIST SPACES

Figure 5.1 Siddharta Hotel, Taj Ganj

the 'mystical East' is echoed in the soundscape of the area. Along with the ubiquitous Hindi film music, are the sounds of the sixties, often extremely scratched and warped by now, which play music by the Beatles, Jimi Hendrix, the Doors and the Rolling Stones. This adds counter-cultural allure to the romance of exploring the realm of the 'other' and historically locates the emergence of practices, aesthetics and desires that continue to inform much backpacker travel in India. The 'sixties' revalorisation of the mystic East drew on colonial representations but recast India in a more positive light. The great exodus of Western youth to India and the establishment of hippy centres, or what are commonly known by Indians as 'freak centres', dates from this time.

Small shops trading in marble products and other crafts are concentrated along the main roads of Taj Ganj but operate alongside the shops serving the

ENCLAVIC AND HETEROGENOUS TOURIST SPACES

Figure 5.2 Treat Restaurant, Taj Ganj

local population. For many backpackers, the attractions of buying are not paramount although they are usually tempted into buying some items to take home. The traders habitually attempt to catch the passing tourists' attention and lure them into their shop. Most backpackers find this initially intimidating but soon become adept at ignoring the appeals or feel comfortable about entering the shop and haggling with the trader. Besides this, unofficial guides and rickshaw drivers tout for custom so there is little chance of passing through Taj Ganj without being accosted.

Most backpackers at some stage do venture into craft shops and the interaction with the trader cannot simply be reduced to that of a commercial relationship, although the trader's aim is primarily to sell. Discussions about many subjects often take place over a cup of tea and tourists staying in the area for a few days will, upon passing the shop again, frequently pop in for a chat. The relationship between buyer and seller is not as contractual and delimited as in the West but allows for wider communicative expression, producing the sensual and congenial etiquette of barter in a convivial setting.

Seeking a spiritual purity and espousing post-materialist values, many backpackers conceive of their journey as being a partial renunciation of consumption and subsequently they can become frustrated at the nature of the relationships established between themselves and locals:

> Gary *(26, former clerical worker, from Montreal, Canada, intends to travel with his partner for three months)*: In Agra, it's hard to meet Indians because you always get approached by one whose brother has a shop; or they want to sell you something. Though every now and then you meet one who will show you around and be open towards you.

The idealised, uncommercial space that tourists imagine evaporates in confronting the brute reality of local economic need for tourist money. As one of the centres of tourism in India, a throng of guides, traders and touts compete for the scraps that backpackers might offer and many tourists comment on the difference between Agra and other places they have visited:

> Liz *(29, nurse, from Cardiff, intends to travel on her own for two months)*: In Agra, it makes you a little bit sad because you want to have contact with people but they think you are a walking dollar note, which is very hard sometimes.

While the budget hotels and the company of other backpackers provides some refuge from the touts, most tourists are doggedly pursued. Many backpackers only initially find this frustrating and worrying, and gradually adapt, suggesting that there is an early stage of the holiday during which the tourist becomes mentally and practically acclimatised to the new environment:

> Greg: There's so many things that drive you crazy but you just know you can't be impatient. I've met so many travellers who have got so het up about the hassle and you think, hang on, that'll get them nowhere. You just have to go with India although it takes a while to sink in.

The necessity for the tourist to haggle creates a form of interaction that involves both participants in mock anger, disbelief and reasonableness amongst other theatrical expressions and postures. To an extent, this draws the tourist into a local world which denies social distance and instigates a level of social performance which many tourists come to enjoy:

Clive *(30, 'jack of all trades', from Wellington, New Zealand, has been travelling for four months and does not know how long he will stay in India)*: It's an adventure, having to fight your way everywhere, especially in Agra. At times, it gets me down but mostly, it's just a laugh, you know, you join in. You've just got to accept it and adapt.

Backpackers use motor and cycle rickshaws as a means of transport and this means that they are forced into negotiating about the cost of the journey and are subject to 'hassle' from those operators touring for business. Such travails are part and parcel of the experience of backpackers but several commented that 'hassle' was particularly fierce in Agra where there is a great deal of competition between rickshaw drivers for the small number of potential Western passengers. Most rickshaw operators attempt to persuade their Western passengers to visit one of the larger emporia where they have a understanding with the proprietor that a small reward will be paid if they convey tourists to the premises, to be supplemented by commission in the event of the tourist buying anything. Most tourists have to withstand the insistent promptings of the driver to 'just have a look, no need to buy' and most demur at the opportunity. Because those backpackers who do buy are unlikely to make a costly purchase, the pickings of the operator are slim unless they strike lucky. However, the opportunity to supplement their small income cannot be overlooked.

The ambition of the rickshaw driver is to take the tourist on a day tour around the sights of Agra and much energy is expended in pressurising the tourist to agree to this. To this end, many operators acquire the photographs and written statements of previously satisfied customers who fulsomely recommend the 'day tour'. If this strategy is successful, the rickshaw driver has a 'captive' passenger who is more likely to agree to visit emporia and eat at the restaurants suggested by the guide/driver. However, most backpackers decline this offer since, in general, they avoid control over their experience of time and space.

Besides this dramaturgical ritual involved in declaiming the excellence of their service, most rickshaw drivers are not afraid to give voice to their opinions about politics, rich tourists and businessmen as they pedal or drive their passengers around. Moreover, the cycle rickshaw particularly precludes transported isolation from the smells, sounds and people of Agra, and does not facilitate swift passage. This contributes to the sensual and communicative interchange.

Although some backpackers are thoroughly disturbed by the hassle, most develop strategies to minimise the annoyance they often feel. Given their strong imperatives towards self-development, after relecting upon the cultural differences they face, they often philosophically compare conditions in their native country:

Margaret *(22, student, from Glasgow, UK, intends to travel with two friends for three months)*: I think you become ruder and harder here but that will go when I return home. You have to become more patient. When I go home I won't shout at a five minute queue in a railway station!

Karl *(see chapter 4)*: In Agra, a lot of people chase you to sell you things. I've got used to it a bit, and you try to ignore them as people, but that's not my way. But it can make you more straightforward. In Europe, people try to take advantage of you in more subtle ways. There's a lot of double-talk and hypocrisy. Perhaps if a little bit of this 'civilisation' was to vanish, it would be a good thing.

This adaptive disposition also manifests itself in the way many backpackers assess the unfamiliar approaches to the management of time in everyday life, again questioning the normativity of conventions back home:

Bob *(27, trainee solicitor, from Devon, UK, intends to travel for one month)*: People here are more relaxed, they have more time. It's another way of thinking completely. In Europe, there's one common sentence, 'I've no time'. But in India, this is a sentence you hardly ever hear. If you open your mind to the Indian way you will see that this is stupid. Of course you have time!

The same can be said insofar as backpackers confront situations where unaccustomed spatial conventions are experienced:

Debbie *(23, recently graduated from university, from Bristol, UK, intends to travel for four months with her partner)*: Things that are a big problem in Europe are no problem here. For example, if there are twenty people on the back of a truck, all squashed together, nobody minds at all, and nobody complains.

Brian *(32, ex-teacher, from Dundee, has 'no idea' how long he will travel around India)*: I was shocked that you have no private sphere about you, but it's not so horrible once you get used to it. People come up and talk to you, and they touch you, and ask you very personal things. But it's not intrusive really, it's just different.

What this highlights is that a willingness to abandon normal spatio-temporal conventions puts tourists in unfamiliar situations to which they must adapt.

The roads in Taj Ganj have no clear pavements, are unmetalled and strewn with potholes and refuse. Various forms of transport – bullock-carts, auto and cycle-rickshaws, horse-carts, cycles, scooters, motorbikes, and other vehicular contraptions – occupy the same arteries as pedestrians, creating a choreography of contingent manoeuvres and evasions. Furthermore, a profusion of animals including buffaloes, cows, monkeys, dogs, cats, pigs, rats and donkeys also share the road space, with large numbers of pedestrians along some stretches. Tourists proceeding on foot through the streets of Taj Ganj must be alert to obstructions and hazards, other people and animals, to the danger caused by traffic, and to the attempts of traders and beggars to attract their attention. Walking here is an activity which is continually subject to disruption and is at odds with the ordered choreographies played out in enclavic tourist space. Moreover, the physical manoeuvres required to elude impediments and hazards, together with the blasts of heat from furnaces and cafés, the inevitable collisions with people and animals, and the irregular surface of roads create particularly interesting geographies of touch and physical sensation.

As well as providing social diversity and contact, Taj Ganj also contains rich sensual elements; visual stimuli, soundscapes, smellscapes and touch experiences are at variance to those in the controlled acres of Agra Cantonment. I have emphasised the visual unpredictability that the proliferation of practices and actors in such spaces present to the passer-by. In Taj Ganj, a wide range of activities is carried out. As a place of residence, a host of domestic tasks are performed by the inhabitants, including washing, collecting water, cooking, childcare, cleaning clothes and hanging them up, and the streets are also a gregarious space where friends meet, neighbours exchange gossip and chat, and individuals and groups dally. There are particular meeting points, such as around water outlets, the *tonga*[3] stand and in cafés. A diversity of passers-by travel through Taj Ganj; travelling salesmen, hawkers, mendicants, preachers, puppeteers, bands of musicians, political orators and saddhus, who supplement the presence of inhabitants, workers and schoolchildren. The streets are also often the location for more collective pursuits such as religious processions, *hartals*,[4] *bandhs*,[5] and political demonstrations. Besides providing a huge playground for children, the street is frequently the location for groups of children and adults playing chess, cards, *karam*[6] and cricket. Besides the tourist establishments, there are a profusion of workplaces where work activities spill out onto the street or where there is no apparent 'backstage', such as engineers, smiths, potters, bookbinders, metal workers. Many services actually ply their trade on the street itself as dentists, fortune-tellers, shoe-shiners, barbers, letter-writers, shoe repairers, bicycle fixers and tea-wallahs attend to the needs of local people.

The sheer diversity of street scenes and the juxtaposition of unfamiliar and familiar elements provide numerous spectacles for onlookers. Residents of Taj Ganj claim to enjoy this form of entertainment – 'just sitting and watching' as they call it – and likewise, many backpackers remark upon their enjoyment of experiencing street scenes as they shared a pot of tea with a trader or sat in a café. One said:

> David: One of the things I love here is that you can just sit and watch the world go by. Nobody's going to say 'move on now'. And there's always something to look at. Look – a camel might go past or a bunch

of Saddhus. There's nothing that's similar in shape, size or form. The diversity is amazing.

In addition to this rich visual panoply, the smellscapes and soundscapes of Taj Ganj are also multi-faceted. The rich fragrance of cafés and sweetstalls mingle with the scented wafts of incense and the more mundane aromas of dung, sewers, sweat and buffaloes. Loudspeakers diversely broadcast current attractions at the cinema, political speeches, or the call to prayer of the muezzins at the local mosques. Travelling street players perform their music, often competing with horns and traffic, animal and bird noises, the shouting of hawkers and loud conversations and arguments, and the soundtrack to the area is provided by the Indian film music emanating from cassette outlets and the 'sounds of 60s' mentioned above. This impressive array of sounds prompted one tourist to remark:

> Derek *(20, student, from London, intends to travel for five weeks)*: Britain's going to seem so dead when I get back. Quiet and boring. Everybody in their houses, and no life on the streets. The only noise you will hear is the rumble of traffic.

The exploration of Taj Ganj by backpackers is often supplemented by wandering around other areas in Agra that are not necessarily constructed for tourists. Kinari Bazaar or the plusher shopping offered at Sardar Bazaar are popular destinations for backpackers although they are apt to 'just wander about' wherever takes their fancy or spend most of their time 'hanging around' the cafés. Conversely, Agra Cantonment is not the sort of space where wandering is rewarding since its long straight roads, landscaped order, lack of pedestrians and roadside cafés and shops delimit the possibility of meeting the unexpected. The range of sights available to backpackers is thus extended:

> Jem: Well of course we've seen the Taj but we've rather enjoyed going round the bazaars. There are other things you can see. Like today we saw the prostitutes shouting out to the men in Kinari bazaar, and all the wee shops and the ordinary buildings, a woman breastfeeding her baby – and that's beautiful as well.

Their excursions through heterogeneous tourist space as well as non-tourist local space supplies backpackers with oblique observations and interesting insights. In summing up their experiences, the most common thread is to remark upon the difference and diversity of the country:

> Michael *(39, strategic consultant, from Melbourne, Australia, travelling in India with his friend for one month)*: It's a shimmering place, all unreal in a way, the holy and the profane next to each other. The sheer amount of

difference — every face, every personality is different. Every day is a different experience. What you experience is all down to chance. There's so many contrasts amongst the people, whereas in Europe you don't get this variety.

Stephanie: You can see anything in India. My impression of India has been the variety. Everything's been different in every town and village that we've visited. You never know what's going to happen or what you're going to see next.

This apparent sheer diversity often overwhelms backpackers and makes it difficult for them to feel they have 'captured' or understood India since the sights and sounds they experience seem bewildering in their variety and are apt to break down conceptual categories:

David *(26, psychologist, from Christchurch, New Zealand, travelling on his own in India for two months)*: I guess my impressions of India are really hard to put into words, it's a land of such contrasts and contradictions. It assaults your senses all the time — the colours, the smells, the tastes, the sights. It's all so different. And underpinning all that, the whole religious, cultural and historical foundations are really quite mind-boggling, impossible to get your head round in three months. But I love how multifarious it is. Each city and state is so different and every place has got its own stories, its own history.

Besides abundance and experiential richness being a narrative trope of travel accounts, this experience of diversity is also partly a consequence of the tour not being over-determined by thematic design, by imperatives to visit particular sites and by rigid spatial and temporal regulation. By wandering, visiting places with no obvious attraction, and by spending lots of time watching and talking, a variety of experiences emerge.

The importance of encountering 'strangeness' is allied to the desire to meet Indians on their own terrain. The possibility for backpackers to become acquainted with locals at more than an economic level is realised by many, especially when they choose to relax in one place for a while rather than constantly travelling. One woman who had stayed in Agra for a while said:

Sandra *(29, office administrator, from Dublin, has been travelling on her own for eighteen months)*: It's good to stay somewhere rather than dashing from place to place. I've been here a few days and being on my own, I've got to know everybody round here. And people have been really good to me. I've only been once to the Taj while I've been here. I've been travelling so much, I'd just rather sit and chat.

Others have surprising and enjoyable experiences:

> Pascale *(28, radio journalist, from Liège, Belgium, travelling in India on her own for one month)*: Yesterday, I met a nine-year-old boy and I spent the afternoon walking round Agra with him, and he showed me all sorts of interesting things. I went to his house and met his family, and had tea and it was really fun.

These encounters with locals in Taj Ganj indicate the wider context of backpacker travel in India. The disposition to travel on local buses, shop in ordinary shops and generally move around in non-enclavic space means that the urge to meet locals can readily be met:

> Gunther: You can't help meeting people. I spent a few days with a real family in Rajasthan – not one employed to put up tourists. People spend time with you here, are so kind and friendly. In Germany it's so different, but here, after two minutes talking to someone, you are in their house, being treated like a god.

The urge of many backpackers to get off the 'beaten track' leads them into encounters with others which although interpreted from a particular cultural position, nevertheless, can be unpredictable and rich experiences. Rather than the famous sites, the most common response was to cite the people or more mundane social aspects as highlights of their trip, which is partly an attempt to acquire a distinct form of cultural capital:

> Gary: In Agra, the local people have been the highlight for me. The Taj seems to me to be a typical tourist site, the kind of building people visit if they are European sightseers. But I'm not very interested in going to such sites and looking at buildings.

An interesting aspect of these local–tourist interactions in Taj Ganj is the participation of local young men who are attracted by the allure of the 'modern' as embodied in the Western backpackers. In a sense, these locals often serve as cultural interpreters, negotiating local meanings with those of the tourists. The common themes in the fascination of these local youths with the Western 'other' that emerged when I witnessed such encounters were pre-marital sex and drug consumption which contrast with 'traditional' domestic attitudes. Thus there seemed to be much curious discussion around issues of sexuality, pleasure, responsibility and drugs in such exchanges.

On the other hand, local men (for this is a highly gendered exchange) in Taj Ganj acknowledge the economic benefits the tourists bring but also stress that they enjoy chatting to the tourists, finding out about their country and sharing ideas. However, there is a strong thread of anxiety concerning the impact of

'Western ways' upon the youth of the quarter, around the same issues of sex and drugs as corrupting factors:

> Pawal *(25, jeweller)*: The tourists are marvellous for the city. We would not have such business if they did not come, and we can also learn a lot from them; their different ways and ideas. One thing though, we are worried about these drugs they bring in – not most of them, we know – but some of our young people have become addicted to heroin. And AIDS too, their view of sex is different.

The construction and experience of 'India' by Western package tourists and backpackers emerges out of different colonial narratives and representations of the 'other'. Package tourists have a particular itinerary shaped for them which pre-selects sites deemed most worthy and representative of India. The package tour imperatives to restrict movement and exploration in non-enclavic space help to confirm the negative 'Third World' stereotypes that persist in the Western media, since part of the strategy to control visitors includes the fostering of fear at what could happen outside the enclave. The short glimpses of what appear to be poverty, squalor and chaos during air-conditioned journeys feed into this disquietude and sustain old colonial notions of deficiency in responsibility and self-help, 'civilised' standards, a lack of 'advancement' and discipline. Thus the space of India, whilst romantic in terms of its past majesty and glamour, is widely perceived as the space of the absolute 'other', chaotic, disorienting and dangerous.

Backpackers also construct India as a realm of 'otherness' but here it is rather more positively evaluated as the land of mysticism, wisdom and authenticity. Crucially, in its contrast with Western space, it provides a realm in which the Western individual, denuded of spirituality, natural impulses and humanity can rediscover these attributes and change. Offering a spatial and temporal freedom to wander, to temporarily dwell, unhindered by the usual constraints, India promises self-discovery and enlightenment. The construction of non-Western space as a playground for the fantasies and desires of Western travellers emerged during colonialism. These discursive formations have taken a peculiar turn wherein Western youth celebrate the mysticism, drugs and knowledge awaiting discovery.

I have suggested that contemporary Western urges to experience unpredictability can be explored in heterogeneous spaces such as Taj Ganj where experimental identifications may be sought, and sensual experiences realised. By strolling through such realms, backpackers may be akin to the early modern flaneur. The random juxtapositions that so stimulated Baudelaire's hero, and movement 'in the ebb and flow, the bustle, the fleeting and the infinite' (Baudelaire, 1972, 399) can be experienced here. Moreover, the freedom to loiter, the 'reprieve from time' (Bauman, 1994, 140) which permits pedestrians to witness the momentary passing scenes is a resource available to most backpackers who move through this space.

Indian space is shaped by itineraries which includes particular sites where there is held to be a drug, rave or religious 'scene', and undeniably is characterised by its apparent authenticity and self-revealing properties. Yet these romantic conceptions at least open up the possibility of their own deconstruction by emphasising movement towards self-discovery and a reflexive approach to the 'other'.

By contrast, the tourists who dwell in the purified tourist space of Agra Cantonment find their encapsulation and directedness frustrating but a combination of their prejudices and the controlling strategies of tour personnel restricts their movement outside the enclave. The tour's concentration on historic specimens of architecture, and the theming of the environments they stay in, limits the scope for experimentation and exploration. Instead, simulacra of India cater for their desire to experience the 'other'. Rebellious urges and 'post-tourist' ironic performances generally occur within the temporal and spatial confines of the schedule and the enclave, yet when these are escaped, the subsequent encounters with a less-regulated space can be thrilling. However, the regulation of locals in Agra Cantonment means that interaction with Indians other than tour employees is rarely more than cursory. The performances of package tourists at the Taj discussed in the previous chapter are similarly rather controlled in the enclave.

However, in heterogeneous tourist space of Taj Ganj, the proliferation of sights, smells and sounds, the movement and interaction of diverse people, animals and forms of transport, the potential for chance visions and 'marvellous encounters', and the juxtaposition of pleasure and danger, provide a space which cannot be packaged. Tourists' modes of walking, consuming and gazing are shaped by contingency and negotiation. Memories cannot be pre-arranged but perceptual memories, aroused by smells and atmospheres, can be provoked. Narratives are ephemeral and disconnected. The experiential approach of backpackers is capacitated in Taj Ganj, and is fuelled by their more dialogic relationship with locals, who often interrupt assumptions and confront prejudices.

Both the itineraries of package tourists and backpackers are largely designed according to particular priorities. Although differently constructed, these distinct strategies by which India can be consumed, and cultural capital can be attained through the acquisition of knowledge, experience, artefacts and memories, are predicated on persistent Orientalist tropes. Likewise, I have shown how the conventions of travel performance and techniques of representation by both groups follow consistent patterns. There are backpacker technologies and practices which are as common-sense in their application as the more directed enactions of package tourists. Both groups experience frustration about the restrictions imposed by their modes of travel. Backpackers bemoan the commercialisation of particular spaces and particularly lament that the commercial concerns of locals come between them and their search for an untainted, authentic 'other'. Package tourists complain about the restrictions placed on their movements by tour guides, the unrepresentative architectural and historical version of India they consume, the homogeneity of the enclaves they stay in, the undisguised schemes to part them from their money, and the hard work that is entailed in consuming places. And as I have shown, they also evoke particular negative views about India based on fears about disease, disorder and hassle. Yet I want to insist upon the difference that temporal and spatial independence makes to the kinds of influences and encounters that tourists experience. The efficacy of stage managers, directors and choreographers in the tourist enclaves exerts a more profound form of control. More importantly, I maintain that the spatial distinctiveness of heterogeneous tourist space, its material and social form, offers at least the potential to engage with an unrepresentable form of 'otherness', an other that cannot be drawn back into colonial discourse.

Notes

1 This information was collected from the visitor books of the Gulshan Lodge, the India Guest House and Jehangir Guest House and the Uttar Pradesh Tourist Office respectively.
2 These figures were compiled from the visitor books of the Gulshan Lodge, the India Guest House and Jehangir Guest House, which are hotels used almost exclusively by Western backpackers.
3 Horse-drawn carriages.
4 Strikes and lock-outs.
5 Close-downs and boycotts.
6 A board game; the closest British equivalent would be shove-ha'penny.

6

TOURIST PLANS FOR AGRA AND THE TAJ

In the previous chapter, I identified two distinct forms of tourist space in Agra and suggested that they differently constrain and enable tourist experiences, meanings and performances. The enclavic tourist space of Agra Cantonment has been superimposed upon a previously colonial space which also served an enclavic function. The maintenance and development of this enclave has gained momentum in recent years with an increase in the number of hotels, large emporia and restaurants being constructed. This testifies to an increase in package tourists coming to and staying in Agra. However, in Taj Ganj, tourist development has not been so spectacular. In fact, the smaller tourist enterprises which principally serve backpackers are, in many cases, operating closer to the margins of viability, according to their owners. In this chapter, I will assess some of the effects of these developments and investigate the proposals for further developing tourism in Agra and the consequences that may follow if these projects are realised. Of course, the Taj is deeply implicated in these proposed schemes, and is at the centre of suggestions to maximise tourist revenue and 'improve' tourist infrastructure. In order to identify the ongoing processes whereby tourist spaces are being produced, I will refer to themes examined in previous chapters: different regimes of spatial regulation, contestation over the representation and meaning of tourist places, and the conditions in which particular tourist practices and performances take place.

However, what I particularly wish to focus on is the ways in which the various plans mooted for tourist development reflect globalising Western conceptions about the production of tourist space and conservation. In the colonial era, as I have shown, the significance of the Taj was classified and described by Orientalist discourses which widely transmitted a set of notions which have proved remarkably stubborn and persist in the normative narratives of Western tourism. As an internationally renowned tourist site, the Taj is also subject to other global discourses around the theme of conservation and ways of producing tourist space. These notions are wielded by Western commentators and politicians and translated by local authorities into policies. These contemporary spatialising discourses in which the Taj is identified (by Western commentators and administrators) as a site for which the whole world is responsible, seem to incorporate the Taj in a global yet neo-colonial space.

As the economic and political power of the prestigious and successful businesses in Agra Cantonment increase with this growth in organised tourism, these proposed and ongoing developments also promote an unequal struggle over space. To examine these processes, I will consider the relationship between the contrasting tourist spaces of enclavic Agra Cantonment and Taj Ganj. These two distinct spaces constitute a dual tourist economy. They are interlinked in several ways, but their economies can be identified by distinct systems of production, consumption, circulation and exchange. Besides these economic distinctions, contesting commercial practices and strategies aimed at different tourists give rise to conflicts over the use and control of tourist space. I will exemplify this duality by looking at the role of the commission system in each sector. I will follow this by examining the influence of the global meta-narrative of conservation upon Agra and the Taj, and will then investigate the plans for developing tourism, notably schemes which aim to extend theming and the production of simulacra to produce a tourist 'experience'. I will conclude by revisiting processes of spatial regulation and the ways in which an intensified control over tourist space in Agra seems to be spreading.

Commission and the dual tourist economy

The commission system, the paying of a percentage of completed sales to agents who deliver purchasing tourists to service and retail enterprises, operates in all sectors of tourist activity in Agra. Indeed, the *Lonely Planet* asserts that, 'of all the cities in India, Agra is the city most seriously entangled in the nefarious activity of giving commission' (Finlay, 1993, 337). An examination of the role of commission and the contrasting strategies between those who work in Taj Ganj and Agra Cantonment highlights huge differences in political and economic power.

It is difficult to get people working in the enclavic tourist space of Agra Cantonment to be candid about the system of commission although they do not deny it exists. This is because they feel that the commission system has brought Agra a certain notoriety for exploiting tourists and they are unwilling to confirm its extent. However, rates diverge widely according to the size of the business paying commission and the power of those asking for commission, instantiating a dual economy wherein, for example, the poorest transport workers earn a small fraction of those who serve wealthier tourists.

The cycle-rickshaw wallahs, as the lowliest and poorest of those involved in this chain of commission, are very willing to discuss what they regard as its inequities. Lal, an old rickshaw operator, listed the differing rates of commission received by those who convey tourists into the large emporia. Allegedly, if tourists complete a purchase, the different transporters conventionally receive the following percentage of the price paid: cycle-rickshaw wallah – 2 per cent; auto-rickshaw driver – 5 per cent; taxi driver – 10 per cent; coach driver and party guide – 10 per cent each.

The great increase in the size and number of large emporia in Agra Cantonment over the past decade has severely affected middle-range traders and small sellers of crafts. Since the big businesses can afford to pay higher rates of commission due to their economies of scale, they attract many more tour parties than these smaller enterprises, having established commission arrangements with tour companies and transporters. The smaller concerns increasingly rely on unchaperoned parties and individuals, tourists who are likely to be less shopping oriented and have smaller disposable incomes than package tourists.

The emergence of a vicious cycle whereby the larger emporia continue to prosper at the expense of the smaller could only be broken by a change in these commission arrangements. Although many successful entrepreneurs disingenuously complain about the extent to which they are 'ripped off' by those charging commission, the system ensures that they have a large and steady flow of customers, and has led to the polarisation of the tourist economy which they increasingly monopolise. The numerous small workshops and shops of Taj Ganj competing for the less lucrative custom of the backpackers and independent travellers remain impoverished, and due to the competition for this small slice of the tourist pie, the area is full of touts pressurising tourists to enter their shops. In contrast, the physical infrastructure of the wealthy outlets and their environs are being progressively upgraded, regulated and enlarged. Whereas there were previously a greater number of independent craft producers in Agra, and correspondingly far fewer large emporia, the larger outlets increasingly contract out work from these small producers, who are reduced to selling work to retailers rather than directly to tourists. Power over prices, distribution and commission therefore propagates in the hands of these large entrepreneurs.

This economic power is reinforced by regulatory policies. I have mentioned how tour personnel dissuade tourists from venturing into areas outside the enclave by promoting fears about hassle and violence, and the ways in which they prohibit small producers and providers of services from setting up stalls in the enclave. This is further reinforced by the registering of selected rickshaw-drivers and guides who are permitted to work in the enclave. This limiting of the right to earn restricts them – along with tea-stalls and small retail outlets selling cheap items as films, sweets and cigarettes – to Taj Ganj and other informal tourist areas. Additionally, these restrictions enable the large enterprises in the enclave to charge high prices without the threat of any competition from these smaller businesses. In the following sections, I will examine further ways in which these large enterprises, by forming a cartel, have developed strategies by which the businesses and environment of Taj Ganj have been further regulated.

The global conservation ethic: the Taj Mahal as a World Heritage Site

I have discussed the way that the Taj came to be seen as the pre-eminent symbol of India and the monument most worthy of preservation during the colonial era. Informed by a classifying mentality, writers on the Taj compared and hierarchically ranked it with other global attractions. Although this discourse and classifying process emerged in colonial times, it has progressively become more globalised. The reification of famous sites continues apace with the proliferation of markers around them, and their widespread use as metaphors and synecdoches by the ever-expanding tourist industry.

Another layer of meaning, reinscribing the Taj as of especial global worth, has been added by its inclusion on UNESCO's World Cultural and Heritage List, instituted in 1972, which establishes that certain sites (presently 378) are of 'universal value' and require international co-operation for their preservation. The adding of another layer of official classification is complemented by much tourist literature which feeds upon these selections, usually suggesting that these 'super attractions' be incorporated into itineraries (for instance, see Jouclas, 1993).

Accompanying this reinscription, and this is notably the case with the Taj's designation as a World Heritage Site, has been an increasingly global and globalising concern with conservation which is articulated at global and national level. As India's Supreme Court declared in its judgment ordering the closure of local factories which are allegedly destroying the Taj through air pollution, 'Heritage cannot be sacrificed. Nor compromised' (Baweja, 1993).

Apparently, the previously milky white complexion of the Taj Mahal has turned partially yellow over the past two decades, signalling the increased threat to the monument from air pollution. There are several purported causes of pollution, notably local industries, the oil refinery at nearby Mathura, glass manufacturers at Firozabad and local vehicular traffic (Baweja, 1993).

There have been several moves to minimise these threats. Some 212 local iron foundries which neglected to install pollution control measures were closed down by order of the Supreme Court in 1993 and further closures were subsequently enforced in Firozabad. Likewise, the refinery was ordered to install pollution control equipment upon threat of a similar penalty. Moreover, it is planned to create a trapezium by planting 100,000 trees to create a green belt around the Taj of 10,400 square kilometres (d'Arcy, 1995) and a ring road is being built around the city to minimise the pollution from car exhausts. In addition, an order from Agra Development Authority ordains the minimisation of damage from polluting electric generators which are frequently started up when Agra's notorious electricity supply fails, by insisting that industries and hotels which use such generators will have to use gas or else face closure. In terms of publicity, the local authority has established an extensive advertising campaign; appended to all billboards and plastered over minibuses is the slogan 'GREEN AGRA, CLEAN AGRA' (see figure 6.1).

TOURIST PLANS FOR AGRA AND THE TAJ

These strict measures have met with substantial resistance from sections of the population. Some owners of local factories forced to close have threatened to destroy the Taj. Estimates of the number of jobs lost range from 200,000 to 300,000 and local opposition to the cuts is considerable, even from those who earn their livelihood from the tourist industry. One young local guide highlighted the local despondency and challenged the hegemonic ideas of conservation:

> Ravi: It is the foreign pressure on our government that is stopping the development of industry in Agra – the IMF and that lot and powerful countries like UK and US. Their experts tell us Indians what is harming Taj and we just accept what they say. They close down all the factories and when a scooter factory was due to be opened in Agra it was not permitted. Where are people supposed to work? What can they do to stop the ageing of the Taj? Stop the wind? Stop the rain? They should put a big glass house around the Taj, that would preserve it.

The tourist industry, by far the largest sector of the local economy, is entirely dependent upon the allure of the Taj. However, these stringent preservation measures are strongly resented by unemployed previous employees and owners of these industries:

Figure 6.1 Green Agra, Clean Agra

> Surender *(42, chemist and inhabitant of Taj Ganj)*: It is terrible for the local economy that factories have been closed down because of concern about the pollution on the Taj. Tourism is not the only industry here. How far will they go? We are now worried that our houses, because they are in the area around the Taj, will be demolished to beautify it. This would be disastrous for us.

The pressure to preserve the Taj is growing and there are further campaigns to prohibit all potentially polluting industry within a circumference of 6,000 square miles. This potentially includes the Mathura refinery, which would lead to many more thousands of job losses, although there are plans by the India Oil Corporation to spend 200 million pounds sterling to cut back on emissions (d'Arcy, 1995). The Supreme Court has ordered the Environment Ministry to supervise the relocation of another 2,000-plus industrial units which are believed to be damaging the Taj (*The Daily Telegraph*, 14/8/95).

This imperative to ensure the survival of the Taj for all of humanity has been especially marked by considerable pressure from Western media. Writing about the decay of the Taj, Bernard Levin captures the neo-colonial sentiments of some Western conservationists in his complaints:

> India cannot hide behind the money and experts that will come to Agra. . . . For this catastrophe was not like an earthquake or a terrible explosion; it was caused by Indians who were too lazy, too indifferent, too wasteful, too ignorant to look after an unimaginably precious treasure . . . the rest of the world cannot leave the Taj to its fate, but must rally to its misfortune, because although India does not deserve the Taj, the world still does. . . . And if it is saved, there should be these words carved on a stone plaque just outside the Taj: 'India would have let it die: the rest of the world saved it'.
>
> (Levin, 1994)

Although notable for its implicit racism and neo-colonial arrogance, Levin also pompously espouses the Western conservationist ethos, the prioritising of which might seem a luxury for relatively impoverished countries such as India. In addition to Levin's campaign, the Indian actor Saeed Jaffrey fronted an impassioned half-hour television documentary on the UK's Channel Four entitled *An Open Letter to India* in which he pleaded for the Taj to be saved.[1] This coincided with a leading article in *The Times* on the same day which lamented that the Taj will soon 'look better in our picture-books than it does to the visitor's smarting eye'. It concludes that 'no-one will forgive the Indian Government if it fails to relocate the oil refinery, and if the Taj is allowed to rot beyond repair' (*The Times*, 2/5/95).

To conclude the programme, Jaffrey emotively manipulates Lear's oft-quoted comment about those who have seen the Taj:

> Henceforth, let the inhabitants of the world be divided into two classes: them who *saw* the Taj Mahal; and them who *never will* [my italics].

An Open Letter to India follows old narratives about the Taj. Adopting a reverential and mournful tone, the usual assemblage of venerable guidebook quotes and snatches of poetry are invoked by the narrator. The chief reason for the decline of the Taj is held to be 'official India's ignorance and depravity', a persistent colonial trope. A discourse emerges where 'development' and 'environmentalism' are considered to be in opposition. Jaffrey accuses the government and the World Bank of regarding environmentalism as 'one more obstacle on the road to development'. Whatever the merits of the argument, the discussion is marked by a significant romantic attachment to the idea of preserving an 'authentic India' in defiance of corrupting global processes. This seems to constitute something of a reworking of (post)imperialist nostalgia (Rosaldo, 1993) whereby the desire for authenticity is transferred onto non-Western culture and space, particularly through processes of tourism and ideas about 'heritage'. Thus the Taj becomes incorporated into a contemporary narrative of conservation and heritage, the assumptions and priorities of which are firmly located in the West, although significant strands of the discourse have been adopted by an Indian middle-class, as evinced by the assertions of bureaucrats and media commentators.

The imperative to conserve wildlife, buildings, artworks can partly be considered a form of contemporary imperialism, along with other globalising meta-notions such as 'democracy', 'human rights' and 'freedom'. Yet these abstract notions cannot be easily rejected by the Indian government since opposition would appear to fly in the face of 'world opinion' and the increasing discursive importance of 'heritage', as well as the significance of the tourist industry as a foreign-exchange earner. As Rojek has commented, the dispute over the Taj 'illustrates the collision between local, national and global citizenship rights in the management of some outstanding heritage sites' (Rojek, 1995, 74). Yet significantly, it is the Taj which continues to stand as a symbol of India and Indian heritage. The Western narratives and aesthetic interpretation detailed in Chapter 3 are reworked into this narrative of conservation ideals. It is the Taj rather than numerous other ancient attractions that is deemed worthy of preservation, and it retains its position in the global ranking of sites.

Plans for improving tourist infrastructure: information, theme parks and simulacra

There are nevertheless elaborate plans to develop the Taj and Agra as a tourist complex, to expand tourist space and extend control over it. Agra Heritage Project was set up in 1987, through the joint efforts of the Indian Department of Tourism and the US National Park Service, to set up an agenda for the development of tourism. An interim report has emerged out of research carried out by Roorkee University in India, in allegiance with American scholars, and is supplemented by a summary of research studies. The final report of this joint project will be submitted for implementation to the Indian Government in the near future.

A common complaint from local entrepreneurs and bureaucrats is that foreign tourists do not stay for very long in Agra. Their main source of anger is that the political and economic power of Delhi ensures that many visitors to the Taj arrive for a day trip from Delhi thus minimising their potential expenditure in Agra. Accordingly, the 'main objective' of the Agra Heritage Project is to extend the stay of tourists in Agra to increase revenue. Other aims include an intensified marketing of 'traditional' culture, 'the enhancement of tourist facilities' and the minimisation of pollution (*Agra Heritage Project Interim Report*, 1993, 1–2). A major thrust is to upgrade facilities to make the city more 'attractive' to tourists: to provide better accommodation and catering, superior guide services at monuments, and improved transport facilities.

Other specific recommendations of the report include an increase in tours that encompass Fatehpur Sikra and other local historical attractions to diversify the tourist base at Agra and extend visitors' length of stay (*AHP Interim Report*, 1993, 11). Further to this aim is also the suggestion that 'there should be an adequate variety of daily cultural shows' (ibid., 13). Clearly, a number of organised entertainments would fill in the gaps in the routines offered to tourists in the Cantonment enclave, supplementing the tourist package in Agra.

Personnel within Agra Development Authority place great stress on developing tourism along particular lines that are more in keeping with the proliferating centres of heritage tourism in the West. Summarising this approach, it is claimed that 'the tourism base of Agra needs considerable diversification from purely "sightseeing" to an "experience".' This will be created by fulfilling, 'the need to add significant elements of human interest and the interpretative explanation of the history and culture of the Moghul period to the overall tourism experience of Agra' (ibid., 15).

The provision of an 'experience' is an increasingly important strategy in tourism marketing (Craik, 1997, 114), and intensifies control over the tourist product. Rather than encouraging tourists to wander and gain their own impressions; the tight management of schedules and information will increasingly resemble an identifiable 'product'. There are specific propositions to provide this 'experience'. The report advises that a source of visitor dissatisfaction is the lack of availability of 'informational and explanatory signboards' and 'tourist information and assistance centres'. The creation of information centres is strongly advocated, one at the East Gate of the Taj where the Western package tourists are admitted. Besides these information services, it is also envisaged that theatrical 'sound and light' shows should be instituted at the major attractions. In the West, information increasingly mediates and shapes the tourist experience of place through the consumption of soundbites and potted histories.

Places are interpreted for the visitor, short narratives are imposed and exploration is directed. The saturation of place with information seems to reduce the potential for imaginative opportunities and reflexivity and diminish possibilities for acquaintance with alternative and local narratives of place. The experience of the Taj for tourists will increasingly become commodified if these measures are adopted.

In addition, there is an increasing tendency for managers to theme tourist space, and to produce simulations and simulacra. In line with the decision to prohibit construction within the orbit of the Taj, Agra Development Authority has also recently ensured that all buildings in the environs of the site are painted a brownish-red in keeping with the red sandstone of the Taj and its outlying structures. This attempt to recreate an 'authentic' design of Moghul times conspicuously introduces an element of theming into the area over which locals have no say and extends regulation over Taj Ganj. This environmental transformation has left many locals unconcerned, but bewildered at the imposition of aesthetic order on their surroundings.

Other plans aim to contribute to the production of a definable 'experience' for tourists to Agra by devising new craft fairs and cultural performances, and building a craft centre. Every February and March for three weeks, there is a festival – 'Taj Mahotsan' – which combines dance, musical displays and other elements of folklore, with stalls selling craft items. This takes place at Schilpgram, a purpose-built entertainment centre half a mile from the East Gate of the Taj, which is situated in a semi-rural area and thus untroubled by urban activities. This shopping experience, seemingly of a more 'authentic' nature than that experienced at the large emporia in Agra Cantonment, will effectively serve as a simulacra of a bazaar. In addition, there is also a proposal to build a craft centre underground which is intended to mimic a bazaar. Carefully controlling prices, design, and modes of selling, these sites will be created to satiate those tourists who would like to explore local bazaars but dare not.

Nevertheless, the conservationist ethos mentioned above is often mobilised to challenge the more playful simulated developments. For instance, it is planned to develop the area on the opposite side of the Jamuna River to where the Taj stands, the mythical site of the fabled 'black Taj'. Currently under excavation, the area was a garden known as Mehtab Bargh, from which local Agrans were able to view the Taj without entering the enclosed area. The garden was never fully developed by Shahjahan but is to be renovated and replanted, thereby further extending the reach of tourist space. This 100 hectares of land is already protected and no structures may be built there that interfere with the famed romantic silhouette of the mausoleum. Currently the haunt of goat herds, local children and dhobis, it has been suggested that it be developed as an area 'with distinct features and facilities' containing various gardens and greenhouses, a swimming pool, amphitheatre, art gallery, aviary, snake park and golf course (*AHP Interim Report*, 1993, 8–9). It is likely that like other proposals, it will be the object of debate, between those who wish to turn it into an entertainment centre and those who wish to renovate and conserve.

Another interesting scheme is to reconstitute the gardens of the Taj to approximate the design and appearance of the grounds in the Moghul era, which were 'densely planted with beds of flowers and and trees of different varieties, and must have had a greater sense of intimacy as well as greater colour' (Leoshko, 1989, 58). The gardening department of the Archaeological Survey of India adjacent to the site told me of their aspirations to landscape the Taj[2] so that rather than the uncluttered vista of today, where tourists are able to gaze upon the mausoleum from the moment they enter, they will gain but a few glimpses of the monument between gaps in the foliage of trees. It is argued, and this seems to be backed up by eighteenth and nineteenth century travel accounts and paintings and photographs of the Taj,[3] that the mausoleum was not designed to be exposed immediately but was to be revealed as visitors progressed towards it (this, of course, hints at the gendered sentiments surrounding the use of the metaphor of unveiling that I discussed earlier). This idea to restore the gardens to their original appearance is informed by notions of authenticity and a distinctive aesthetic which contests Westernised ideals about the desirability of uncluttered prospect. This redesign will, if realised, disable the enaction of a romantic gaze and reconfigure the spatial movements described in Chapter 4. Apparently, the gardens were replete with fruit trees which provided sustenance for the surrounding population. It is intended to replant fruit trees in the garden but staff are worried that they may provide a hiding place for local children and lovers, so concerns about effectively regulating the site may prevail.

A rather more spectacular proposal was that envisaging the creation of a nine-kilometre light rail transportation system, or alternatively, a chair-lift, to connect the Taj, the Fort, Itmad-ud-Daula and Mehtab Bargh. Whilst the report concedes that this will be expensive, it asserts that the benefits in reducing congestion and 'increasing transport convenience' for tourists would justify the cost. However, conservation bodies are likely to veto the plan on the grounds that it will impair the skyline and mar the view from the Taj.

Other planned simulated experiences have met a similar fate. It is proposed to create a weir on the Jamuna two kilometres downstream from the Taj to avoid seasonal low levels of water in the river so as to produce 'increased aesthetic beauty' at the Taj and the proposed park opposite. The river by the Taj will be pleasingly full. It has been proposed that this would enable two theme boats to ply the waters in front of the Taj. The two themes envisaged were designed to entertain domestic and foreign tourists respectively as they sailed down the river. The former was to be based around a commentary and dramaturgical re-enaction of the heroic deeds and actions of Lord Krishna, since his birthplace is traditionally believed to be at nearby Mathura. The latter was to be designed around the life and times of the Moghul Emperor Akbar, and similarly include simulations of events and culture from this period. In addition, it was proposed that there should be a ferry across the Jamuna connecting the Taj with the gardens upon which it was recommended that 'the tourists should be accorded Moghul style hospitality. The bearers should be dressed in Moghul styles' (*AHP Interim Report*, 1993, 9).

I have discussed above the ways in which there has been a long-standing tradition of gazing at the Taj at particular times of the day and night. The presumed danger of terrorism has resulted in entrance being denied after 7 p.m. and this has thwarted the desire to gaze at what are usually considered the most romantic conditions, during a full moon. It was recently proposed that special hidden lights ought to be set up to 'mimic the lunar glow as it moves across the sky from dawn to dusk' (*The Independent*, 29/12/94). Thus the moon could be simulated on each and every night of the year irrespective of the prevailing climatic conditions, thereby satisfying the tourist urge to romantically gaze. One tourist manager was reported to have said, 'In the future tourists will know that there will always be moonlight over the Taj whether it is cloudy or not' (Lees, 1995). It is difficult to assess what the response from Western tourists to this 'inauthentic' light might be. In any case, the project was scrapped because members of the Archaeological Survey of India believed the building's marble might be damaged and that it would be 'sacrilegious' to impose artificial light since unique moods correspond with the natural light at particular times (Bedi, 1995).

The plans for a ropeway, themed boats and simulated moonlight all foundered in the face of the conservationist ethics of the Archaeological Survey of India and elements within Agra Development Authority who insisted that such commercialised entertainments would tarnish the atmosphere and integrity of the Taj. The playing out of these debates around a notion of conservation informed by the notion of gazing upon the sublime and romantic, and the commercial objectives of creating simulated forms, are staged locally amongst business and administrative elites.

Yet if plans for theming the site do come to fruition, the area around the Taj will become ever more like a theme park with increasing regulation, simulacra, interpretative and informational overload, dramaturgical enactments and themed personnel and spaces. As Saeed Jaffrey contends in *An Open Letter to India*:

> Beyond the cash, the theme park idea has one main advantage for the government. It will prepare the ground for simulated antiquity, so when the Taj does finally collapse, they can just put up a very good likeness.

What is likely is that a proliferation of subsidiary attractions and services around the Taj will considerably alter the nature of this space and the experience of visitors. If we take literally the injunction that it should provide an 'experience' for tourists; a packaged and regular commodified collection of homogenised sensations and information, the potential for remembering, reflection and imagination will be reduced. The control, selection and packaging of experience and information would appear to reach its apotheosis, however, not in this physical transformation of the built environment, nor through the provision of themed experiences, information centres and heightened luxury but in its ultimate extension, the application of virtual reality to tourist ,attractions. This potential further shift into the hyperreal is appositely postulated by Rohan, who writes about the potential for virtual reality technology to conjure up an 'immersing, involving experience rivalling that of the real world':

> Affordable VR . . . opens up a host of more serious possibilities. . . . Increasingly realistic graphics will make the experience more vivid: imagine stepping from a virtual Hagia Sophia into a virtual Taj Mahal.
> (Rohan, 1994)

Regulating the Taj and Agra

Conservationist and commercial theming practices have impacted, and will continue to impact, upon the less-regulated areas of Agra as tourist space expands. Particularly affected thus far has been Taj Ganj, in which several regulatory initiatives have been imposed.

Firstly, a Supreme Court order in August 1996 supported a decree proposed by M.C. Mehta, a Delhi lawyer, who has been the guiding force behind many of these judgments, which states that no new constructions may be erected within 200 metres of the Taj Mahal's boundaries. This same document contains the sentence, 'We direct that all those who are occupying any part of land within 200m of the Taj Mahal shall be removed from that area by force, if necessary' (*Supreme Court Decision*, 9/8/96, 6). This caused great consternation amongst many inhabitants and entrepreneurs in Taj Ganj who regarded this as a direct threat to their livelihood. Petitions were organised and campaigners mobilised. In fact, the structures referred to concerned only what were termed 'encroachers', and this necessitated only the destruction of one uninhabited building. Nevertheless, this 'preservation' of a large part of the dynamic bazaar area of Taj Ganj restricts development by curbing any plans to physically expand businesses, and curtailing the opportunities of entrepreneurs who rely on those tourists who emerge from the monument to explore its immediate environs. Again, it is the smaller businesses which suffer as a result of this zeal for preservation.

This is further highlighted by the restrictions on the selling techniques practised by traders from Taj Ganj. There is a constant struggle over space around the Taj between the large economic interests generally located in the Cantonment area and the denizens and traders of Taj Ganj. The pressures from the local bureaucracy and the Agra Tourist Guild, which represents most of the large tourist commercial concerns, to regulate the activities of peddlers around the

Taj is a popular focus of concern within Taj Ganj. Recently, steps were taken to debar traders from working the large ornamental courtyard at the entrance to the Taj since it was considered that this would 'upset' package tourists who were waiting to enter the monument.

The Northern Gate of the courtyard leads directly out of the Taj complex to small craft shops. A central strategy of the traders here was to solicit for business inside the courtyard, attempting to lure Western package tourists into this part of Taj Ganj to sell their goods. Although only a few package tourists would venture into Taj Ganj, as the tourists with the greatest disposable income, they were a vital source of revenue to these traders. Now that the tourist police have forbidden the practice of 'hassling' tourists inside the courtyard, these small businesses are suffering economic hardship. This both reflects the desire of the large emporia and hotels to maximise their income at the expense of these small traders and the bureaucratic attempt to control particular spaces in accordance with a set of disciplinary ideals. One of these traders said to me in dismay, 'I think they want to turn Taj Ganj into a Cantonment area'.

This purification of the courtyard is further demonstrated by the excising of any retail practices. Inside the West Gate of this courtyard, various outlets representing a range of Indian states used to be installed in the chambers bordering the thoroughfare. Recently, these have been relocated to a complex some 400 yards away, again to preserve the atmosphere in the courtyard, and prevent the hustling of tourists. Formerly, their prime location ensured that these outlets survived, but with their removal to a more marginal area, their livelihood seems less assured.

Besides these specific measures, there are also plans to discipline tourist space in Agra as a whole, as well as adjoining areas, proposals which will have a considerable impact on the tourist experience of Agra and will reconstitute tourist space. An intensified regulation of space is proposed by the Report and the Summary of Research Studies of Agra Heritage Project. A central aim of the project is to create a

> clean environment for the tourist where there is free flow of traffic, a noise and air pollution free atmosphere, so the tourists will know the real beauty of the Taj as in bygone eras.
>
> (*AHP Interim Report*, 1993, 2)

To reconstitute spaces in accordance with these aims, it is deemed necessary to control traffic and the use of roads, the activities of informal and small tourist entrepreneurs, the behaviour of locals and the management of sites.

The proposals concentrate at length on the congestion and noise pollution caused by traffic. It is envisaged that the whole Agra traffic system be transformed. As well as supporting the ring road, it is advised that key arterial roads 'to and between attractions' should be improved by repairing, creating verges and pavements and lighting (*AHP Interim Report*, 1993, 14). Importantly, the rather chaotic traffic situation in Agra is only seen as a problem insofar as it impacts upon the tourist trade and thus the focus is restricted to further beautifying the roads between the Taj and Agra Cantonment. The emphasis on upgrading the roads *between attractions* seems to aim at the creation of pristine corridors to minimise visual disruption, and create an illusory spatial network of order.

Even more drastically, to alleviate traffic congestion, the study suggests that fourteen parking lots with 450 parking spaces should be created around Agra Fort and the Taj and that marble and transport companies should be relocated away from those areas contained within the national park (*AHP Summary of Research Studies*, 1993, 32). This reductive designation of the city as seen by tourists as purely a space containing and facilitating heritage tourism would remove the sights and sounds of Indian city life.

Furthermore, the report complains about the heterogeneity of the traffic; 'bicycles, rickshaws, three-wheeler scooters, two-wheeler scooters, cars, buses, trucks and pedestrians all vie for a piece of the road', as well as the added problem of 'the continual encroachment along the roadside by small shops, stalls, taxi and three wheeler stands' (*AHP Summary of Research Studies*, 1993, 21). It is suggested that this situation requires more intense regulation. I have described how in the tourist enclave of Agra Cantonment, local people, traffic and structures are tightly controlled. With the extension of these regulated spaces to incorporate more of Agra, possibly including areas of Taj Ganj, the construction of a larger organised tourist space will further minimise tourist encounters with the life of the city and marginalise heterogeneous tourist space. As routes between attractions become more seamlessly convenient and regulated, ordinary aspects of Indian life are further drained out of the tourist picture and removed from the attention of the tourist gaze.

To further emphasise this point, the report considers measures to curtail and regulate small entrepreneurs by alleging that the highest degree of dissatisfaction for tourists is with 'the presence of hawkers and peddlers' (*AHP Interim Report*, 1993, 12). In this, they support the contentions of another report on developing tourism in Agra by Kumar who reports that:

> several historic monuments are situated in the crowded areas of town. Immoral and antisocial elements are always sprawling there not to miss an opportunity for pickpocketing, eve-teasing[4] and other nefarious activities.
>
> (Kumar, 1991, 169)

The report recommends an increase in tourist police to minimise hassling and makes the impractical suggestion that touts and small traders 'should be licensed and assigned small kiosks some distance from the entrance to the monument' (*AHP Interim Report*, 1993, 13), a proposal that would again create a pristine and disciplined tourist space and also restrict the livelihood of those whose economic *modus operandi* involves touting for business.

Overall, the extraction of all extraneous elements out of the tourist environment that are considered distracting to the packaged tourist experience is conceived as desirable. A major problem identified for tourists visiting Agra is that noise and bustle 'reduces the possibility for calm enjoyment of the beautiful grounds and . . . monuments' (*AHP Summary of Research Studies*, 1993, 22).

As far as the grounds of the Taj are concerned, it is alleged that the major disturbance:

> results from the loud conversations between tourists and their guides, and even more so from the shouting of and between the guides and photographers. This report recommends that the guides and photographers be properly educated to respect the serenity and quiet in and around the monument.
>
> (*AHP Summary of Research Findings*, 1993, 24)

Moreover, there is a proposition to limit the number of entrants to best facilitate the 'calm enjoyment' advocated (*AHP Interim Report*, 1993, 14–15). In effect this has already been partly achieved by the cheapest price of admission now increased to 15 rupees, shortly to be raised to 20 rupees. This debars many Indians from the monument and most groups of villagers are now forced to arrange their visit for Friday, when the site remains free for everybody. Obviously, admissions will decrease although revenue is likely to multiply. This form of class discriminatory regulation effectively restricts admission to those able to afford it and is the cause of considerable resentment amongst locals who argue that entrance to a national monument should not be exclusive. The stage of the Taj will be transformed by this removal of poorer visitors and become a more purified space.

In order to further the aim of achieving a quiet atmosphere conducive to contemplative enjoyment, it is suggested that loudspeakers which play loud music around monuments should be removed to 'increase the serenity of the site'. This is not a proposal that is likely to be welcomed by the locals affected, for the soundscape of the typical Indian street is not usually controlled by noise abatement strictures, there being a widespread tolerance for music playing; indeed, Bollywood[5] soundtracks are a continuous aural feature. Tellingly, the report uses as evidence of noise pollution the fact that the volume in some areas is 'far above the level recommended by the US Federal Highways Administration' (*AHP Interim Report*, 1993, 2), thus importing a Western standard test to measure noise in a different environmental and cultural context. This highlights how notions of regulating public space, and particularly tourist space, are becoming disembedded from localities and Western, globalising standards are used to define and measure spatial 'quality'.

The importation of nineteenth-century Western imperatives that regard uninterrupted and contemplative gazing at romantic sights as the epitome of appropriate tourist practice is both an absorption of, and a response to, such tourist values. In order to achieve the standards that are imagined will best please Western tourists, a number of other 'modernising' measures are proposed which conflict with local customs and habits. For instance, a new electric crematorium has recently opened in Agra and it is hoped that this will prevent the discharge of incompletely burnt bodies into the Jamuna, which are apt to float past the Taj, disrupting the romantic tourist gaze. It seems unlikely that many locals will readily change their funerary customs of burning the deceased on pyres. Also, the custom of defecating in the open by the river is to be challenged by the provision of 80 community toilets. Again, it seems unlikely that this will change the open-air toilet habits of many Agrans which are thought of as healthy and communal.

Finally, the rights of tourists, rather than locals, to certain facilities and standards is most glaringly highlighted in one of Kumar's recommendations where he advocates that a 'separate hospital with all modern facilities and proper ambulance service for the exclusive use of tourists may be set up in Agra' (Kumar, 1991, 247).

Power over the production of tourist space overwhelmingly concentrates wealth in the hands of the few, marginalises further small traders and providers of services, and alters the spatial and social relationship between locals and tourists. However, the process is an uneven one; in Agra, distinct spaces are built for domestic tourists, backpackers and package tourists. An exemplary contrast in the regulation and production of tourist space and the spatial experience of different tourists is provided by the disparity between two coach parks for visitors to the Taj Mahal; one for the coaches bringing domestic tourists, and the other delivering Western package tourists.

Previously situated at a site closer to the Taj, the large domestic coach park has been relocated to a site a quarter of a mile away to minimise disruption. On an average day there are 60 buses parking at this site. The coach park is surrounded by some 90 small stalls selling food and souvenirs of the Taj and large numbers of tourists spend time haggling over prices. In addition, there are several other casual peddlers and rickshaw drivers touting for business. There is considerable noise and much bustle as tourists arrive, eat and make their way to the West Gate to enter the Taj. Their meandering progress contrasts sharply with the guide-led, urgent march of the package tourists.

Also recently relocated is the coach park for organised tours to the Taj carrying Western tourists. Formerly some 300 yards from the East gate, coaches now stop about half a mile from the East Gate. To minimise pollution and contact with the local population, particularly the hustlers who surround the gate, Agra Development Authority have introduced electric-battery-operated minibuses which convey tourists the remaining half mile to the site. Although there are eight or nine marble shops and eating houses lining the short walk to the Gate, guides ensure that few tourists stop at these businesses. The largest shop is, rather incongruously, a Benetton outlet which beckons tourists with the claim that it sells similar goods at 25 per cent of their retail cost in the West (perhaps this is the first installation in the future production of a Western retail landscape). The package tourists are shielded from the vast numbers of tourists who crowd in at the West Gate and once inside the courtyard, rapidly make their way to the entrance unencumbered by touts, retailers or unofficial guides. Although comparatively quiet, the surrounds of the East Gate still disturb some tourists, especially when they see roaming pigs devouring rubbish:

> Courtney *(55, factory inspector, from New York, on a three-week tour with his partner which incorporates China, India and the UK)*: We came into the Taj this morning and the first thing we saw was a mangy, rabid dog and then a band of pigs scrubbing around in the filth and garbage. Disgusting. The last thing you expect to see at the Taj Mahal!

The separation of these facilities, with their different organisation of regulation and tourist practice testifies to the material conceptualisation of distinct forms of tourism. Practice in one space can be typified as lively, convivial, hectic and commercial whilst the other is systematic, organised and individualistic.

Another interruption in the seamless progression towards regulated, commercialised and themed tourist space in Agra has been the local controversy over who has the right to seek employment as a guide. There are three sorts of *official* guides at the Taj; those who exclusively tout for business at the Taj itself, those regularly employed by tour companies who accompany large groups to the Taj, and a casual group who are on call to provide a service for companies when required and provide a flexible labour force. Besides these official guides, however, there has been a substantial growth in the number of unofficial guides, a situation the official guides complain bitterly about. This has arisen because although they had been debarred, a recent local court ruling found in favour of an unregistered guide bringing a party of tourists into the Taj on the grounds that to restrict him would have denied his livelihood. These unofficial guides have undercut the charges of the official guides, prompting some tour operators to prefer them. Now a third group has entered the picture who provide their services free on the basis that they can earn money through the receipt of commission by taking tour parties to emporia. To enforce quality control in these conditions is impossible because of the necessity to find employment, particularly since the hardship experienced by small traders in Taj Ganj and the closure of factories in Agra has greatly increased rates of unemployment in the city. There are undoubtedly problems about a skilled workforce being undercut by cheap, unskilled workers. However, the process of marginalisation, whereby an elite strata of registered guides who serve wealthy tourists consign those falling outside the system to search for scraps has been challenged. The power to control who should work in tourist space has been successfully contested by a group of marginalised workers, demonstrating that the vested commercial interests do not always have things their own way, despite the underlying trends towards marginalisation, regulation and thematisation.

I have shown how the imperatives to develop tourism seem increasingly to be informed by Western, globalising discourses of conserving, theming and regulating space. Whilst these discourses are translated to frame the processes of tourist development in Agra, there is considerable competition between them. Thus, commercial desires and notions about designing themed spaces conflict with aims to conserve 'authentic' features, and desires to conserve have to mediate directives to regulate space. As an ensemble, however, these ideals are increasingly evident in the inscription of power on tourist space, both at the Taj and in Agra.

The proposed reconfigurations of space in Agra will result in more spaces being brought under central control, subject to a more systematic and centralised form of regulation, and a spatial purification whereby exclusionary policies will eliminate supposedly distracting and 'unsightly' local features and activities from tourist space. The tourist product will constitute a mediated 'experience' which will excise any 'clutter' from the potted versions of India and the Taj.

Although I have shown that there are instances where small entrepreneurs have successfully challenged the strategies of the vested interests who attempt to curtail their social and economic activity, the implications for the livelihood of these informal traders and providers of services are grim, as they become increasingly marginalised and their economic strategies subject to regulation. I envisage that the extension of an enclavic, highly commodified form of tourist space will be matched by the shrinkage, marginalisation or even disappearance of heterogeneous tourist space. The proximity of Taj Ganj to the Taj Mahal raises the prospect that the area will be coveted for large-scale, capital-intensive tourist developments. Such spatial colonisation will result in the impoverishment of the enterprises in Taj Ganj or they will have to develop strategies whereby they provide services for large businesses based in Agra Cantonment. Increasingly, craft workers based in Taj Ganj are forced to supplement their income by supplying items for the large outlets in Agra Cantonment. The sub-contracting schemes of large emporia usually involve recruiting the services of hundreds of isolated workers whose lack of collective power means that prices offered for their work tend to be kept low.

It is also likely that any decline in heterogeneous tourist space will lead to Agra becoming a less attractive destination for backpackers. The extent of backpacker networks in India means that there are plenty of alternatives vying for inclusion in their itineraries. As global 'super-attractions' such as the Taj Mahal become surrounded by enclavic tourist space, they draw more organised, package tours but, at the same time, force others to look for ways to escape the design codes, reduced social contact and intensive forms of regulation they produce. Thus the ongoing production of tourist space proceeds, stimulated by the desire of tourists both to experience familiarity and encounter otherness.

Notes

1. The programme was broadcast on 2/5/95 at 8 p.m. on the *Without Walls* series.
2. Interview, May 1997.
3. See Pal's illustrated chapter 6 in his edited collection, *Romance of the Taj Mahal*, where photographs and paintings clearly show the profusion of foliage in contrast to the unobstructed contemporary prospect.
4. Common Indian euphemism for the sexual molestation of women.
5. Bollywood is the term used to denote the film industry based in Mumbai.

7

CONCLUSION

By portraying a range of culturally situated tourist narratives and performances, I have tried to side-step the ethnocentric, functionalist and over-generalised concepts present in most theories of tourism. The sheer variety of identifiable narrative tropes and performative conventions examined here seems to deny that tourism can be typified and classified. Instead, tourism is a set of contesting and ever-changing performances, focusing in this work on narration, walking, gazing, photographing and remembering. This is not intended to be an exhaustive list but designed to stress the ongoing, embodied, active nature of tourism as process.

This work has been guided by the notion of a 'progressive sense of place', which disavows the idea that places have some essential identity. Rather, places are continually reconstituted by the activities that centre upon them. The Taj Mahal and Agra are the centre of diverse practices which are organised locally, nationally and globally. They are produced at different scales by local, national and international entrepreneurs and administrators; represented in contrasting ways by tourist marketers, media and tourists; and are located in diverse itineraries. By identifying the most popular (and some subaltern) narratives about the site, it is apparent that the Taj has contrasting symbolic values, and is located in different 'imaginary geographies' which I have identified as colonial, sacred, exclusive and inclusive national, and local. These diverse spatial imaginaries impact upon performance and meaning *in situ*, and are practically articulated by their manifestation as itineraries which link symbolic places together. To conceive the Taj as having some essential character is to ignore the polyphonous interpretations and diverse practices that centre upon it.

My aim is to show how the meaning of particularly symbolic sites are rarely totally determined by official or commodified versions, although the power to impress meaning upon a place is always evident, here through (neo)colonial and commodifying hegemonies. Power is concerned with fixing representation and framing interpretation yet the Taj is revealed as a site where a range of identities is articulated. To invoke Neumann's words once more, tourism is 'a metaphor for our struggle to make sense of our self and world within a highly differentiated culture' directing us to symbolic sites 'where people are at work making meaning, situating themselves in relation to public spectacle' (Neumann, 1988, 22).

These touristic narratives and performances which articulate identities can indicate some of the diverse cultural practices that emerge out of processes of globalisation. The massive development of tourism on a global scale has resulted in the proliferation of tourist destinations and the kind of infrastructure evident in large capital developments in Agra. In this competitive environment, cultural heritage is increasingly a resource which corporations, nations and regions repackage to lure tourists. Like other aspects of globalisation, this has resulted in a certain degree of homogeneity: the mediascapes broadcast in travel magazines and throughout popular cultural forms transmit stereotypical representations, tours are organised according to predictable time–space patterns, and, as I have shown here, forms of tourist space emerge which are characterised by distinctive modes of regulation, design and management. Yet whilst it may seem that in the hotels, emporia and restaurants of these spaces, one could literally be 'anywhere in the world', it is always the case that apparently homogenising formations are always worked out 'in, and through, specificity' (Hall, 1991, 28–9) – informed by the particular interests of local entrepreneurs, bureaucrats and politicians, and according to particular capital–labour relationships.

I have already mentioned that the production of enclavic space in Agra Cantonment and the future plans for conserving, regulating, commodifying and theming tourism characterise the production of leisure spaces in the West, and increasingly, non-Western bounded realms. The escalating numbers of tourists searching out proliferating tourist spaces are an important strand in global ethnoscapes (Appadurai, 1990). Moreover, ways in which representations of famous cultural symbols are incorporated into global 'mediascapes' by travel and advertising industries seem to exemplify the 'disembedding' processes whereby the production of meaning about culture and places becomes detached from locality (Giddens, 1991).

Tourism at the Taj started in the colonial era, the 'take off phase for global capital' (Robertson, 1992, 180). I have shown how the world was classified and incorporated into European systems of knowledge by colonial practices and representations. Thus at the Taj, certain dominant processes emerge from this colonial tourism, for as King remarks:

> In certain locations and certain cultural contexts, even indeed for certain cultural actors and practices, the relevant cultural space to which the discourse belongs is [the] historically and culturally inscribed space of post-colonialism.
>
> (1991, 9)

However, as Appadurai has convincingly asserted, globalisation is not an inevitable and remorseless extension of power but is more accurately characterised as a range of 'complex, overlapping and disjunctive processes' (1990, 296)

– as the diversity of imaginary geographies which incorporate the Taj testify. More contemporary key globalising concepts such as 'secular national democracy' and 'conservation' are focused on the Taj, but so are defensive reactions to globalising processes, such as recursive nationalism and religious nostalgia, as well as narratives and practices which subvert hegemonic praxis and the 'imagined worlds of the official mind' (Appadurai, 1990, 296).

Globalisation in this context is not only typified by disembedding processes but the repatriation of cultural elements which co-exist with national and local cultural continuities. Furthermore, sites of international tourism are exemplary points of dialogue and negotiation between tourists and locals. Hybrid narratives are articulated alongside somewhat serially reproduced, culturally situated stories, and new cultural forms and practices may emerge out of the interchange of knowledge and ideas. It is true that while much tourism at the Taj concerns insular, self-contained groups and activities, other tourist practices are more concerned with interaction, exchanging ideas and experiencing cultural difference. Important roles are played by local cultural intermediaries, much like the denizens of Taj Ganj, who skilfully translate and negotiate meanings with tourists, and by those tourists, who exchange their political beliefs and cultural impressions with locals. This diversity, within the context of a dominant regime which reinforces normative tourist patterns and produces regular forms of tourist space, exemplifies 'the simultaneous production of cultural homogeneity and cultural heterogeneity' (Robertson, 1992, 173) which typifies globalisation.

The meaning and purpose of space is reproduced, or contested, by what I have termed tourist performances. The notion of performance has been neglected recently and despite its limitations is useful as a way of theorising the diverse acts which people accomplish in particular spaces. The notion distinguishes the spatial contexts of social action: whether stages are clearly bounded or not, the degree of regulation over what acts are permissible, and the extent to which actors are managed, choreographed and directed. Whilst performance is able to highlight the characteristics of particular spaces in this way, it also identifies the disposition of actors as they enter specific realms. The extent to which actors are familiar with roles and procedures, their desire to conform to group behaviour and peer-group pressure, their willingness to transgress routine enactions and improvise, and their ability to act ironically to undermine or mock performative codes, all cannot be determined by the codes and conventions of powerful regulatory agencies and the disciplinary structure of certain spaces.

However, particular 'stages' are organised and regulated in ways that *potentially* constrain or enable improvised enactions. The Taj Mahal is neither a wholly enclavic or heterogeneous tourist space and there are a multitude of tourist performances, each articulating a distinct praxis and disposition. In the bazaar area of Taj Ganj, a heterogeneous tourist space, the potential to escape from conventional tourist activity is facilitated by the absence of any directors, stage managers, the variegated patterns of movement, diversity of activities and elements, and the pervasive sensual stimuli. The performative codes and enframing conventions brought by backpackers are no less structured than those of other tourists: the focus on looking at and moving towards particularly valorised aspects of the 'other', the need to maintain status and individuality, the search for mystical experiences and drug-related revelations to achieve 'self-realisation'. Yet a combination of the qualities of the space and the greater reflexivity engendered by a lack of temporal and spatial constraints increase the possibility of improvisational performances, along with the prospect of disorientation. In the more systematically regulated enclavic space of Agra Cantonment, where stage managers and directors wield power over their troupes, improvisation is more conditional and yet even here, the conventions of tourist performance can be undermined by rebellious and cynical acts.

Whilst I have found the notion of performance useful to a study of tourism, I believe it is more widely applicable to exploring diverse cultural and social actions. The idea that spaces, while always liable to change, are diversely managed, regulated and bounded provides an important context within which groups and individuals may manoeuvre. The discursive and practical assumptions of actors about what enactions are appropriate in specific situations are another vital context. Together, these constitute the parameters of social performance, and provide the context within which conventions of space and identity might be redefined or transformed.

I have mentioned that the production of single-purpose, purified, regulated, commodified and policed tourist space indicates wider processes of spatial production. It may well be that the ordering conventions of purified space actually mask the ambiguities and arbitrary juxtapositions of difference that constitute heterotopias. However, the power of these techniques to regulate unorthodox performances and create common-sense norms powerfully constrain alternative meanings and practices.

Simmel (1995) highlighted the juxtaposition of multiple cultural forms and social practices that characterised the early modern metropolis. Yet these dynamic elements are increasingly being extinguished from the urban realm, or pushed out to marginal locations. Late capitalism has rendered urban life increasingly predictable and marked by sensual deprivation by incorporating difference through commodification. The erasure of functionally and culturally diverse urban spaces has thwarted human contact, the desire for difference, and the need to wallow in the obscure and confusing. As a corollary, those spaces assigned marginal status are increasingly imagined and depicted as sites of disorder, poverty, filth, over-population and chaos. At the same time, as such spaces always have, they serve as realms of desire where 'others' can be encountered.

Equally, the leisure spaces now being produced in the West and elsewhere, such as shopping malls and theme parks, are characterised by their intensified regulation. Whereas the early modern spaces described by Baudelaire and Benjamin were protean and variegated, contemporary leisure spaces channel movement, regulate aesthetics, replace social life with its simulation, debar certain people and are generally organised so as to maximise consumption and minimise other activities (Benjamin, 1973). Yet heterogeneous spaces and the experiences they provoke are increasingly sought by tourists who generally need to move outside the West, to India for example, to find them.

This desire for otherness and heterogeneity is stimulated and served by the tourist industry and across Western popular culture. Non-Western cultures and spaces are consistently represented as 'exotic' in tourist brochures, films and advertisements. This is a way of confining difference, of ordering knowledge. Similarly, the package tour is designed to contain alterity while gazing upon selective aspects of it. The sensual, the chaotic and the unquantifiable are alluring but this heterogeneity is contained by the kind of heterotopia that Foucault typified as classificatory and systematically organised. And yet the desire stems from the radical lack of heterogeneous space in the West, or at least space that can be easily decoded and unpicked so as to reveal its ambivalences and contradictions. Thus the alternative movement towards heterogeneous tourist space signifies the dearth of a particular form of space in the tourist's country of origin where playfulness and imagination can be stimulated and indulged. It is this unbalanced distribution of order and pleasure in Western spatial economies which leads to the deflection of desire towards more variegated spaces.

BIBLIOGRAPHY

Adler, J. (1989a) 'Origins of sightseeing', in *Annals of Tourism Research*, 16: 7–29
—— (1989b) 'Travel as performed art', in *American Journal of Sociology*, 94: 1,366–91
Agnew, J. and Duncan, J. (1991) *The Power of Place: Bringing Together Geographical and Social Imaginations* (Routledge, London)
Agra Heritage Project Interim Report (1993) (Roorkee University, India)
Agra Heritage Project Summary of Research Studies (1993) (Roorkee University, India)
Ahmed, M. (1924) *The Taj and Its Environs* (R.G. Bansard, Delhi)
Albers, P. and James, W. (1988) 'Travel photography: a methodological approach', in *Annals of Tourism Research*, 16: 134–58
Alexander, M. (ed.) (1987) *Delhi and Agra: A Traveller's Companion* (Constable, London)
Anderson, B. (1983) *Imagined Communities* (Verso, London)
Anderson, K. and Gale, F. (eds) (1992) *Inventing Places: Studies in Cultural Geography* (Longman Cheshire, Melbourne)
Appadurai, A. (1990) 'Disjuncture and difference in the global cultural economy', in M. Featherstone (ed.) *Global Culture: Nationalism, Globalisation and Modernity* (Sage, London)
Arora, R. (1937) *The City of the Taj* (Hibernian Press, Calcutta)
Auge, M. (1995) *Non-Places: Introduction to an Anthropology of Supermodernity* (Verso, London)
Ayala, H. (1991) 'Resort hotel landscapes as an international megatrend', in *Annals of Tourism Research*, 18: 568–87
Bachelard, G. (1969) *The Poetics of Space* (Beacon Press, Boston)
Bajaj, J. (1993) *Ayodhya and the Future India* (Centre for Policy Studies, Madras)
Barber, B. (1995) *Jihad vs the World* (Times Books, New York)
Barnes, T. and Duncan, J. (eds) (1992) *Writing Worlds* (Routledge, London)
Barthes, R. (1977) *Image, Music, Text* (Collins, Glasgow)
Basu, T. *et al.* (1990) *Khaki Shorts, Saffron Flags* (Orient Longman, New Delhi)
Baudelaire C. 1972, *Selected Writings on Art and Artists*, P.E. Charvet (trans. and ed.) (Penguin, Harmondsworth)
Baudrillard, J. (1981) *For a Critique of the Economy of the Sign* (Telos, St Louis)
Bauman, Z. (1994) 'Desert spectacular', in K. Tester (ed.) *The Flaneur* (Routledge, London)
Baweja, H. (1993) 'Taj Mahal: acid rain pours down', in *India Today*, 15/10/93, 74–7

Bayly, C. (ed.) (1993) *The Raj: India and the British 1600–1947* (National Portrait Gallery Publications, London)
Bedi, R. (1995) 'India "reveres tourism more than temples"', in *The Daily Telegraph*, 25/2/95
Bender, B. (ed.) (1993) *Landscape: Politics and Perspectives* (Berg, Oxford)
Benjamin, W. (1973) *Charles Baudelaire* (Verso, London)
Bennett, T. (1995) *The Birth of the Museum* (Routledge, London)
Bhabha, H. (ed.) (1990) *Nation and Narration* (Routledge, London)
—— (1994) *The Location of Culture* (Routledge, London)
Bhardwaj, S. (1987a) 'Single religion shrines, multireligion pilgrimages', in R.L. Singh and R.P.B. Singh (eds) *Trends in the Geography of Pilgrimages* (Banares Hindu University, Varanasi)
—— (1987b) 'Geography and the hereafter', in V.S. Datye (ed.) *Explorations in the Tropics* (Prof. K. Dikshit, Pune)
Bird, J., Curtis, B., Putnam, T., Robertson, G. and Tickner, L. (eds) (1993) *Mapping the Futures* (Routledge, London)
Bohle, H. (1987) 'Spatial planning and ritual politics: the evolution of temple towns and urban systems in medieval South India', in V.S. Datye (ed.) *Explorations in the Tropics* (Prof. K. Dikshit, Pune)
Boorstin, D. (1964) *The Image: A Guide to Pseudo-Events in America* (Harper, New York)
Boyarin, J. (1994) *Remappping Memory: The Politics of Time Space* (University of Minnesota Press, Minneapolis)
Britton, S. (1991) 'Tourism, capital and place: towards a critical geography of tourism', in *Environment and Planning D: Society and Space*, 9: 451–78
Bruner, J. (1991) 'Transformation of self in tourism', in *Annals of Tourism Research*, 18: 238–50
—— (1994) 'Abraham Lincoln as authentic reproduction: a critique of postmodernism', in *American Anthropologist*, 96: 397–415
Buie, S. (1996) 'Market as mandala: the erotic space of commerce', in *Organisation*, 3(2): 225–32
Caillois, R. (1961) *Man, Play and Games* (Free Press, New York)
Cannadine, D. (1983) 'The context, performance and meaning of ritual', in E. Hobsbawn and T. Ranger (eds) *The Invention of Tradition* (Blackwell, Oxford)
Carlson, M. (1996) *Performance: A Critical Introduction* (Routledge, London)
Carroll, R. (1972) *The Taj Mahal* (Newsweek, New York)
Carter, E., Donald, J. and Squires, J. (eds) (1993) *Space and Place: Theories of Identity and Location* (Lawrence and Wishart, London)
Chakrabarty, D. (1991) 'Open space/public space: garbage, modernity and India', in *South Asia*, 16: 15–31
Chandhoke, N. (1993) 'On the social organiation of urban space – subversions and appropriations', in *Social Scientist*, 21: 63–73
Chandra, B. (1993) 'Historians of modern India and communalism', in R. Tharpar, H. Mukhia and B. Chandra, *Communalism and the Writing of Indian History* (People's Publishing House, Delhi)
Chaney, D. (1993) *Fictions of Collective Life* (Routledge, London)
Classen, C. (1997) 'Foundations for an anthropology of the sense', in *International Social Science Journal*, September, 153: 401–12

BIBLIOGRAPHY

Clifford, J. (1988) *The Predicament of Culture: Twentieth Century Ethnography, Literature and Art* (Harvard University Press, Cambridge, Mass.)

Clifford, J. and Marcus, G. (1996) *Writing Culture: The Politics and Poetics of Ethnography* (University of California Press, Berkeley)

Cohen, A. (1985) *The Symbolic Construction of Community* (Tavistock, London)

Cohen, E. (1972) 'Towards a sociology of international tourism', in *Social Research*, 39

—— (1979) 'A phenomenology of tourist experiences', in *Sociology*, 13: 179–202

—— (1988) 'Traditions in the qualitative sociology of international tourism', in *Annals of Tourism Research*, 15: 29–46

Cohen, S. and Taylor, L. (1992) *Escape Attempts* (Routledge, London)

Cohn, B. (1984) 'The census, social structure and objectification in South Asia', in *Folk*, 26 (Copenhagen)

Connerton, P. (1989) *How Societies Remember* (Cambridge University Press, London)

Craik, J. (1995) 'Is cultural tourism viable?', in *Smarts*, 2: 6–7

—— (1997) 'The culture of tourism', in C. Rojek and J. Urry (eds) *Touring Cultures: Transformations of Travel and Theory* (Routledge, London)

Crang, M. (1994) 'On the heritage trail: maps of and journeys to olde England', in *Environment and Planning D: Society and Space*, 12: 341–55

Crang, P. (1997) 'Performing the tourist product', in C. Rojek and J. Urry (eds) *Touring Cultures: Transformations of Travel and Theory* (Routledge, London)

Crawshaw, C. and Urry, J. (1993) 'Tourism and the photographic eye', Department of Sociology Paper, Lancaster

—— (1997) 'Tourism and the photographic eye', in C. Rojek and J. Urry (eds) *Touring Cultures: Transformations of Travel and Theory* (Routledge, London)

Cresswell, T. (1996) *In Place/Out of Place: Geography, Ideology and Transgression* (University of Minnesota Press, London)

Crick, M. (1991) 'Tourists, locals and anthropologists: quizzical reflections on "otherness" in tourist encounters and in tourism research', in *Australian Cultural History*, 10: 6–19

Crooke, W. (1906) *Things Indian* (John Murray, London)

Culler, J. (1981) 'The semiotics of tourism', in *American Journal of Semiotics*, 1: 127–40

D'Arcy, S. (1995) 'Silver lining for India's favourite monument', in *The Times*, 5/3/95

Datye, V. (ed.) (1987) *Explorations in the Tropics* (Prof. K. Dikshit, Pune)

Dawson, G. (1994) *Soldier Heroes: British Adventure, Empire, and the Imagining of Masculinities* (Routledge, London)

De Certeau, M. (1984) *The Practice of Everyday Life* (University of California, Berkeley)

Denzin, N. (1997) *Interpretative Ethnography: Ethnographic Practices for the 21st Century* (Sage, London)

Desai, M. (1993) 'Towards a syncretic vision of India', *Times of India*, 28/12/93

Deshpande, S. (1994) 'Evaluating Hinduvta', *Times of India*, 4/1/94

Dubashi, J. (1990), in S.R. Goel (ed.) *Hindu Temples: What Happened to Them? A Preliminary Survey* (The Voice of India, New Delhi)

Dubey, D. (1987) 'Sacred complex of Pragaya: the myth of Triveni', in R.L. Singh and R.P.B. Singh (eds) *Trends in the Geography of Pilgrimages* (Banares Hindu University, Varanasi)

BIBLIOGRAPHY

—— (1990) 'Kumbh Mela: origin and historicity of India's greatest pilgrimage fair', in L. Gopal and D.P. Dubey (eds) *Pilgrimage Studies: Text and Context* (Society of Pilgrimage Studies, Allahabad)
Duncan, J. (1989) 'The power of place in Kandy, Sri Lanka, 1780–1980', in J. Agnew and J. Duncan *The Power of Place: Bringing Together Geographical and Social Imaginations* (Routledge, London)
Eade, J. and Sallnow, M. (eds) (1991) *Contesting the Sacred* (Routledge, London)
Eagleton, T. (1983) *Literary Theory: An Introduction* (Blackwell, Oxford)
Eck, D. (1991) 'Kashi: city of all India', in T.N. Madan (ed.) *Religion in India* (Oxford University Press, Delhi)
Eco, U. (1986) *Travels in Hyper Reality* (Picador, London)
Edensor, T. and Kothari, U. (1994) 'The masculinisation of Stirling's heritage', in D. Hall and V. Kinnaird (eds) *Tourism: A Gender Analysis* (Wiley, Winchester)
Edensor, T. (1997a) 'National identity and the politics of memory: remembering Bruce and Wallace in symbolic space', *Environment and Planning D: Society and Space*, 29, 175–94
—— (1997b) 'Reading *Braveheart*: representing and contesting Scottish Identity', in *Scottish Affairs*, 21, Autumn, 135–58
—— (1998) 'Moving through the city', in Bell, D. and Haddour, A. in *City Visions* (Longman, London)
Elias, N. (1978) *The Civilising Process, vol. 1: The History of Manners* (Oxford, Blackwell)
Elst, K. (1992) *RamJanbhoomi vs Babri Masjid* (Voice of India, New Delhi)
Featherstone, M. (1991) *Consumer Culture and Postmodernism* (Sage, London)
Feifer, W. (1985) *Going Places* (MacMillan, London)
Finlay, H. et al. (1993) *India: A Travel Survival Kit* (Lonely Planet, London)
Fishman, R. (1987) *Bourgeois Utopias: The Fall and Rise of Suburbia* (Basic Books, New York)
Forster, E.M. (1924) *Passage To India* (Penguin, London)
Foucault, M. (1977) *Discipline and Punish: the Birth of the Prison* (Allen Lane, London)
—— (1978) *The History of Sexuality: an Introduction, Volume 1* (Penguin, London)
—— (1986) 'Of other spaces', in *Diacritics*, Spring, 16(1) pp 22–7
—— (1988) 'The subject and power', in H. Dreyfus and P. Rabinow, *Michel Foucault: Beyond Structuralism and Hermeneutics* (Harvester, Brighton)
Freitag, T. (1994) 'Enclave tourist development: for whom the benefits roll?', in *Annals of Tourism Research*, 21: 538–54
Game, A. (1991) *Undoing the Social* (Open University Press, Milton Keynes)
Geertz, C. (ed.) (1963) *Old Societies and New States: the Quest for Modernity in Africa and Asia* (Free Press of Glencoe)
—— (1973) *The Interpretation of Cultures* (Basic Books, New York)
—— (1993) 'Deep play: notes on the Balinese Cockfight', in Geertz, C. *The Interpretation of Cultures: Selected Essays* (Fontana, London)
—— (1994) 'Primordial and civic ties', in J. Hutchinson and A. Smith (eds) *Nationalism* (Oxford University Press, Oxford)
Genocchio, B. (1995) 'Discourse, discontinuity, difference: the question of "other" spaces', in S. Watson and K. Gibson (eds) *Postmodern Cities and Spaces* (Blackwell, Oxford)
Giddens, A. (1984) *The Constitution of Society* (Polity, Cambridge)

BIBLIOGRAPHY

—— (1985) *A Contemporary Critique of Historical Materialism, Volume 2: The Nation-State and Violence* (Polity, Cambridge)

—— (1991) *Modernity and Self-Identity* (Polity, Cambridge)

Goel, S. (ed.) (1990) *Hindu Temples: What Happened to Them? A Preliminary Survey* (Voice of India, New Delhi)

Goffman, E. (1959) *The Presentation of Self in Everyday Life* (Doubleday, New York)

—— (1961) *Asylum* (Anchor Books, New York)

Gopal, L. and Dubey, D. (eds) (1990) *Pilgrimage Studies: Text and Context* (Society of Pilgrimage Studies, Allahabad)

Gottdiener, M. (1997) *The Theming of America: Dreams, Visions and Commercial Spaces* (Westview Press, Oxford)

Gottlieb, A. (1982) 'American vacations', in *Annals of Tourism Research*, 9: 165–87

Graburn, N. (1983) 'The anthropology of tourism', in *Annals of Tourism Research*, 19: 9–33

Gregory, D. (1994) *Geographical Imaginations* (Blackwell, Oxford)

Gregson, N. and Crewe, L. (1997) 'The bargain, the knowledge, and the spectacle: making sense of consumption in the space of the car boot sale', in *Environment and Planning D: Society and Space*, 15: 87–112

Gurumurthy, S. (1993) 'The inclusive and the exclusive', in J. Bajaj (ed.) *Ayodhya and the Future India* (Centre for Policy Studies, Madras)

Hall, D. and Kinnaird, V. (eds) (1994) *Tourism: A Gender Analysis* (Wiley, Winchester)

Hall, S. (1991) 'The local and the global: globalisation and ethnicity', in A.D. King *Globalisation and the World System* (MacMillan, London)

Hamilton, J. (1937) *The Taj Mahal of Agra* (Liddell's Press, Simla)

Harvey, D. (1989) *The Condition of Postmodernity* (Blackwell, Oxford)

Hetherington, K. (1992) 'Stonehenge and its festival: spaces of consumption', in R. Shields (ed.) *Lifestyle Shopping* (Routledge, London)

—— (1996) 'The utopics of social ordering: Stonehenge as a museum without walls', in S. Macdonald and G. Fyfe (eds) *Theorising Museums* (Blackwell, Oxford)

Hewison, R. (1987) *The Heritage Industry* (Methuen, London)

Hobsbawm, E. and Ranger, T. (eds) (1983) *The Invention of Tradition* (Blackwell, Oxford)

Howes, D. (ed.) (1991) 'Sensorial anthropology', in D. Howes (ed.) *The Varieties of Sensory Experience: A Sourcebook in the Anthropology of the Senses* (University of Toronto Press, Toronto)

Howes, D. and Classen, C. (1991) 'Sounding sensory profiles', in D. Howes (ed.) *The Varieties of Sensory Experience: A Sourcebook in the Anthropology of the Senses* (University of Toronto Press, Toronto)

Hutchinson J. (1992) 'Moral innovators and the politics of regeneration: the distinctive role of cultural nationalists in nation-building', *International Journal of Comparative Sociology* 33 (1–2): 101–17

—— (1994) 'Cultural nationalism and moral regeneration', in J. Hutchinson and A.D. Smith (eds) *Nationalism* (Oxford University Press, Oxford)

Hutchinson, J. and Smith, A.D. (eds) (1994) *Nationalism* (Oxford University Press, Oxford)

Jameson, F. (1991) *Postmodernism, or the Cultural Logic of Late Capitalism* (Verso, London)

Jash, P. (1990) 'Pilgrimage, an avenue for salvation', in L. Gopal and D.P. Dubey (eds) *Pilgrimage Studies: Text and Context* (Society of Pilgrimage Studies, Allahabad)

Johnson, N. (1995) 'Cast in stone: monuments, geography and nationalism', in *Environment and Planning D: Society and Space*, 13: 51–65

Jouclas, S. (1993) 'Universal treasure', in *High Life*, Winter 1993: 21–8

Judd, D. (1995) 'The rise of the new walled cities', in H. Liggett and D. Perry (eds): *Spatial Practices* (Sage, London)

Kabbani, R. (1986) *Europe's Myths of Orient* (Pandora, London)

Kapoor, B. (1962) *Glimpses of Agra* (Gaya Prasad and Sons, Agra)

Kasinitz, P. (ed.) (1995) *Metropolis: Centre and Symbol of Our Times* (Macmillan, London)

Kay, J. (1991) 'Landscapes of women and men: rethinking the regional historical geography of the United States and Canada', in *Journal of Historical Geography*, 17: 435–52

Kearns, G. and Philo, C. (1993) *The City as Cultural Capital; Past and Present* (Pergamon, Oxford)

Keay, J. (1989) *India Discovered* (Rupa, Calcutta)

Keith, M. and Pile, S. (1993) *Place and the Politics of Identity* (Routledge, London)

King, A. (1976) *Colonial Urban Development: Culture, Social Power and Environment* (Routledge, London)

—— (1990) *Urbanism, Colonialism and the World Economy* (Routledge, London)

—— (1991) *Globalisation and the World System* (MacMillan, London)

Klugman, K. (1995) 'The alternative ride', in Klugman, K., Kuentz, J., Waldrep, S. and Willis, S. *Inside the Mouse: Work and Play at Disney World* (Rivers Oram Press, London)

Klugman, K., Kuentz, J., Waldrep, S. and Willis, S. (1995) *Inside the Mouse: Work and Play at Disney World* (Rivers Oram Press, London)

Kracauer, S. (1995) *The Mass Ornament* (Harvard University Press, Cambridge, Mass.)

Kramrisch, S. (1991) 'Space in Indian cosmogony and architecture', in K. Vatsyayan (ed.) *Concepts of Space* (Indira Gandhi National Centre for the Arts, New Delhi)

Krishna, S. (1994) 'Cartographic anxiety: mapping the body politic in India', in *Alternatives*, 19: 507–21

Kumar, P. (1991) *Tourism Develpment in Agra* (Agra University, Agra)

Kundra, R. and Bawa, S. (1991) *The History of Ancient and Medieval India* (Neelam, Delhi)

Kusy, F. (1989) *Cadogan Guide to India* (Cadogan, London)

Lash, S. and Urry, J. (1994) *Economies of Signs and Space* (Sage, London)

Law, J. (1994) *Organising Modernity* (Blackwell, Oxford)

Lear, E. (1874) *Indian Journals*,

Lees, C. (1995) 'Taj Mahal to bask in electric moonlight', in *The Times*, 22/1/95

Lees, L (1997) 'Ageographia, heterotopia, and Vancouver's new public library', in *Environment and Planning D: Society and Space*, 15: 321–347

Lefebvre, H. (1991) *The Production of Space* (Blackwell, Oxford)

Leoshko, J. (1989) 'Mausoleum for an Empress', in P. Pal (ed.) *Romance of the Taj Mahal* (Thames and Hudson, London)

Levin, B. (1994) 'A monumental problem: Taj Mahal', in *The Times*, 20/12/94

Little, K. (1991) 'On safari: the visual politics of a tourist representation', in D. Howes (ed.) *The Varieties of Sensory Experience: A Sourcebook in the Anthropology of the Senses* (University of Toronto Press, Toronto)

Loker-Murphy, L. and Pearce, P. (1995) 'Young budget travellers in Australia', in *Annals of Tourism Research*, 22: 819–43

Low, G. (1993) 'His stories? Narratives and images of imperialism', in E. Carter, J. Donald and J. Squires (eds) *Space and Place: Theories of Identity and Location* (Lawrence and Wishart, London)
Lowenthal, D. (1985) *The Past is a Foreign Country* (Cambridge University Press, Cambridge)
Lynch, K. (1973) *What Time is This Place* (MIT Press, Boston)
Lyotard, J. (1984) *The Postmodern Condition* (Manchester University Press)
MacCannell, D. (1976) *The Tourist* (Macmillan, London)
Madan, T. (ed.) (1991) *Religion in India* (Oxford University Press, Delhi)
Martin, L. et al. (1988) *Technologies of the Self: a Seminar with Michel Foucault* (Tavistock, London)
Massey, D. (1993) 'A progressive sense of place', in J. Bird et al. *Mapping the Futures* (Routledge, London)
—— (1995) 'Places and their pasts', in *History Workshop Journal*, 39: 182–92
May, T. (1993) *Social Research: Issues, Methods and Process* (Open University Press, Milton Keynes)
McClintock, A. (1994) *Imperial Leather* (Routledge, London)
McKay, G. (1996) *Senseless Acts of Beauty: Cultures of Resistance Since the Sixties* (Verso, London)
Middleton, D. and Edwards, D. (1990) *Collective Remembering* (Sage, London)
Mitchell, D. (1995) 'The end of public space?: People's Park, definitions of the public, and democracy', in *Annals of the Association of American Geographers* 85(1): 108–33
Mitchell, W. (1986) *Iconology: Image, Text, Ideology* (University of Chicago Press, Chicago)
Moin-ud-Din, M. (1924) *The Taj and its Environs* (R.G. Bansal and Co., Delhi)
Monk, J. (1992) 'Gender in the landscape: expressions of power and meaning', in K. Anderson and F. Gale (eds) *Inventing Places: Studies in Cultural Geography* (Longman Cheshire, Melbourne)
Morinis, E. (1984) *Pilgrimage in the Hindu Tradition* (Oxford University Press, Delhi)
Morley, D. and Robins, K. (1992) 'No place like heimat', in E. Carter, J. Donald and J. Squires (eds) *Space and Place: Theories of Identity and Location* (Lawrence and Wishart, London)
Nath, R. (1972) *The Immmortal Taj Mahal* (D.B. Taraporevala and Sons, Bombay)
Nelles Guide to Northern India (1990) (Robertson-McCarta, London)
Neumann, M. (1988) 'Wandering through the museum: experience and identity in a spectator culture', in *Border/Lines*, Summer: 19–27
Nicholson, L. (1989) *Collins Illustrated Guide to Delhi, Agra and Jaipur* (Collins, London)
Nolan, M. and Nolan, S. (1992) 'Religious sites as tourist attractions in Europe', in *Annals of Tourism Research*, 19: 68–78
Nora, P. (1989) 'Between memory and history: les lieux de memoire', in *Representations*, Spring issue: 7–25
Noyes, J. (1992) *Colonial Space: Spatiality in the Discourse of German South West Africa 1884–1915* (Harwood Academic Publishers, Reading)
Oak, P. (1979) *The Taj Mahal is a Tejo Mahalaya* (Jagti Press, New Delhi)
—— (1989) *Taj Mahal: The True Story: The Tale of a Temple Vandalised* (A. Ghosh, Houston)
Oppermans, M. (1993) 'Tourism space in developing countries', in *Annals of Tourism Research*, 20: 535–556
Pal, P. (1989) *Romance of the Taj Mahal* (Thames and Hudson, London)

Palmer, G. and Jankowiak, W. (1996) 'Performance and imagination: toward an anthropology of the spectacular and the mundane', in *Cultural Anthropology*, 11(2) 225–258

Pandey, G. (ed.) (1993) *Hindus and Others: The Question of Identity in India Today* (Viking Penguin, New Delhi)

Pandey, P. (1993) 'The civilised and the barbarian: The new politics of late twentieth century India and the world', in G. Pandey (ed.) *Hindus and Others: The Question of Identity in India Today* (Viking Penguin, New Delhi)

Park, C. (1994) *Sacred Worlds* (Routledge, London)

Parry, B. (1993) 'The contents and discontents of Kipling's imperialism', in E. Carter, J. Donald and J. Squires (eds) *Space and Place: Theories of Identity and Location* (Lawrence and Wishart, London)

Pawson, E. (1992) 'Two New Zealands: Maori and European', in K. Anderson and F. Gale (eds) *Inventing Places: Studies in Cultural Geography* (Longman Cheshire, Melbourne)

Pearce, D. (1988) 'Tourist time budgets', in *Annals of Tourism Research*, 15: 106–21

Pearce, D. and Moscardo, G. (1988) 'The concept of authenticity in tourist experience', in *Australian and New Zealand Journal of Sociology*, 22: 121–32

Phillips, R. (1997) *Mapping Men and Empire: A Geography of Adventure* (Routledge, London)

Porteous J. (1990) *Landscapes of the Mind: Worlds of Sense and Metaphor* (Toronto University Press, Toronto)

Pratt, M.L. (1992) *Imperial Eyes: Travel Writing and Transculturation* (Routledge, London)

Pred, A. (1990) *Making Histories and Constructing Human Geographies* (Westview Press, Boulder, Colorado)

Rai, R. (1986) *Taj Mahal* (Times Books, London)

Riley, P. (1988) 'Road culture of international long-term budget travellers', in *Annals of Tourism Research*, 15: 313–28

Rinschede, G. (1992) 'Forms of religious tourism', in *Annals of Tourism Research*, 19

Ritzer, G. and Liska, A. (1997) '"McDisneyization" and "post-tourism": complementary perspectives on contemporary tourism', in C. Rojek and J. Urry (eds) *Touring Cultures: Transformations of Travel and Theory* (Routledge, London)

Rizvi, S. (1987) *The Wonder That Was India: vol 2* (Sidgwick and Jackson, London)

Robertson, R. (1991) 'Social theory, cultural relativity and the problem of globality', in A.D. King (ed.) *Globalisation and the World System* (MacMillan, London)

—— (1992) *Globalization* (Sage, London)

Robins, K. (1991) 'Tradition and translation: national culture in its global context', in J. Corner and S. Harvey (eds) *Enterprise and Heritage* (Routledge, London)

Rodaway, P. (1994) *Sensuous Geographies* (Routledge, London)

Rodman, M. (1992) 'Empowering place: multilocality and multivocality', in *American Anthropologist*, 94: 640–56

Rohan, V. (1994) 'Welcome signs of unreality: future visions', in *The Times*, 21/5/94, 6

Rojek, C. (1993) *Ways of Escape: Modern Transformations in Leisure and Travel* (Macmillan, London)

—— (1995) *Decentring Leisure* (Sage, London)

—— (1997) 'Indexing, dragging and the social construction of tourist sites', in C. Rojek and J. Urry (eds) *Touring Cultures: Transformations of Travel and Theory* (Routledge, London)

Rosaldo, R. (1993) *Culture and Truth* (Routledge, London)
Said, E. (1978) *Orientalism* (Routledge, London)
—— (1985) 'Orientalism reconsidered', in F. Baer et al. *Europe and Its Others* (University of Essex, Colchester)
Samuel, R. and Thompson, P. (1990) *The Myths We Live By* (Routledge, London)
Samuel, R. (1994) *Theatres of Memory* (Verso, London)
Sarkar, T. (1994) 'Educating the children of the Hindu rashtra: notes on the RSS schools', in *South Asia Bulletin*, 14: 10–15
Saunders, N. (1995) *Ecstasy and the Dance Culture* (Nicholas Saunders, London)
Schimmel, A. (1991) 'Inner and outer space in Islam', in K. Vatsyayan (ed.) *Concepts of Space* (Indira Gandhi National Centre for the Arts, New Delhi)
Schutz, A. (1964) *Collected Papers: vol 2* (Martinus Nijhoff, the Hague)
Sennett, R. (1994) *Flesh and Stone* (Faber, London)
Shearer, A. (1989) *The Traveller's Key to Northern India* (Harrap Columbus, London)
Shields, R. (1991) *Places on the Margin* (Routledge, London)
—— (ed.) (1992) *Lifestyle Shopping* (Routledge, London)
Short, J. (1991) *Imagined Country* (Routledge, London)
Shourie, A. (1993) 'The buckling state', in J. Bajaj (ed.) *Ayodhya and the Future India* (Centre for Policy Studies, Madras)
Sibley, D. (1988) 'Survey 13: purification of space', in *Environment and Planning D: Society and Space*, 6: 409–21
—— (1992) 'Outsiders in society and space', in K. Anderson and F. Gale (eds): *Inventing Places: Studies in Cultural Geography* (Longman Cheshire, Melbourne)
Siebers, T. (1994) *Heterotopia: Postmodern Utopia and the Body Politic* (University of Michigan Press, Ann Arbor)
Simmel, G. (1995) 'The metropolis and mental life', in P. Kasinitz (ed.) *Metropolis: Centre and Symbol of Our Times* (Macmillan, London)
Singh, R.L. and Singh, R.P.B. (eds) (1987) *Trends in the Geography of Pilgrimages* (Banares Hindu University, Varanasi)
Singh, R.P.B. (1987) 'Time and Hindu rituals in Varanasi', in R.L. Singh and R.P.B. Singh (eds) *Trends in the Geography of Pilgrimages* (Banares Hindu University, Varanasi)
—— (1990) 'The pilgrimage manadala of Varanasi (Kashi) A study in sacred geography', in L. Gopal and D.P. Dubey (eds) *Pilgrimage Studies: Text and Context* (Society of Pilgrimage Studies, Allahabad)
Smart, B. (1994) 'Digesting the modern diet: gastro-porn, fast food and panic eating', in K. Tester (ed.) *The Flaneur* (Routledge, London)
Smith, A. (1991) *National Identity* (Penguin, London)
Smith, N. (1993) 'Scaling places', in J. Bird et al. *Mapping the Futures* (Routledge, London)
Smith, V. (1989) 'Introduction', in V. Smith (ed.) *Hosts and Guests: The Anthropology of Tourism* (2nd edition) (University of Pennsylvania Press, Philadelphia)
—— (1992) 'The quest in guest', in *Annals of Tourism Research*, 19: 1–17
Soja, E. (1995) 'Heteropologies: a remembrance of other spaces in the citadel-LA', in S. Watson and K. Gibson (eds) (1995) *Postmodern Cities and Spaces* (Blackwell, Oxford)
Somers, M. (1994) 'The narrative constitution of identity: a relational and network approach', in *Theory and Society*, 23: 605–49
Sontag, S. (1979) *On Photography* (Penguin, Harmondsworth)
Sopher, D. (1986) 'Place and landscape in Hindu tradition', in *Landscape*, 29: 1–9

BIBLIOGRAPHY

—— (1987) 'The message of place in Hindu pilgrimage', in R.L. Singh and R.P.B. Singh (eds) *Trends in the Geography of Pilgrimages* (Banares Hindu University, Varanasi)

Spivak, G. (1990) *The Postcolonial Critic* (Routledge, London)

—— (1998) 'Can the subaltern speak?', in C. Nelson and L. Grossberg (eds): *Marxism and the Interpretation of Culture* (University of Illinois, Chicago)

Spurr, D. (1993) *The Rhetoric of Empire* (Duke University Press, London)

Srivastava, V. (1990) 'Suryatirthas: a review', in L. Gopal and D.P. Dubey (eds) *Pilgrimage Studies: Text and Context* (Society of Pilgrimage Studies, Allahabad)

Stallybrass, P. and White, A. (1986) *The Politics and Poetics of Transgression* (Methuen, London)

Steevens, G. (1909) *In India* (Blackwood, London)

Stoddard, R.H. (1987) 'Pilgrimages along sacred paths', in R.L. Singh and R.P.B. Singh (eds) *Trends in the Geography of Pilgrimages* (Banares Hindu University, Varanasi)

Stoller, P. (1989) *The Taste of Ethnographic Things: The Senses in Anthropology* (Philadelphia University Press, Philadelphia)

Tester, K. (ed.) (1994) *The Flaneur* (Routledge, London)

Thapar, R. (1993) *Communalism and the Writing of Indian History* (People's Publishing House, Delhi)

The Times (1995) 'Marble Cancer', leading article (2/5/95)

Thomas, N. (1994) *Colonialism's Culture* (Polity, Cambridge)

Thornton, S. (1995) *Club Cultures: Music, Media and Subcultural Capital* (Polity, Cambridge)

Tillotson, G. (1993) 'The Indian picturesque: images of India in British landscape painting 1780–1880', in C.A. Bayly (ed.) *The Raj: India and the British 1600–1947* (National Portrait Gallery Publications, London)

Tilly, C. (1994) 'Afterword: political memories in space and time', in J. Boyarin (ed) *Remapping Memory: The Politics of Time Space* (University of Minnesota Press, Minneapolis)

Turner, V. and Turner, E. (1973) *Image and Pilgrimage in Christian Culture* (Columbia University Press, New York)

Urry, J. (1990) *The Tourist Gaze* (Sage, London)

—— (1992) 'The tourist gaze "revisited"', in *American Behavioural Scientist*, 36: 172–86

—— (1994) 'Cultural change and contemporary tourism', in *Leisure Studies*, 13: 233–8

—— (1995) *Consuming Places* (Routledge, London)

Vatsyayan, K. (ed.) (1991) *Concepts of Space* (Indira Gandhi National Centre for the Arts, New Delhi)

Virilio, P. (1991) *Lost Dimension* (Semiotext(e), New York)

Wang, N. (1996) 'Logos-modernity, Eros modernity, and leisure', in *Leisure Studies*, 15: 121–35

Warner, M. (1996) *Monuments and Maidens* (Vintage, London)

Watson, S. and Gibson, K. (eds) (1995) *Postmodern Cities and Spaces* (Blackwell, Oxford)

Weightman, B. (1987) 'Third world tour landscapes', in *Annals of Tourism Research*, 14: 227–39

Wood, R. (1994) 'Hotel culture and social control', in *Annals of Tourism Research*, 21: 65–80

Wright, P. (1985) *On Living in an Old Country* (Verso, London)

Yuval-Davies, N. (1997) *Gender and Nation* (Sage, London)

Zukin, S. (1992) *Landscapes of Power* (University of California Press, Berkeley)

NAME INDEX

Adler, J. 63, 69, 105, 119–20, 138, 163
Agra Heritage Project (AHP) Interim Report 188, 189, 191, 193, 194, 195
Agra Heritage Project (AHP) Summary of Research Studies 194, 195
Albers, P. 128–9
Alexander, M. 76
Anderson, B. 38
Appadurai, A. 14, 201–2
Arora, R. 74, 76
Asthana, P. 88
Auge, M. 47, 49, 141
Ayala, H. 46

Bachelard, G. 145
Bajaj, J. 92
Barber, B. 49
Barnes, T. 18, 19
Barthes, R. 143
Basu, T. 91, 92
Baudelaire, C. 60, 178–9, 203
Baudrillard, J. 5
Bauman, Z. 60, 178
Bawa, S. 86–8
Baweja, H. 184
Bedi, R. 191
Bender, B. 16, 17, 140
Benjamin, W. 203–4
Bennett, T. 42, 65
Bhabha, H. 6, 82
Bhardwaj, S. 30–1, 139
Bohle, H. 32
Boorstin, D. 5
Boyarin, J. 38
Britton, S. 5, 11, 12
Bruner, J. 3, 16
Buie, S. 55

Caillois, R. 67
Carlson, M. 64
Carroll, R. 74, 81, 97
Chakrabarty, D. 47, 54, 59–60
Chandhoke, N. 56, 57
Chandra, B. 85, 91
Chaney, D. 140; performance 62, 63, 64, 66; photography 129, 132, 138
Classen, C. 18, 58
Clifford, J. 2, 69
Cohen, A. 136
Cohen, E. 4, 51, 61
Cohen, S. 5, 44
Cohn, B. 39, 72–3
Connerton, P. 139–40, 141
Craik, J. 52, 188
Crang, M. 70, 141
Crang, P. 62, 63, 121
Crawshaw, C. 119, 129
Cresswell, T. 42
Crewe, L. 53
Crick, M. 2, 45, 82
Crooke, W. 78, 79
Culler, J. 13, 120

D'Arcy, S. 184, 186
Dawson, G. 77
De Certeau, M. 43–4, 106
Denzin, N. 2, 103
Desai, M. 85
Deshpande, S. 91
Dubashi, J. 93
Dubey, D. 31–2
Duncan, J. 18, 19, 39

Eade, J. 4
Eagleton, T. 15

215

NAME INDEX

Eck, D. 31
Eco, U. 5
Edensor, T. 3, 15, 19, 37, 38, 60
Edwards, D. 138
Elias, N. 48

Featherstone, M. 5, 48
Feifer, W. 66
Finlay, H. 30, 75, 164, 182
Fishman, R. 47
Foucault, M. 41, 42
Freitag, T. 46

Game, A. 38, 106, 143
Geertz, C. 35, 62, 64
Genocchio, B. 42
Giddens, A. 15, 35, 70, 201
Goel, S. 93
Goffman, E. 49, 62, 65
Gottdiener, M. 14, 48, 49
Graburn, N. 3, 4, 5
Gregson, N. 53

Hall, S. 15, 201
Hamilton, J. 76, 78, 123
Harvey, D. 5, 11
Hetherington, K. 38, 42, 53
Hewison, R. 37
Howes, D. 18, 58, 119
Hutchinson, J. 39, 82

Jaffrey, S. 186–7, 191
James, W. 128–9
Jameson, F. 5
Jankowiak, W. 61, 66, 69
Jash, P. 29
Johnson, N. 38
Jouclas, S. 184
Judd, D. 47

Kabbani, R. 23, 24, 77
Kapoor, B. 140
Kay, J. 82
Kearns, G. 11, 15
Keay, J. 24, 73
Keith, M. 15
King, A. 24, 25, 55, 201
Klugman, K. 52, 67
Kothari, U. 37
Kracauer, S. 50
Krishna, S. 40, 86

Kumar, P. 194, 196
Kundra, R. 86–8
Kusy, F. 75

Lash, S. 5, 14
Law, J. 20
Lear, E. 72
Lees, C. 191
Lees, L. 42, 68
Lefebvre, H. 15, 49, 53
Leoshko, J. 190
Levin, B. 186
Liska, A. 49, 50, 52
Little, K. 2, 14, 16
Loker-Murphy, L. 162
Low, G. 26, 77
Lowenthal, D. 135
Lynch, K. 145
Lyotard, J. 6

MacCannell, D. 3–4, 63, 120
Marcus, G. 2
Martin, L. 41
Massey, D. 7, 20, 138
McClintock, A. 24
McKay, G. 53
Middleton, D. 138
Mitchell, D. 48
Mitchell, W. 16
Moin-ud-Din, M. 78
Morinis, E. 30, 32
Morley, D. 36
Moscardo, G. 3

Nath, R. 88
Nelles Guide to Northern India 75, 79
Neumann, M. 6, 49–50, 121, 137, 200–1
Nicholson, L. 75
Nolan, M. 4
Nolan, S. 4
Noyes, J. 22

Oak, P. 93–4
Oppermans, M. 45

Pal, P. 1, 104, 142, 199; colonial narratives 72, 73, 74, 76
Palmer, G. 61, 66, 69
Pandey, G. 91
Park, C. 29
Parry, B. 26

NAME INDEX

Pawson, E. 37
Pearce, D. 3
Pearce, P. 162
Phillips, R. 77
Philo, C. 11, 15
Pile, S. 15
Porteous, J. 58
Pred, A. 21

Riley, P. 162–3
Rinschede, G. 4
Ritzer, G. 49, 50, 52
Rizvi, S. 96–7
Robertson, R. 14, 201, 202
Robins, K. 36
Rodaway, P. 51, 58
Rodman, M. 20
Rohan, V. 192
Rojek, C. 12, 14, 16–17, 45, 52, 96, 187;
    Apollonian and Dionysian culture 43
Rosaldo, R. 26, 187

Said, E. 6, 22, 24, 26
Sallnow, M. 4
Samuel, R. 71, 82, 84, 135, 138
Sarkar, T. 92
Saunders, N. 53
Schimmel, A. 29, 32
Schutz, A. 64
Sennett, R. 47, 52
Shearer, A. 75, 97
Shields, R. 6, 17, 21, 45, 48, 50, 105
Short, J. 38
Sibley, D. 42, 52
Siebers, T. 42
Simmel, G. 203
Singh, R.P.B. 31
Smart, B. 60
Smith, A. 35, 37, 38, 84
Smith, V. 61
Soja, E. 42

Somers, M. 69, 70
Sontag, S. 138
Sopher, D. 28, 29, 32
Spivak, G. 6
Spurr, D. 22, 24, 76
Srivastava, V. 30
Stallybrass, P. 26, 45
Steevens, G. 80–1, 121
Stoddard, R.H. 30
Stoller, P. 18

Taylor, L. 5, 44
Thapar, R. 91
Thomas, N. 16, 17, 26
Thompson, P. 71, 82, 84, 138
Thornton, S. 53
Tillotson, G. 23
Tilly, C. 138
Times, The 186
Turner, E. 4
Turner, V. 4

Urry, J. 5, 6–7, 14, 61, 66; gazing 119,
    120, 125, 128; photography 129, 130;
    remembering 135, 136

Virilio, P. 50

Wang, N. 48
Warner, M. 138
Weightman, B. 47, 51, 54, 150–1
Wheeler, J.T. 77–8
White, A. 26, 45
Wood, R. 46
Wordsworth, W. 136–7
Wright, P. 37

Yuval-Davies, N. 37

Zukin, S. 5

SUBJECT INDEX

activities, social: enclavic tourist space 49; heterogeneous tourist space 54–6, 174–5; *see also* performances
administrative power 10–13
admission prices 123, 195
aesthetic control 51–3
aesthetic value 101–2
Agra 148, 149–80; backpackers in Taj Ganj 162–80; regulation 192–9; *see also* tourist plans
Agra Cantonment 175, 203; commission 182–3; package tourism 150, 150–62, 178–80
Agra Development Authority 123, 184, 188, 189, 191, 196
Agra Fort 155
Agra Heritage Project (AHP) 187–8, 193
Agra Tourist Guild 152, 192
Ajmer pilgrimage 31, 33, 98
Akbar, Emperor 86, 190
Allahabad 30, 31–2
Annual Indian History Congress 1993 85
anthropological gaze 128
Apollonian culture 44–5
Archaeological Survey of India 72–3, 190, 191
architecture, Hindu 32
astrologer, hotel 160–1
authenticity 3, 164; staged authenticity 3, 153–5

Babri Masjid 93
Bharatiya Jamata Party (BJP) 91, 92
backpackers 28, 45; gazing 123–5; narratives of the Taj Mahal 100–1; photography 131–2; reasons for visiting India 165–7; Taj Ganj 150, 162–80; walking 111–13
bang lassi 124, 169
bazaar 55
Benetton 197
Bentinck, Lord 74
biographical narratives 70
boats, themed 190–1
Braj Bhoomi 34–5
Britain: colonial narratives of the Taj Mahal 72–4; colonial space 25; Criminal Justice Bill 58; national space 37–8, 38–9; tourists and photography 131
buildings: control/theming 189
bureaucratic power 10–13

cafés 168–9
cantonment area 25; *see also* Agra Cantonment
capitalism 10–13
childhood play 145–6
Chisti, Shaikh Salim 33
cities 25
coach parks 196–7
collective gaze 125–7
colonialism 201; ethnography, tourism and 2; narratives of the Taj Mahal 71, 72–82, 103; space 22–8
commission 110, 182–3
commodification 188–9; memory 141–3; space 47–8
Congress Party 85, 93
conservation 24–5; colonialism and 72–4; global conservation ethic 184–7
contestation 37–8
continuity 145–6

218

SUBJECT INDEX

cosmological symbolism 32, 97
Cottage Industries 155
counter-narratives 100–2, 103
courtyard 193
craft centre 189
crafts: emporia 109–10, 155, 183; souvenirs 141–3; small traders 155, 170–2, 183
crematorium 196
Criminal Justice Bill 58
cruelty 79–81
cultural habits 16–17, 63–4
cultural integration 87
Curzon, Lord 74

death 139
defining events 84
design codes 52
despotism 79–80
destabilisation 67
development 187
Diana, Princess of Wales 1, 131
differerence *see* otherness
Dionysian culture 44–5
Disneyland 67
disorder 156–7; *see also* heterogeneous tourist space
diversity 175–6
domestic tourists: coach park 196; gazing 125–8; model Taj Mahals 139, 142–3; photography 133–5; walking 114–16
drugs 28, 124, 165, 166–7, 177–8
dual city 25
dual tourist economy 182–3

economy: dual tourist economy 182–3; economic significance of the Taj Mahal 100
emporia 109–10, 155, 183
enclaves, European 25
enclavic tourist space 45–53, 149, 201; movement 50–1; package tourists in Agra Cantonment 150–62; performance 62, 64–8; regulation 49–50; sensual experience 51–3; social activities 49; *see also* Agra Cantonment
enframing conventions 132–3
England *see* Britain
entrance charge 116, 123, 195
'environmental bubble' 51
environmentalism 187

erotic fantasies 77–8
ethereality 76–7
ethnocentric bias 2–3
ethnography 2
European enclaves 25
exclusivist national narratives 84
'experience': provision of 188–92
'expert' narratives 99, 100

factory closures 184–6
Fatehpur Sikra 31, 155, 188
femininity 77–9
films 127
flaneurie 60
flexible positional superiority 27
footwear, removal of 111
foreign dignitaries 118
foreign independent travellers 150
formal sector 45; *see also* enclavic tourist space, package tourists
'freak centres' 28, 170
Fridays 116–17
frustration: package tourists and 110–11, 157–9

garden parties, themed 154–5
gardens of the Taj Mahal 190
gazing 51–2, 119–28, 131, 146–7
gendered spatial imaginary 77–9
globalisation 201–2; conservation ethic 184–7; tourist space 10–13
'Golden Triangle' 27
groups 114–15
guidebooks 75, 104
guided tours 107–10, 141
guides: regulation of 197–8
Guptas, the 85

'hassle' 171–3
heroic narratives 82, 85
heterogeneous tourist space 53–60, 149, 202–3, 204; backpackers in the Taj Ganj 150, 162–80; movement 57–8; performance 62, 64–8; regulation 56–7; remembering 143; sensual experience 58–60; social activities 54–6; *see also* Taj Ganj
heterotopias 42–3
Hinduism 73–4; and death 139; 'fundamentalist' nationalist narratives 85,

219

SUBJECT INDEX

90–6; Hindu-Muslim riots 168; sacred space 28–35
history: remembering 135–6, 138–9; *see also* narratives
holidays 136–7
'homeland' 37
hotels: Agra Cantonment 152–5, 159–61; Taj Ganj 168–9

identity: articulation of a range of identities at the Taj Mahal 200–1; Indian national identity 39–40, 85–90, 99, 125–6; narratives of the self 70
'imaginary geographies' 7–8, 200
immersion 67
improvisation: backpackers 163–4; more complete 66–7; partial 66
Independence 85
India Oil Corporation 186
individualism 113
informal sector 45; *see also* back-packers, domestic tourists, hetero-geneous tourist space
information 188–9
infrastructure 187–92
insubstantiality 76–7
integration, national 85–90
involuntary memory 143–5
ironic performances 66, 133
Islam 29, 73, 139; *see also* Muslims
Italy 4
Itmad-ul-daulah 155

Jamuna River 139; theming 190–1
Jones, Sir William 24
journals 138

Kaaba 29
Kandy, Sri Lanka 39
Kashi (Varanasi) 30, 31
Khadims 114
Kinari Bazaar 175
Krishna, Lord 34–5, 190
Kumbh Mela 30

landscaping 190
Leader 127
leisure spaces 48–9
length of stay 111, 150, 163, 188
light rail transportation system 190

lighting 191
linear perspective 16
local production 14–15
locals: cultural intermediaries 202; forms of remembrance 145–6; interactions with backpackers 176–8; package tourists' contact with 159–61; use of the Taj Mahal 116–18
Lonely Planet Travel Survival Kit 164, 167, 168, 169
love 102

marble inlay crafts 155; *see also* crafts
marginalisation 203; guides 197–8
Mathura-Vrindaban-Gokul complex 34–5
Mecca 29
mediascapes 14
mediatised gaze 127
Mehta, M.C. 192
Mehtab Bargh 189–90
memory 135; *see also* remembering
mixed tourist spaces 60
mobile enclaves 51
model Taj Mahals 139, 142–3, 144
Moghul Sheraton Hotel 150
'Moghul' theme night 154
Moghuls 22; cruelty 81; Muslim narratives of the Taj Mahal 98; 'Second Golden Age' of India 86–8
moonlight, simulated 191
movement: enclavic tourist space 50–1; heterogeneous tourist space 57–8; walking *see* walking
Mumtaz, Mr 100
Mumtaz Mahal 1, 94, 140
Muslims 29; destruction of Hindu temples 91, 93; Hindu-Muslim riots 168; local Muslim worshippers 116; narratives of the Taj Mahal 72, 96–9, 103; remembering 140–1; visitors to the Taj Mahal 114, 128; *see also* Islam
mysticism 28, 76, 123–4; *see also* sacred space, spiritual experience

Nagma 127
narratives 17, 69–104, 137–8, 200–1; colonial 71, 72–82, 103; Hindu 'fundamentalist' nationalist 85, 90–6; Muslim 72, 96–9, 103; nationalist 71,

SUBJECT INDEX

82–96, 103; other narratives 100–4; 'secular' nationalist 85–90
national identity 39–40, 85–90, 99, 125–6
national pride 89–90, 115–16
national space 35–40
national subject 37
National Trust 37–8
nationalist narratives 71, 82–96, 103; Hindu 'fundamentalist' 85, 90–6; 'secular' 85–90
'native' quarter 25–6
necral landscapes 139
networks, spatial 19–40
New Zealand 38
noise control 195
novelty photographs 133, 134

oil refineries 184–6
Open Letter to India, An 186–7, 191
order 42–5; see also enclavic tourist space
Orientalism 75–82
Oswal emporium 155
otherness 44–5, 52, 204; backpackers and 167, 175–6, 178–80; colonial space and 22–4; package tourists and 157–9, 178–80; simulated in Agra Cantonment 153–5

package tourists 45, 193; Agra Cantonment 150, 150–62, 178–80; gazing 121–3; mobile enclaves 51; perception of contemporary India 27–8; photography 129–31; regulation of visit to the Taj Mahal 196–7; walking 106–11
partial improvisation 66
paths around the Taj Mahal 107–9
pedestrian 'tactics' 43–4; see also walking
performances 8, 104, 105–48, 200–1, 202–3; gazing 119–28, 131, 146–7; photographing 128–35, 138, 146–7; regulation of tourist space 61–8; remembering 135–46, 147; walking 105–19, 146; see also narratives
personal occasions 70, 133–4
photography 128–35, 138, 146–7
picnicking 115
pilgrimage 3–4, 98, 140–1; sacred space 28–35
plans, tourist see tourist plans
play, childhood 145–6

policing 117–18
political power 10–13
pollution 184–6
post-colonial theories of tourism 6
postmodern theories of tourism 5–6
post-tourist performances 66, 133
poverty 57, 156–7
power: capital, bureaucratic and political 10–13; regulation and 41–5; representations and 17; the Taj Mahal as representation of 101
Pratap, Rana 85
Prayaga (Allahabad) 30, 31–2
preservation see conservation
prices, admission 123, 195
pride, national 89–90, 115–16
privatisation 47–8
prostitution 161
psychedelic gaze 124; see also drugs
public space 47–8
purified spaces 42–5

Quamar, Dr 100
Quran: extracts from 97

Radah Soami sect 33
ranking perspective 74–5
Rashtriya Swayamsevak Sangh (RSS) 85, 91, 92
reflexivity 113, 162–3
regular visitors to India 166–7
regulation 41–68, 203–4; Agra 192–9; and dual economy 183; enclavic tourist space 45–53; heterogeneous tourist space 53–60; modes of 49–50, 56–7; tourist performances 61–8; the Taj Mahal 117–18, 192–9
remembering 135–46, 147
representations of space and place 13–19
reverential gaze 127–8
rickshaws 172, 182–3
risk 59–60
ritual inversion 4–5
rituals 114, 138, 139–41
romantic gaze 120–5

sacred space 28–35
Sardar Bazaar 175
Schilpgram 189
'Second Classical Age' 86–7
'secular' nationalist narratives 85–90

SUBJECT INDEX

security: continuity and 145–6
self-discovery 113, 162–3, 165–6, 167
self-expression 42–5
selling ('hassle') 171–3
sensual experience 18; enclavic tourist space 51–3; heterogeneous tourist space 58–60; remembering 143–5; Taj Ganj 174–5
sex tourism 161
sexuality 177–8
Shahjahan, Emperor 1, 138, 140; narratives of the Taj Mahal 79–80, 86–7, 94
Shiva 94
Shivajii 85
shopping/shops 155, 170–1; emporia 109–10, 155, 183; *see also* small traders
sight sacralisation 120
simulacra 189–92
Singh, Guru Gobind 85
small traders 55, 155, 170–2 183; regulation 192–3, 194–5, 198
social activities *see* activities, performances
social habit memory 139–40
solitude 122
souvenirs 141–3; *see also* crafts
space *see* tourist space
spatial conventions 173
spatial networks 19–40
specialisation of tourist space 14
spiritual experience 113, 165, 166–7; *see also* mysticism, sacred space
Sri Lanka 39
staged authenticity 3, 153–5
Stonehenge 38, 140
streets 152, 173–5
strongly classified space 42–5
students 166
Sufi saints 31
super-sacred sites 30
surveillance 117–18
symbol of India 75, 88–90, 121

'tactics', pedestrian 43–4
Taj Ganj 183, 202–3; backpackers in 150, 162–80; regulation 192–9 passim
Taj Mahal 1–2, 21–2, 146–8, 200–1, 201–2; economic significance 100; gazing 119–28; inclusion in pilgrimages to other sites 32–3; infrastructure proposals 187–8, 190–1; model Taj Mahals 139, 142–3, 144; narratives of *see* narratives; photography 128–35; regulation 117–18, 192–9; remembering 135–46; symbol of India 75, 88–90, 121; walking 105–19; World Heritage Site 184–7
'Taj Mahotsan' festival 189
team performance 65–6
Tejo Mahalaya 94
temples: destruction of Hindu 91, 93
theme parks 189–92
theming 49; garden parties 154–5
time: length of stay in India 111, 150, 163, 188; spent at the Taj Mahal 112, 114, 115; temporal conventions 173; time of day and visit to the Taj Mahal 123
tirthas (river-crossing places) 31–2
toilets 196
tour representatives 160; *see also* guides
tourism: colonialism, ethnography and 2; theories of 3–6
tourist economy, dual 182–3
tourist performances *see* performances
tourist plans 181–99; commission and dual tourist economy 182–3; global conservation ethic 184–7; improvement of infrastructure 187–92; regulation of the Taj and Agra 192–9
tourist space 7, 10–40; colonial space 22–8; enclavic *see* enclavic tourist space; in a global frame 10–13; heterogeneous *see* heterogeneous tourist space; national space 35–40; place and spatial networks 19–40; regulation *see* regulation; representations of space and place 13–19; sacred space 28–35
traffic 193–4
transgression 42–5
travel narratives 70
travel writing 24

UNESCO 184
unity, national 85–90
universal cultural space 12
unpredictability 59–60
urban poverty 57
Urs (annual ritual) 140–1

Varanasi 30, 31
'Village' theme night 154–5
virtual reality (VR) 192
Vishwa Hindu Parishad (VHP) 91

walking 105–19, 146; pedestrian 'tactics' 43–4; *see also* movement

weakly classified space 42–5

World Bank 187

World Heritage Site 184–7

young local men 177–8